Designing Interactive Hypermedia Systems

Digital Tools and Uses Set

coordinated by
Imad Saleh

Volume 2

Designing Interactive Hypermedia Systems

Edited by

Everardo Reyes-Garcia
Nasreddine Bouhaï

WILEY

First published 2017 in Great Britain and the United States by ISTE Ltd and John Wiley & Sons, Inc.

ISTE Ltd
27-37 St George's Road
London SW19 4EU
UK

www.iste.co.uk

John Wiley & Sons, Inc.
111 River Street
Hoboken, NJ 07030
USA

www.wiley.com

© ISTE Ltd 2017
The rights of Everardo Reyes-Garcia and Nasreddine Bouhaï to be identified as the authors of this work have been asserted by them in accordance with the Copyright, Designs and Patents Act 1988.

Library of Congress Control Number: 2016956786

British Library Cataloguing-in-Publication Data
A CIP record for this book is available from the British Library
ISBN 978-1-78630-063-8

Printed and bound by CPI Group (UK) Ltd, Croydon, CR0 4YY

Contents

Chapter 2. Training in Digital Writing
Through the Prism of Tropisms: Case
Studies and Propositions. 37

Stéphane CROZAT

Introduction

The terms "hypertext" and "hypermedia" were introduced in scientific literature 51 years ago, in the description by the visionary computer engineer Ted Nelson of his Evolutionary List File (ELF) file structure. The main idea of the system was to make computers more user-friendly for personal and creative use. Nelson believed that information required an environment that was not only flexible but also able to support "idiosyncratic" arrangements that were modifiable and in a transitory state if final or definitive alternative organization methods had not been determined [NEL 65]. As we will see in this book, hypermedia systems are still very much a relevant and timely topic[1]. Different perspectives have evolved over the years, and we can identify schools of thought that have emerged (in the United States, France and the northern European countries, to cite a few examples[2]), but the main thing is that we continue to exploit (and have not yet exploited all of) the possibilities offered by these systems.

Introduction written by Everardo REYES-GARCIA.

1 Readers can get a more complete idea of recent issues via the actions of two pioneering international conferences in the field, which continue to exist: HT, by the Association for Computing Machinery (ACM), launched in 1987 in North Carolina, and H2PTM, organized by the Laboratoire Paragraphe of the Université Paris 8, first held in Paris in 1989.

2 The main contributors, to name just a few, are George Landow [LAN 06], Jay Bolter, Michael Joyce, Mark Bernstein and Stuart Moulthrop in the United States; Jean-Pierre Balpe, Imad Saleh, Jean Clément, Marc Nanard and Sylvie Leleu-Merviel in France, and Uffe Wiil, Peter Nürnberg and Espen Aarseth in northern Europe. We also cite the edited volumes [WAR 03], [SAL 05], [BER 09] and [ANG 15].

The study of hypermedia includes all of the problems, methods, tools, uses and ideologies associated with it. In the literature, these studies have addressed, at various points in time: man–machine interaction, documentation systems, digital literature and poetry, online teaching, new forms of media, the Web, social networks, and, most recently, digital humanities and the Internet of Things (IoT). This ubiquity and persistence can be explained by the fact that hypermedia systems are a specific type of software oriented toward linking digital information within a graphic environment.

Hypermedia systems are productions that exist onscreen, a property that raises questions having to do with display support. Unlike texts that are printed or engraved on solid surfaces, digital texts are represented in the form of two basic components – links and nodes – and their integration follows rules drawn from disciplinary fields of application. In other words, they require a structuring model in order for the linked information to be usable and understandable for users.

Together, nodes and links create a hypertextual structure. In the computer environment, the screen is the reference location within which the content of nodes and link relations is updated and refreshed. Additionally, the rhetoric of hypertexts tells us that meaning is given by the understanding of the structuring of ideas, and this understanding is attained not only by choices of navigation (from one node to another) but also by constant backtracking within the content itself (that is, within the structuring model). Therefore, the problem is one of having reference points in the structure, much like section and chapter titles, footnotes and numbering are used in printed texts, but this time for electronic formats.

Historically, we can differentiate between two interdependent axes in hypermedia research: systems and models. The former refers to the technical and engineering aspects of software (data architectures, formats and structures). From this point of view, the technical evolution of systems is often perceived as going from monolithic hypermedia (in which the components are located in a single place) to open systems by means of the abstraction of services (in which functionalities and content of information can exist as independent blocs and on demand).

The second axis focuses on navigation models, types of structures, ergonomics and cognitive problems. With regard to navigation models, we have a repertoire and vocabulary of hypertextual structural models. Petersen [PET 11] summarizes five of these:

– associative structures: used to associate pieces of information (nodes) in an arbitrary fashion (with links);

– spatial structures: their use is based on visual attributes (such as colors, shapes, dimensions and positions in space) representing relationships;

– taxonomic structures: support multiple tasks of categorization. Relationships are represented by inclusion and exclusion rather than by association;

– argumentative or problem-based structures: used to "type" entities (nodes or links) according to the problems being discussed, positions with regard to these problems and the evidence supporting or refuting these positions;

– annotation and metadata structures: can be used to add comments or descriptive information to entities or to the overall information structure.

These models are used in various domains supporting aid with decision-making above all else; however, it is also possible to use and detect hypertextual structures in an artistic context. The well-known term "ergodic literature" [AAR 97], for example, looks at systems from the perspective of the work done by a reader to find his way in the text. This work can not only be composed of a traditional reading process, but may also begin with a corpus in which everything is linked; these links are then progressively deleted until a satisfactory point is reached (what Bernstein calls "structural hypertexts"), or it may be done via "fractal narratives", suggesting that two adjacent nodes can be amplified by adding a third node between them and replicating the process recursively [HAR 12]. The term "strange hypertexts" is generally used to evoke the need for exotic tools in the search for new alternative spaces [BER 01].

As we have emphasized, these models are implemented and represented in graphic form onscreen. Let us go back to Ted Nelson. While his ELF system was at a general level, almost like an operating or middleware system encompassing multiple existing services and file formats on a machine (texts, images, videos, sounds), other systems have since appeared with a more specific motivation or vocation: NLS by Douglas Engelbart, HyperCard by

Apple, Director by Macromedia, Xanadu by the same Ted Nelson, Hyperties by Ben Schneiderman, and Storyspace and Tinderbox by Eastgate Systems[3].

More recently, with the arrival of the Web, browsers have become the preferred development platform for experimenting with, adapting and implementing hypermedia functionalities. Let us clarify here that the "Web" is not synonymous with the Internet, or with a hypermedia system. The Web is a medium of information and communication that uses networked technologies (such as the HTTP protocol) to access information distributed (and localized by URLs) in a specific format (HTML language). During its 25 years of existence, the Web has become the most widespread and omnipresent medium in the world; however, its technical capabilities remain limited compared to those of a robust hypermedia system. Moreover, its "media language"[4] has undergone an evolution that can be characterized by the logic of "remediatization" [BOL 00], meaning that most of its modes of functioning and representation have been inspired by existing mass media (books, television, film and radio).

At the present time, we believe conditions are favorable for a new wave of hypermedia systems. First, this is because the technical possibilities of the Web have expanded (with innovations such as SVG, WebGL, WebRTC and Web Audio API), while retaining the same technical basis (the trinomial of HTML, CSS and JavaScript), which has helped to develop a Web culture with a stable base.

Second, the Web continues to maintain its free and open aspect, supported by communities of developers (professional, scientific, artistic and amateur) who share their computer codes, create libraries, and publish manuals and tutorials. This is a collective intelligence, a participative ecology that is self-regulated and based on respect for practices.

Third, the Web is able to communicate with other technical objects (software, physical interfaces, everyday personal devices) as well as with organic ones (the living world). The development of hypermedia systems makes it necessary to think beyond the screen and to consider the cognitive and perceptive aspects, spatiotemporal contexts, preservation and social consequences of these systems.

---

3 Tinderbox and Storyspace, developed by Eastgate Systems, are still maintained for new versions of OS X: http://www.eastgate.com/

4 To paraphrase an idea put forth by [MAN 13]. The language of a medium is related to "the ways in which this organizes media data and access to and modification of this data" (p. 169).

Finally, human and social sciences, in turning to digital technologies, have been completely turned on their ear. Computer environments are no longer just tools to process and analyze data obtained using quantitative and qualitative methods; they have themselves become objects of study. To give an example, think about software studies, digital studies and digital methods. Software studies examine the way in which software influences culture, as well as the power relationships between systems, designers and humans [FUL 08]. Digital studies emphasize the types of exchange, production and work created by new information technologies [STI 14]. Digital methods use the characteristic elements of the Web (links, sites, engines and social networks) as a footprint and a resource for the study of social culture [ROG 13]. In short, these perspectives can be associated with that of digital humanities [BER 12], in which the central focus becomes the uncertain, polysemous, and permanently transitory nature of interpretations, functions and representations of digital technologies.

This book belongs to that context. It is more than a technical analysis of the implementation of algorithms or development environments; rather, it offers the reader a group of texts in which the authors of these systems themselves show the complexity of the factors behind the design, implementation and maintenance of tools. Through these reflections, we address questions which put not only the "user" at the heart of systems, but also society, modern concerns, scientific disciplines and culture. In other words, studying hypermedia via the design of tools and functionalities is another way of understanding modern and future man.

Authors and chapters

The texts which form this book have been selected for their richness, originality and scientific rigor. They all share the characteristic of addressing hypermedia systems from a theoretical and practical perspective. The authors of these texts [CRO 15, CUN 14, DEM 15, DES 15, LAI 15, LAT 12, LEC 11, MAT 14, RIC 15] have participated in, conducted, developed and/or tested their own tools and methods. These hypermedia systems are also featured in doctoral theses and research which have public or private financial support.

In the next few pages, instead of introducing each chapter traditionally, we will offer readers three diagrams that graphically show the relationships between the texts. Figures I.1 and I.2 are network diagrams of the authors and their bibliographical references. We have grouped the nodes into four categories: chapter author, cited author, co-author (of the chapter or the cited author) and subject (field of study according to the university documentation system[5]). The idea of the diagram is to get an overall view of the book from its metatexts; that is, texts that refer to other texts. In these figures, we can see nodes that play the implicit role of "bridge" between other nodes. We can also see links (and the complexity generated by them), which are the same color as their starting node. If readers identify an author or discipline familiar to them, they can then more easily find the chapter in which this author or discipline is cited.

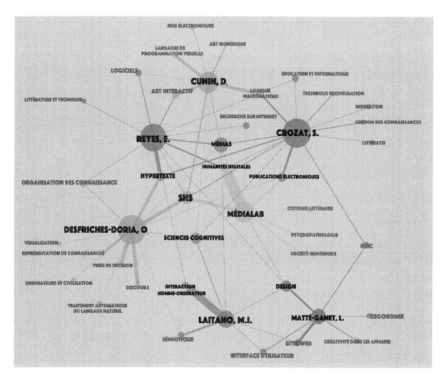

Figure I.1. *Diagram of authors and fields featured in chapters. For a color version of this figure, see www.iste.co.uk/reyes/hypermedia.zip*

---

5 http://www.sudoc.abes.fr/

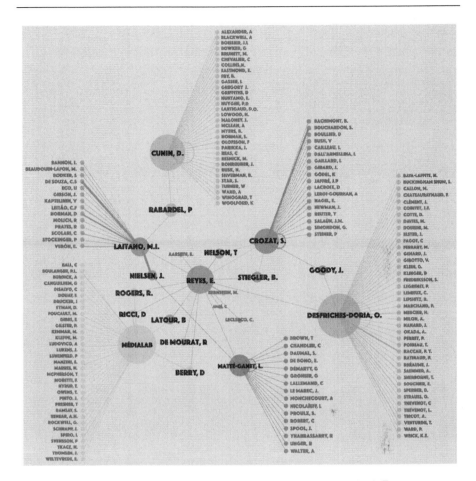

Figure I.2. *Diagram of authors and names of authors cited. For a color version of this figure, see www.iste.co.uk/reyes/hypermedia.zip*

The third diagram, Figure I.3, offers a graphic depiction of the relationships between the keywords in the texts and the authors who write about them. To produce it, we first analyzed all of the texts using the lexicometric tool of word frequency. Each word is weighted according to the number of repetitions (in a chapter and in the entire book). This quantification can be done in a basic way with software platforms such as Wordle and Voyant, but other, more complex analyses can be carried out with topic modeling tools such as Mallet. After the qualifications, we grouped the words most frequently used, bearing in mind that the total number of words contained in this book is around 57,000 (320 thousand symbols). The color code used in the figure is as follows: red for "general issues", blue for "methods" used by the authors, green for "theoretical and/or practical tools" they use and yellow for "usages" in which the issue plays a role. In a way, the columns can be read as follows: The [*author*] addresses the [*issue(s)*] from the perspective of the [*method(s)*] using the [*tool(s)*] in the context of the [*usage(s)*].

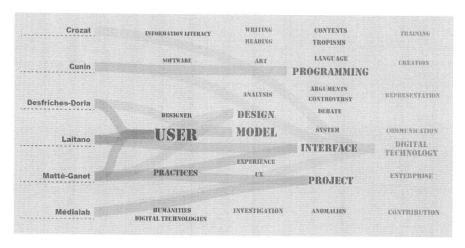

Figure I.3. *Keywords in this book organized in columns. Left to right: author name, issues, methods, tools (theoretical or practical) and usages. The size of the text corresponds to the number of occurrences of the word in the whole text. The vertical position of the words corresponds to their author. For a color version of this figure, see www.iste.co.uk/reyes/hypermedia.zip*

We hope that these images will help readers to track relationships between the bibliography, problems, methods, tools and usages of hypermedia systems as they have been addressed by the authors in this book. The final interpretation remains the responsibility of the readers, of course, and the idea is that they will be able to complete, update, modify and question it on an ongoing basis.

Acknowledgments

We would like to thank Imad Saleh, director of the Laboratoire Paragraphe at the University of Paris 8, for his encouragement and advice during the writing of this book. We are also grateful to the authors who accepted our invitation to enrich this book with their research and reflections.

Bibliography

[AAR 97] AARSETH E., *Cybertext: Perspectives on Ergodic Literature*, Johns Hopkins University Press, Baltimore, 1997.

[ANG 15] ANGÉ C. (ed.), *Les objets hypertextuels*, ISTE Editions, London, 2015.

[BER 01] BERNSTEIN M., "Card shark and thespis: exotic tools for hypertext narrative", *Proceedings of the 12th ACM Conference on Hypertext and Hypermedia (HT'01)*, New York, pp. 41–50, 2001.

[BER 09] BERNSTEIN M., GRECO D. (ed.), *Reading Hypertext*, Eastgate Systems, Watertown, 2009.

[BER 12] BERRY D., *Understanding Digital Humanities*, Palgrave, New York, 2012.

[BOL 00] BOLTER J., *Remediation: Understanding New Media*, MIT Press, Cambridge, 2000.

[CRO 15] CROZAT S. "Les tropisms du numérique", in SALEH I. *et al.* (eds) *H2PTM'15*, ISTE Editions, London, 2015.

[CUN 14] CUNIN D., Pratiques artistiques sur les écrans mobiles: création d'un langage de programmation, Doctoral Thesis, University of Paris 8, 2014.

[DEM 15] DE MOURAT R., OCNARESCU I., RENON A.L. *et al.*, "Méthodologies de recherche et design: un instantané des pratiques de recherche employées au sein d'un réseau de jeunes chercheurs", *Sciences du Design*, 1.1, PUF, Paris, 2015.

[DES 15] DESFRICHES O., FAGOT C., "Visualisation d'information à base de modèles pour l'argumentation", in SALEH I. *et al.* (eds), *H2PTM'15*, ISTE Editions, London, 2015.

[FUL 08] FULLER M. (ed.), *Software Studies: A Lexicon*, MIT Press, Cambridge, 2008.

[HAR 12] HARGOOD C., MILLARD D., DAVIS R., "Exploring (the poetics of) strange (and fractal) hypertexts", *Proceedings of the 23th ACM Conference on Hypertext and Hypermedia (HT'12)*, New York, pp. 181–186, 2001.

[LAI 15] LAITANO M.I., Le modèle trifocal: une approche communicationnelle des interfaces numériques: Contributions à la conception d'interfaces accessibles, Doctoral Thesis, University of Paris 8, 2015.

[LAN 06] LANDOW G., *Hypertext 3.0: Critical Theory and New Media in an Era of Globalization*, Johns Hopkins University Press, Baltimore, 2006.

[LAT 12] LATOUR B., *Enquête sur les modes d'existence: une anthropologie des Modernes*, La Découverte, 2012.

[LEC 11] LECLERCQ C., GIRARD P., "The experiments in art and technology digital archive", *Rewire: 4th International Conference on the Histories of Media Art, Science and Technology*, Liverpool, available at: http://inha.revues.org/4926, September 2011.

[MAN 13] MANOVICH L., *Software Takes Command*, Bloomsbury, London, 2013.

[MAT 14] MATTÉ-GANET L., "Pourquoi l'UX Design va s'éteindre en France, heureusement pour nous", *Conférence FLUPA UX-Day 2014*, available at: http://tinyurl.com/matte-ganet-ux2014, Paris, 2014.

[NEL 65] NELSON T., "A file structure for the complex", *ACM 20th National Conference*, New York, pp. 84–100, 1965.

[PET 11] PETERSEN P., WIIL U., "Hypertext structures for investigative teams", *Proceedings of the 22nd ACM Conference on Hypertext and Hypermedia (HT'11)*, New York, pp. 123–132, 2011.

[RIC 15] RICCI D., "Clues. Anomalies. Understanding. Detecting underlying assumptions and expected practices in the digital humanities through the AIME project", *Visible Language*, available at: http://bit.ly/dhanomalies, vol. 49, no. 3, 2015.

[ROG 13] ROGERS R., *Digital Methods*, MIT Press, Cambridge, 2013.

[SAL 05] SALEH I. (ed.), *Les hypermédias: conception et réalisation*, Hermès Science-Lavoisier, Paris, 2005.

[STI 14] STIEGLER B. (ed.), *Digital studies: organologie des savoirs et technologies de la connaissance*, Fyp Paris, 2014.

[WAR 03] WARDRIP-FRUIN N., MONTFORT N. (ed.), *The New Media Reader*, MIT Press, Cambridge, 2003.

From Controversies to Decision-making: Between Argumentation and Digital Writing

1.1. Introduction

As part of the Vesta Cosy research project (*Vers un ESpace Tactile d'Argumentation, COllaboratif et Symbolique*, or Toward a Tactile, Collaborative, and Symbolic Argumentation Space), financed by the DGA (*Direction Générale de l'Armement*), we work in collaboration with the companies Intactile Design and Syllabs on methodological and conceptual principles and a computer application for symbolic mapping to be used in the visualization and analysis of complex systems, based on knowledge models in the field. One of Vesta Cosy's major applications is in the area of decision-making. In this context, the objective of the application is to provide people involved in the analysis and simulation of these complex situations with a space that will allow them to focus exclusively on their decision-making issue. In this chapter, we will offer a reflexive analysis of the benefits for the tool design process of comparing two fields of experimentation: decision-making and controversy analysis. We will begin by discussing traditional hypermedia approaches, and then examine decision-making and controversy analysis as well as possible connections between the two. Next, we will give a brief report on current methods and tools used in controversy representation, followed by a detailed introduction to Vesta Cosy. Reflections on argument representation that have emerged

Chapter written by Orélie DESFRICHES-DORIA.

during the course of the project will be discussed, as will the theoretical context used regarding argumentation, which we will use to examine the issues involved in rethinking hypermedia design. We will then describe the general methodology we use in controversy analysis and which we developed during the project. Finally, an original approach to new digital writings is given, which will benefit from these reflections on argumentation and the work carried out during the Vesta Cosy co-design process.

1.2. Hypertexts and hypermedia

The idea of hypermedia was preceded historically by the invention of the concept of hypertext, which, according to Rhéaume [RHÉ 93], dates from the 1940s, when Vannevar Bush designed MEMEX, which was intended to function on the model of human thought and seen as associative. The term "hypermedia", which appeared subsequent to "hypertext", initially had mainly to do with learning environments and innovative teaching methods. These environments function on the same principle as hypertext, that of non-linear and non-sequential navigation between the elements of an item or items of content, but, in the case of hypermedia, this content also includes images, videos, graphics, audio and animations.

In 1998, Tricot and Nanard [TRI 98] proposed an inventory of hypermedia categories: "applications dedicated to learning (EAO), to information extraction (SGBD), to the exchange of information (Internet), the provision of information (interactive terminals), and assistance with writing (…), planning, or the study of documents (…). The only commonality shared among all these systems is that they support a usage or alternate activities of selection, comprehension, and evaluation".

What are the characteristics of these hypermedia systems in terms of functioning?

According to Rhéaume [RHÉ 93], the node is the minimum unit of information in a hypertext, and the multiple nodes in a sequence are connected to one another by links. A node is intended to correspond to an idea or concept, also called a "chunk" according to cognitive approaches. Thus, a node can correspond to a textual fragment or to an image, graphic or video clip.

Links can be referential (a link establishes a relationship between a node and a reference element that is inscribed in a recipient node, such as a bibliographical reference, for example) or organizational. They therefore involve hierarchization, a direction of reading between two nodes [RHÉ 93].

The most widely recognized flaws in this type of structure are information fragmentation and the loss of overall vision, which can disorient the user, and cognitive overload, which can make it necessary to remember the path taken between the nodes in the hypermedia network.

The view given up to this point has to do with the function initially defined by the principle of hypertext and applied to different types of information simultaneously in hypermedia. However, technologies and the Web have been developed, resulting in an increase in power of today's massive use of hypertext on the Web, and also accompanied by the emergence of new principles of interaction with tactile or sound interfaces, for example. We believe that the view presented above of hypermedia design can be revisited not only through the lens of application principles such as Vesta Cosy, but also in terms of the design of hypernarrativity and digital writing. We will return to this subject in section 7. The following sections will introduce the areas of experimentation that have accompanied the development of the Vesta Cosy tool, and then we will discuss the functioning of the tool in detail.

1.3. From decision-making to the study of controversies

1.3.1. *Definition of the concept of controversy*

According to C. Lemieux [LEM 07], conflicts that are presented as controversies have a triadic structure: "they refer to situations in which a dispute between two parties is conducted in the presence of a public third party which is thus placed in the position of judge". Lemieux also characterizes controversies by the symmetry of principle applied to the parties with regard to their right to put forth their arguments. Next, he emphasizes the role of the organizational and media device of debate, which imposes constraints on the attitudes and argumentations of the actors, on the one hand, and determines the "degree of confinement" of exchanges, which must itself shift from a private conflict to a controversy and then to an institutional crisis according to a continuum, on the other. The gradation of this degree of confinement is connected to the insertion into the conflict of actors with varying degrees of expertise. Thus, according to Lemieux's analysis [LEM 07], if non-specialist actors, as is the case in our area of experimentation, come to participate in the debate, this debate will slide toward institutional crisis. This definition of controversy evokes questions of the legitimacy of lay actors and their power of action and argumentation in the context of a controversy.

1.3.2. *Shifts from one situation to another*

The shift from a decision-making scenario to a controversy-representation scenario can present certain difficulties of understanding at first glance.

One of the aims of this chapter is to study how shifts from one situation to another (decision-making to controversy representation, and vice versa) have allowed us to move forward in the process of designing the Vesta Cosy tool, which is considered to be representative of a new generation of hypermedia, and to discuss the residual design difficulties that remain.

First, it is clear that these two distinct situations show certain similarities. Decision-making situations put the decision makers in a position of comparing possibly divergent views of the conduct and actions to be taken. Their search for a consensus takes place through the exchange of arguments that may take their legitimacy of authority from actors. We believe that controversies and debates constitute an especially rich ground for observing exchanges of arguments, and that questions having to do with the legitimacy of the actors in these processes are vital in the power plays and arguments that take place on these occasions. Additionally, the approach to argumentation put forth by Chateauraynaud [CHA 07] and focused on the study of the transformations caused by the device of public debate examines the way in which actors are involved in debates, as well as the influence of context of utterance on the presentation and reception of an argument. This conception of the study of argumentation appears to us to be linked to the contextualization of arguments.

With regard to systems intended to aid in decision-making and the contextualization of arguments, we suggest, like Lipshitz and Strauss [LIP 97], that expert decision-making support systems are guided and limited by underlying conceptions of decision-making. Likewise, a controversy-representation device contains a conception of controversy, as well as a definition of the objectives of this representation.

These authors show that the definition of uncertainty is subjective, and also that it depends on the decision model used. Weick's approach [WEI 79], which concedes that multiple meanings may be imposed on a situation, goes in the same direction.

Additionally, the theory of mental models "is based on a hypothesis first formulated in 1943 by the Scottish psychologist Kenneth Craik: in order to understand and anticipate reality, the human mind will create miniature mental representations of it that enable this mind to simulate its functioning" [THE 09]. In this "mental models" approach, Legrenzi and Girotto [LEG 96] show that decision-making is more difficult when a situation is represented with multiple options. In controversy, the definition of risks and uncertainties is composed of subjective elements, and thus constitutes a preferred entry point.

Finally, we believe the decision-making approaches proposed by Klein and Klinger [KLE 91, KLE 93] are also pertinent, particularly because they emphasize the context of decision-making in terms of pressure, urgency and the possibility of having to decide in situations where goals are poorly defined, with objectives that may evolve and change.

1.3.3. *Controversy representation*

There are several approaches, according to Lemieux [LEM 07], that may be taken to the analysis and representation of controversies: a classic controversy approach which acts "to reveal" sociohistoric reality, and an approach initiated by science studies, which considers controversies as "*sui generis* phenomena" that enable the study of the transformations they produce in the social world.

This latter approach is the source of the school of thought known as sociology of proof (or pragmatic sociology), which includes two main sub-branches: anthropology of science and technology, known as actor–network theory, developed by Bruno Latour and Michel Callon, and sociology of action regimes, developed by Luc Boltanski and Laurent Thévenot [LEM 07]. The work we are discussing here has benefited from these two branches of sociology of proof, but does not agree with all of their theoretical approaches and devices.

Actor–network theory is the fruit of studies conducted in the fields of science and innovation. It studies interaction and mediation between the human and non-human actors which form a collective, that is, a network (or sociotechnical organization). In this approach, objects and humans are put on the same level and considered to be actors or mediators, a theory based on the concepts of attachment and translation [CAL 06]. This alignment of human and non-human actors corresponds to a conjunctive paradigm that can be seen in the epistemology of human sciences and is characterized by the act of "no longer looking objectively at subjects, but by looking subjectively at objects" [GEN 08], and corresponds to the emergence of systemic approaches.

In the sociology of action regimes, non-humans acquire actor status when they are involved in a stable social dynamic, while humans act with subjective skills and capacities [GEN 08] and implement actions according to regimes of engagement [THE 06].

Other approaches tend to analyze the frameworks constraining argumentation within the device of debate itself [CHA 07, ELS 05], that is, the way in which the organization and proceeding of a debate influences the expression of its arguments.

What is of particular interest to us is the way in which the representation of controversies can contribute to reflection on the analysis framework of arguments as well as the on-the-spot questions asked of actors, that is, the issue of points of view in these representations.

Throughout the Vesta Cosy project, it has seemed relevant to employ a testing ground related to a controversy   and formulated as follows: "Controversial expertise on risk and vulnerability of karstic massifs subjected to drilling in Haut-Bugey (1989–2014)". This includes a section that examines the legitimacy of controversy actors and the structure of lay knowledge and expertise in the proceeding of a debate. This testing ground is drawn from the context of the RisCom Shale Gas project (ISCC/CNRS-Cnam)[1], piloted by M. Letté[2]. We will discuss part of the work carried out in this project in detail later in this chapter.

---

1 "Shale Gas and Sociotechnical Controversy: An expert study of environmental risk and its communication in the karstic environment (1989-2014)" – financed by *PEPS Risque et communication: Innovation, expertise, controverse* (RisCom).
2 Financed by the HT2S-CNAM laboratory.

1.3.4. *Some controversy visualization and processing tools and methods*

There are several families of tools in the succinct panel that we will now present: qualitative and quantitative textual analysis tools, data visualization tools and mapping tools. The subject of controversy analysis is strongly marked by a textual component; thus, there are several subtypes of textual analysis tools. Qualitative textual analysis tools of note include the following:

– the Prospero textual data analysis tool[3], designed by Francis Chateauraynaud and Jean-Pierre Charriau to describe and analyze complex files;

– text mining tools such as Calliope[4], which are used to extract terms and analyze trends via the word-association method;

– qualitative text analysis tools such as Cassandre[5], which makes it possible to analyze texts collaboratively using semi-automatic tagging and then compare interpretations, or Agorae[6], which is based on sociosemantic approaches to the Web and enables multiperspective corpus analysis.

Notable quantitative textual analysis tools include the following:

– Iramuteq[7] (developed by Pierre Ratinaud), used, for example, in computer-aided speech analysis (lexicometry and morphosyntactic analysis) in order to show the interactive dynamics and sequences of debates or crises in visual form [MAR 12]; it should be noted that this application does not show only quantitative dimensions.

– CorTexT[8], which is a technological platform for the analysis of textual data, oriented toward bibliometrics and relational distribution (for co-citations in scientific corpuses, for example).

---

3 http://prosperologie.org/?sit=22#5
4 http://www.calliope-textmining.com/index.html
5 http://www.cassandre.ulg.ac.be/
6 http://hypertopic.org/
7 http://www.iramuteq.org/
8 http://www.cortext.net/

Poibeau [POI 14] offers an analysis of the functionalities and limits of automatic language processing tools for social sciences, specifying that the pertinence, prioritization and interpretation of information must still be carried out by a human analyst. In the analysis of controversies, the processing of a corpus with these types of tools as a precursor to controversy visualizations is a fairly widespread method, used in particular when applying actor–network theory. In this vein, Venturini [VEN 10, VEN 12] presents an application methodology for actor–network theory's use in controversy representation in an educational context.

Worth citing among the tools available for the visualization of data applied to controversy representation is Gephi[9], which is a tool for the visualization of network graphs. It enables the user to establish links between sources, taken from the Web or from social networks, which include opinions on current debates, and to represent the positions of the actors with spatialization algorithms. Combined with a storytelling tool such as Manylines[10], Gephi makes it possible to account for controversy in presenting successive states of graphs.

Baya-Lafitte and Cointet [BAY 14] discuss a trial involving controversy representation using Gephi, based on the theme of climate negotiations and starting with a material that takes into account the whole of the official process of climate negotiations. The technical nature and complexity of the method are clear, as is the need for expert knowledge on the subject of the controversy in order to achieve a pertinent reading of the graphs produced.

Mapping tools can also be divided into several types: mind mapping, concept mapping, argument mapping and issue mapping (for an overall view of the differences between these tools, we refer readers to Okada *et al.* [OKA 08]; and Davies [DAV 10]. We will focus here on two tools: Compendium and Rationale.

Compendium is defined by Buckingham Shum and Okada [BUC 08] as a hypermedia concept mapping tool. The program contains IBIS (Issue-Based Information System) deliberation language, which translates the base

---

9 http://gephi.github.io/
10 http://tools.medialab.sciences-po.fr/manylines

concepts of this model (Problems raised, Positions, and Arguments) in the hypertext network and categorizes nodes and links semantically. The analytic framework used for categorization is described by top-level categories that are instantiated into tags, and a code is then assigned to each tag. This code is then transferred onto conceptual maps in order to describe the entities shown on them. Visually, arguments are composed of fragments taken from texts connected to one another, tagged and linked to the actors who have enunciated them and for whom it is possible to indicate the agreement or disagreement of others. Besides the inherent difficulty of reading lecture text fragments out of context, even though they are linked to their texts of origin, the binary positions associated with judgments on the arguments are regrettable. In reality, it often happens in debates that actors do not yet know how they will position themselves in an argument, or whether they are neutral, or whether they even wish to make their judgments public. Moreover, this tool does not allow any other possibilities of judging other qualities of the information used in an argument.

Rationale[11] is presented by Davies [DAV 10] as a relatively recent (developed in 2000) computer-aided argument mapping tool. Facts displayed on its argument maps are linked to one another by means of logic connectors such as "but", "because" and "however". Relationships between propositions are limited for the moment to logical inferences; the tool does not cover cause-and-effect relationships or other types of associations such as reasoning by analogy, or argumentation calling on universal values. Rationale has two major characteristics of interest: one, the possibility of contributing to the exercise of critical thinking, and two, the ability to describe where a proposition comes from, for example, from an expert, from common sense or from a statistic or citation.

1.4. Detailed presentation of Vesta Cosy

The Vesta Cosy[12] application can be described according to the dimensions arising from the development of complex models and systems in the field of complex systems engineering, as well as that of expert systems engineering. For more detail, we refer readers to Desfriches Doria *et al.* [DES 16].

---

11 http://rationale.austhink.com/
12 The project is managed by Mr Christophe Fagot of Intactile Design, whom we wish to thank for his careful rereading.

In this section, we will describe the various modules of the application and how they are connected to one another.

Vesta Cosy enables the user to model problematic situations, that is, to create a graphic and symbolic schematization which is itself based on a model of the pertinent components of the field, in order to evaluate simulation scenarios.

In this vein, we have several kinds of knowledge models which we have made to interact in Vesta Cosy (though the design methodologies of these models do not fall within the scope of this chapter).

A business knowledge model presents all of the types of entities in the profession modeled (as well as their attributes), where predetermined instances are used to address a contextual situation and their relationships. The role of this business knowledge model is to provide the user with semantic support used to populate symbolic mapping with the aid of the entities presented in this model, or to create entities absent from the model on the basis of a predetermined semantic framework. Each entity present in the model and/or deposited in the mapped space is equipped with a set of properties proper to its type, represented in an information record (see Figure 1.1), the parameters of which can be set, and which may be only partially filled out.

Each one is also equipped with a set of inference related to the field, which makes it possible on the fly to:

– produce new information or relationships relative to the entities present in the contextual situation;

– request information from the user by indicating missing data that are necessary to the field reference sources being modeled;

– detect potential disagreements between users and inferred information, or between pieces of information inferred by different rules.

– The business model: this model is proper to a field of knowledge; it can be a model having to do with controversies over food additives, which could be instantiated in the context of a study on aspartame or monosodium glutamate, for example. Figure 1.1 shows the display of the knowledge model pertaining to the analysis of a controversy over shale gas, as well as an information record for an actor in the controversy.

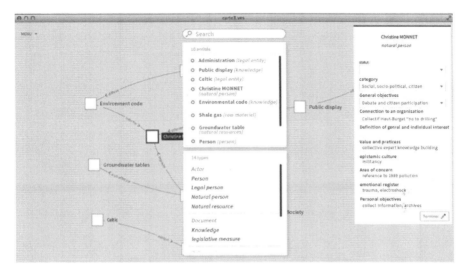

Figure 1.1. *Display of model on controversy over shale gas and information record on an actor*

– The argument model: this model uses the same principles as the business knowledge model does to represent arguments. It is intended generally to take into account the functioning of arguments so as to be able to represent them on symbolic maps and to understand their functioning and the connection of arguments to one another in the context of the question being considered or the contextual situation. It is considered at the same level as a business knowledge model, but is based on the fields of argumentation and debate. The general nature of this model means that its use can be easily adjusted to fit any of the situations represented on symbolic maps. Like the business knowledge model, it also includes general rules for reasoning and decision-making. We have applied our two testing grounds in parallel to this aspect of Vesta Cosy in order to design versions of this model, as well as to determine what is relevant for display on a map involving entities and arguments.

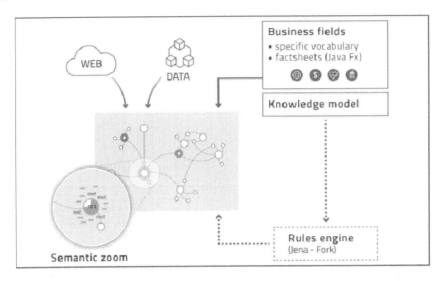

Figure 1.2. *Illustration of the connection of different modules in Vesta Cosy*

– Symbolic mapping (or set or scene): this is used to instantiate the knowledge model relative to a contextual situation that we wish to represent in order to study it or create simulations. Its role consists of visually representing points of view constructed from inserted entities taken from the business knowledge model, or added based on professional reference sources. Mapping is used to lay out an issue contextually, and it could serve to archive the analysis of a question, though issues of archiving have not yet been addressed in the project. It is composed of entities that rely on the knowledge model and displays points of view that are argumentary threads constructed through the identification of arguments and actors which converge on these arguments. The map also plays a pivotal role between the instantiation of a knowledge model with regard to a target issue, and the additional information required in this knowledge model with regard to the target issue.

Figure 1.2 illustrates the functioning and connection of the various models introduced above. Figure 1.3 shows the Vesta Cosy mapping interface.

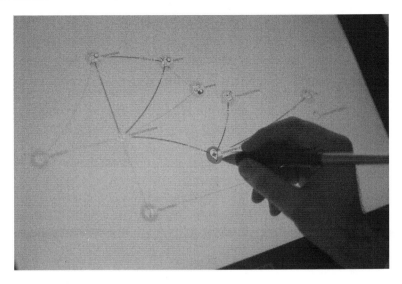

Figure 1.3. *Vesta Cosy mapping interface (plateau)*

There are three other Vesta Cosy modules:

1) Semantic zoom: this is available in the symbolic mapping board and allows the user to interact with symbolic representations. It is used to switch from a detailed view of the business model (of the instantiation of the general business knowledge model) on the map to a more general view. It enables the processing of levels of granularity of perspectives. Depending on the degree of zoom chosen, the display of information and graphic details, which contain elements describing the entities in the knowledge model, varies. Thus, when the user zooms in using the mouse's scroll wheel or by swiping on a touchscreen, it does not mean that this user only wants to enlarge graphic objects. Rather, it means the user wants to get more details concerning entities located on the periphery of the enlargement point. Conversely, zooming out using the mouse or a touchscreen is more than a simple request to reduce the size of graphic objects, but rather an indication of the desire to have less detail concerning the entities described, and to move toward broader visualization of the density of entities. The different levels of details and information offered depend on their semantic description and the level of zoom. This is a major new design contribution within the project.

2) Extraction module: this is a functionality which the user can choose to activate or not, and which carries out automatic searches for information

concerning one or more entities positioned on the symbolic map. Requests can involve the Web or, eventually, specialized databases, and each piece of information can be weighted according to its "importance" with regard to the entity being analyzed and to other information brought up. These information requests are represented on the map according to various details, such as a tag cloud, for example, showing current search trends on the Web regarding an actor placed on a map. In a manner consistent with semantic zoom, the tag cloud display is dependent on the degree of generality chosen through semantic zoom. Thus, by going from a very high-detail zoom to a low-detail zoom, the visualization of the information retrieved changes from a cloud of variably sized tags, to a more or less colored disk surrounding the entity on the plateau, and finally, to a simple coloration of the outline of the entity.

3) Rules engine module: this is a rules engine similar on many points to the existing ones (Apache Jena, Pellet, Drools), but with two very specific characteristics. First, it is used in real time, which means that it produces inferences as information is added or withdrawn by the user to the entities on his or her symbolic map (whether these are descriptive records of entities or relationships between entities). Second, it accepts disagreements, which means:

– that the business rules it exploits can infer contradictory information (which happens in real cases with which experts are confronted, in sectors such as defense, medicine, law and taxation);

– that the user can be in disagreement with the information produced by the rules applied and, in this case, it is the user's opinion that takes precedence (and not the information taken from business rules) for the inferences that may result.

1.5. What is the content of argument representations?

To begin this section, which presents the work completed and still in progress on argument representation, it is useful to specify the functioning adopted in the back-and-forth between the various dimensions of the application and the two fields mobilized.

1.5.1. *Interactions between the two fields*

We have used an iterative method to study the constraints of the field of decision-making simultaneously with our study of a controversy over shale gas. These two fields have served to alternatively evaluate the propositions that have progressively emerged from each field. If one of the fields does not allow a proposition to be validated, it is not eliminated; rather, alternatives are then sought. However, the design of the argument model has been inspired mainly by the controversy model. As shown in Figure 1.4, the design of hypermedia falls at the confluence of the following elements:

– graphic modules related to data visualization and already developed in the project;

– the progressively developed controversy analysis framework presented in section 3.3;

– the knowledge model that instantiates entities proper to the area of controversy over shale gas;

– theoretical approaches adopted from argumentation (which we will discuss in the next section), and which guide us in the design of the argument model .

The concentric circles indicate circles of actors that we have identified as being present in the study of the controversy over shale gas.

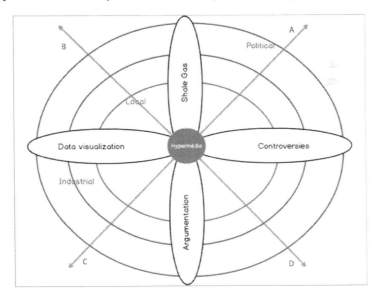

Figure 1.4. *Representation of the position of hypermedia in the design process of the argument model. For a colour version of this figure, see www.iste.co.uk/reyes/hypermedia.zip*

The blue arrows indicate the axes of development upon which this layout has enabled us to work; they are to be considered one by one. Thus, axis A (on the upper right of the diagram) concerns the determination of a general knowledge model based on the study of controversies and the instantiation of this model for the study of this controversy over shale gas. Axis B (on the upper left of the diagram) consists of determining the elements to be represented on a map when this knowledge model is used for this controversy, and more generally, to evaluate which graphic dimensions of knowledge models are pertinent for mapping. Axis C consists of determining which elements should be represented on a map when the argument model is used. Finally, axis D concerns the study of interactions between the two models on the following levels: how the knowledge model can rely on the characteristics of the argumentation model; the division of elements between the two models and the mutual enrichment of the two models. Numerous questions have arisen regarding the application of the Vesta Cosy project to the representation of a controversy. First, we should ask ourselves about the objectives of this representation, and the place or role of the user who carries out controversy mapping. We may wish to gain an understanding of a controversy, with varying levels of detail, by studying, for example, the convergences of actors or the connections between arguments. However, the user may also wish to explore a specific point of the controversy, or the position of one or more groups of actors within this controversy. We may also wish to research the levels of contribution by the actors in quantitative terms. It may also seem pertinent to prepare a summary or an analysis of the controversy. Thus, the question of controversy representation is closely linked to the question of the perspective adopted, the objective and the role of the user.

1.5.2. *Theoretical approaches to argumentation*

First of all, it should be mentioned that the design of our argument model is not based solely on reasoning modeling; we have also followed the example of Mercier [MER 11], who, rather than studying reasoning as decontextualized syllogisms, proposes a focus on arguments. In this way, Mercier demonstrates that if performances in the application of classic reasoning to decision-making are unconvincing, this is due to a lack of argumentative contextualization.

Next, we have mobilized various argumentation approaches, notably those of Chateauraynaud [CHA 07] and Raccah [RAC 90, RAC 05]. Chateauraynaud proposes a pragmatic sociology of transformations induced by the device of public debate. In this approach, he proposes to enter into analysis through arguments because these are "elementary units of meaning", which delineate and crystallize three dimensions in the device of public debate. These three dimensions are the enunciative framework of arguments; the entities or objects they affect and their impact. He writes: "it is through the use of arguments that we give ourselves the greatest chance of seizing upon the power of the conviction or dedication of an entity or network of entities" [CHA 07]. He then proposes that argumentation should be thought of in terms of impact:

– who delivers the impact of an argument? (actor, speaker);

– what does it impact? (its object or theme);

– what is its impact? (its extension or consequences).

What is remarkable in this approach is that we cannot separate an argument from the actor who delivers it, or from what it impacts (what we call the object of the argument, that is, the conceptual or concrete nameable object with which it is concerned, and which we consider as the object to be represented on a map), and it is precisely this that Vesta Cosy will enable us to do.

Next, Chateauraynaud recommends the use of topoi (singular: topos), which are also used by Raccah [RAC 90, RAC 05] to take into account the scales of values implicitly engaged in arguments.

Pierre-Yves Raccah is the author of a polyphonic theory through a scientific approach of meaning. It is aimed at bringing out the implicit or ideological elements contained in word usage. This theory is based on the presupposition that languages impose constraints on the subjective operations of meaning construction; this is also known as the field of language semantics. This affirmation stems from Bakhtin's concept of "inhabited words". Thus, words in a statement are always the words of others, already used, which suggests a divided, multiple, and inter-relational subject and its dialogism. Raccah also applies this conception of the significance of words to sentences, since the base unit of his analysis is the sentence. Thus: "The statement is an occurrence of a sentence in a situation made by a Speaker".

He proposes a method to bring out the ideological aspects of statements based on the following principle: "statements contain traces of their conditions of statement". Thus, he differentiates between the significance of words and the meaning of words, and, simultaneously, the significance of sentences and the meaning of sentences. The indications (or constraints) of the argumentative orientations of statements are thus contained in the very language itself [RAC 97], and also, significantly, in the connectors used (such as "but", "yet" and "so", for example).

Raccah's approaches are used in two major fields: automatic language processing and reasoning simulation [RAC 90]. These consist of breaking down a statement into topic fields, which correspond schematically to a "way of seeing" an entity, property or relationship. This way of seeing is itself determined by the way in which another entity, property or relationship is seen, that is, by another topic field. A process of gradual inference then takes place [RAC 97].

We can thus represent a topic field by a chain of topic fields interlocked with one another, so that each topic field is characterized both by a conceptual field (entity, property or relationship) and by the topic field it contains, which is itself characterized by a conceptual field and by the topic field it contains, and so on until a fundamental topic field is reached.

A fundamental topic field allows us to stop a series of embedments, which give rise to subjective, unjustified and binary judgments (such as good/bad, I like/I don't like, etc.), that are made by the members of a community on conceptual fields:

– The generic form of a topic field F1 is: $F1: CT1 = <CC1,CT2>$.

For example, for the statement "This baby is wealthy", the topic field of wealth is evoked by the word "wealthy".

– The fundamental topic field of "Ability" can be defined as a binary judgment on the conceptual field of "Capacity for action" and is noted depending on the person who uses this word in a statement positively or negatively:

Ability: <capacity for action, positive> OR Ability:<capacity for action, negative>

– The description according to this approach of the statement "This baby is wealthy" concerns "wealth" and will be as follows (for more detail we refer readers to Raccah [RAC 90, RAC 05]:

Wealth: <POSSESSION, <CAPACITY FOR ACTION, POSITIVE>>

This approach is of particular interest to us because it is based on the acknowledgment of the following principle: the form of the sentences (and the terms or vocabulary used in these sentences) incorporates indications about the argumentative potential of their statements. Thus, it can be used to model and systematize a set of interpretations classically accepted in a language and considered non-exhaustive, corresponding to the use of a term, or to systematize the argumentative functions associated with logic connectors in an iterative manner. Finally, this principle is of interest to us for other reasons; it implies inseparability between the form of the statement and the content of the statement an aspect to which we will return in section 1.7. In addition, this operation through compartmentalization also makes it possible to diagram the functioning of the argument model and its connection to the knowledge model and, overall, the hypermedia model of which Vesta Cosy is composed.

1.5.3. *Hypermedia structure in the process of decision-making map construction with Vesta Cosy*

As we noted in section 1.2, the structure of a hypermedia system is based on the functioning of hypertext, which is used to create associations between elements of information, and thus to access functions such as citing a source, aggregating content and documenting a fact through a non-linear and non-sequential way of organizing information. This operation relies on the activity of navigation conducted by a user between the linked elements.

With Vesta Cosy, it appears that a new generation of hypermedia has emerged. In addition to the navigation process, the user is in the information design field, which is seen as a process aimed at giving meaning to the data: "Information design results from a state of equilibrium between relevant issues of scientific exactitude, aesthetics, cognitive effectiveness, and accessibility, determined by a context. It constitutes a language resulting from the joining together of these major principles, mobilizing work on form, size, color, and orientation by causing relational mechanisms to appear: continuity, similitude, proximity, order, and proportionality" [FRE 15].

Though the graphic qualities present in Vesta Cosy, such as semantic zoom, polymorphic icons and mapping itself, were inspired by the approaches of Jacques Bertin, the association between data and these graphic parameters are taken from information design. Jacques Bertin, who has inventoried eight graphic different variables (the two dimensions of the plan, size, value, grain, color, orientation, and form) and their dimensions of variation (quantitative, qualitative, and ordinate), has proposed a summary of the set of variables used by Vesta Cosy to represent salient or pertinent aspects of data for a user. This means that these graphic variables are limited in number and can therefore constitute a "grammar of (available visual) forms" [MIL 04], while the angles of analysis are potentially infinite. This conception implies that it is just as much the reader as the author who constructs the analysis of a text or a graphic. Though the possible combinations between graphic variables and dimensions of data remain numerous, they nonetheless constitute a finite set. In any case, the user must make choices within the dimensions he wishes to represent his data, and which stem from his framework of analysis. It is the potentially empty structure adaptable to this analysis framework that Vesta Cosy makes possible for models. Thus, certain dimensions of data are contained in the models, and the dimensions most useful for decision-making are the ones associated with graphic variables. This approach is underpinned by cognitive approaches and aimed at saving cognitive time and effort.

Figure 1.5 shows the different levels of structuring of the hypermedia made up by Vesta Cosy. Users can access multiple levels of conceptualization of the issues they wish to represent. The first level, at the top of Figure 1.5, corresponds to a factual view of the elements of the content of the situation being presented, and which can have its objects included in a professional model, that is, the instantiation of a business knowledge model (such as medical, controversy or military). At the second level, located in the middle of Figure 1.5, users can place themselves at the level of the statement or opinion in order to represent the positions of actors regarding a given issue. They can also work on points of view, considering that the actors who converge on part or all of their arguments will define points of view. Finally, at the third level, at the bottom of Figure 1.5, the Vesta Cosy user carries out his own analysis of the problematic situation. He thus finds himself in the role of designer of the information described above and can thus also interact with these associations between visual variables and data to simulate scenarios or envision solutions that are inaccessible or difficult to access without the help of the tool.

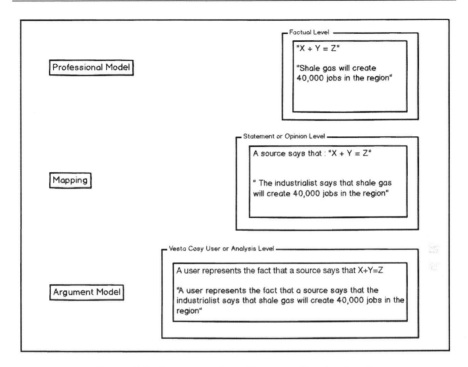

Figure 1.5. *Representation of hypermedia structure in the process of decision-making aid maps using Vesta Cosy*

The originality of this type of hypermedia lies in the user's ability to interact at all of the levels shown in Figure 1.5, across all supports and at the same time. Thus, this hypermedia system is not limited to creating a citation link or reference to an item of content, though it enables the user to act on the factual level, which we consider to be at the same level as classic hypertext. It also allows the user to act at the level of speech and its interpretation, and on their relationship with other items of speech and interpretations, which in some cases may be included in the models to be implemented in Vesta Cosy.

The question of a static representation of debates and of the dialogic and dynamic aspects of exchanges takes on its full meaning here. Is a static representation of exchanges capable of measuring the variety of definitions of the ideas, values and arguments mobilized in exchanges during a controversy?

Vesta Cosy, while not offering the ability to represent in real time the exchanges produced during a debate, seems to offer a dynamic and interactive alternative to take into account or analyze the terms of a debate using asynchronous details.

1.6. Application of Vesta Cosy to controversy analysis

We will begin this section by presenting the dimensions of controversy characterization that have emerged iteratively during the course of the study of the controversy testing ground and the design of Vesta Cosy. Next, we will propose methodological principles for controversy analysis.

1.6.1. *Characterization of the nature of a controversy*

After studying multiple controversies, we have concluded that the subject of "controversy" itself is a complex concept that can involve variable processes depending on one or more dominant features that can vary with the passage of time, and can determine the characteristics of what might be called the nature of a controversy. These characteristic features are enumerated below and must have graphic correspondence points when included in the representation of a controversy:

– *Degree of maturity of the controversy*: This has to do with its duration, the number of actors involved and its degree of advancement. This aspect involves being able to archive the different versions of a map, a functionality that has not yet been developed.

– *Degree of technicality of the controversy*: Some controversies are characterized by the necessity of mastering an area of technical or scientific know-how before being able to enter into argumentation. This technical nature may concern objects of debate such as drilling techniques or ranges of arguments, still over shale gas; for example, arguments presenting this technique as a job creator linked, in particular, with the employment situation in the USA, must be tied in to the policy of subsidizing jobs having to do with shale gas in the USA, and with variations in gas flow (political and economic arguments). Thus, we must be able to present ranges of arguments in this type of controversy (we will discuss these features in more detail in the next section).

– *Rhythm:* A controversy may die down at one moment, lose its intensity and then be reactivated when a new innovation emerges. This feature has not yet been addressed in the Vesta Cosy project.

– *Problems of definition:* Coming to an agreement on the definition of certain subjects of debate is part of the debate itself. Some controversies are characterized by difficulties or clashes over the definition of the terms serving to designate the subjects of debate. This fact implies that subjects of debate can be described, and described differently depending on the actor, in the representation of a controversy in which one of the characteristics is the difficulty experienced by its actors in agreeing on a common definition of the terms designating the objects being debated, particularly in terms of the properties of these objects.

– *Clashes over for/against:* Other controversies are marked by for-or-against binary opposition, on questions of ethics, for example, this may be compared to the topos/topoi approaches of Raccah [RAC 90, RAC 05], discussed in section 5.2. This seems to indicate, if the debate is as clearly positioned, that it has a high degree of maturity, and that these binary oppositions are the result of a process in which argumentation has taken place upstream, and that the oppositions stem from ideology.

– *Degree of opacity:* This is linked to the degree of technicality, and is used to describe a state of opacity of the debate for neophyte actors before they gain the technical knowledge necessary to participate in a debate characterized by its technical nature. This aspect of a controversy implies that it must be able to shift from a state of simplified representation to that of more detailed representation in order to proceed in a back-and-forth manner according to the evolution of users' knowledge. This type of functionality is offered to Vesta Cosy users through semantic zoom, presented in section 1.4.

– *Geographic aspects:* In some debates, a shifting of arguments can be seen, when these arguments are deployed on a local or global scale. Here, the shift from a local to a global vision of the geographic eras concerned by the questions raised in the controversy appears to be decisive. It is possible not to confine ourselves to a geographic representation, but to look at questions conceptually, with the shift from a local conception to a global conception taking place through a declination of the semantic zoom principle discussed in section 4.4:

– *Temporality:* Same as above, but for temporal aspects including relative time scales (long-term versus short-term).

– *Cultural/linguistic variables:* The content of arguments can be very different if the debate is moved over geographic areas, or if cultural or even linguistic variables underlie the different values. This can also be connected to the approaches used by Raccah [RAC 97], discussed in section 5.2. For example, in health, issues change easily if we situate ourselves in the western world or if we transpose the same questions to developing countries. This observation indicates that it seems necessary to be able to pinpoint and represent the values that underlie actors' assertions in order to be able to interact with different interpretations of the meaning of a term designating elements of a debate [DES 16].

– *Quality of data and methods of data production:* In this case, this has to do with searching for sources, analysis methodology, accuracy of interview transcriptions, and, overall, methods of observation and data collection. It can occur in the study of a controversy that an actor who is theoretically concerned does not express himself; this is already a piece of information. It can also occur that the person creating the map is not able to set aside his own convictions on the subject of the controversy. Finally, it can occur that the parties collecting data do not find it, or are missing data. Thus, we must be able to represent degrees of investment in the debate, from the absence of intervention to a representation of the frequency of interventions by an actor (the quantitative aspect). With regard to the role of the user and his critical distance, this is the challenge faced by the method of analysis proposed, as well as the design of Vesta Cosy. We will return to this subject in the next section.

We consider that these characteristics aimed at showing a trend in the state of a controversy at a given time t can have an influence on the representation of this controversy.

1.6.2. *Methodological principles of controversy analysis*

We will now propose our original methodology for the analysis and representation of controversies, the conception of which was not only inspired by the functionalities of Vesta Cosy, but also available online thanks to mapping tools such as GraphCommons[13].

---

13 https://graphcommons.com/

We consider it necessary to begin by contemplating how far the granularity of representation of a controversy will extend. To clarify this point, we have provided a non-exhaustive list below of the different degrees of potential granularity for a mapping situation:

– an overall view of the issues running through the controversy;

– an overall view of the exchanges on a point of the controversy;

– the point of view of an actor or group of actors within the controversy;

– a representation of exchanges in the form of propositions on one or more salient points of the controversy : this option implies questions on the dynamic aspects of exchanges occurring throughout the debate and of contributions, as well as on the form of propositions (verbatim summaries, extracts of verbatim accounts, thematic categories, a summary, who writes it?);

– a representation of the elements of convergence/divergence for actors in the content of arguments.

A second preliminary question consists of noting the position of the person who makes the map. Several cases are possible with regard to the collaborative aspects of this work, in objective terms, and, finally, in terms of role. A representation can be constructed:

– for oneself;

– for someone else;

– individually;

– collectively.

Objectives can include:

– supporting the development of simulation scenarios;

– evaluating the pertinence of these scenarios;

– evaluating risks;

– quantifying and describing elements of a decision;

– arguing for/against a decision;

– bringing new options to light;

– characterizing risks and perspectives on risks;

– characterizing uncertainties and perspectives on uncertainties;

– bringing common/differing elements to light;

– making comparisons based on mapping;

– representing in order to understand;

– representing in order to summarize or report;

– representing in order to explain.

Similarly, the actor who creates a map may play one or more roles at the same time:

– the role of mediator/organizer;

– the role of secretary (with a reporting objective);

– the role of observer;

– the role of decision maker.

Next, with reference to the argumentative approaches adopted and introduced in section 5.2, we recommend entering into the analysis of a controversy through arguments, since they are considered to be inseparable from their instance of statement. To break down the work, this stage consists of listing the human and non-human actors involved in the debate (for example, in the case of a controversy over nuclear energy, the Chernobyl accident could appear as a non-human actor in the debate which influences the debate itself and encompasses a set of representations). Next, we suggest listing the subjects of the debate (considered here to be the subjects of the arguments), with reference to Chateauraynaud's approach.

Finally, the last stage required for readiness to work with hypermedia in all its dimensions consists of defining the properties of the human and non-human actors and the subjects of the debate. The definition of these properties can itself constitute a part of the debate, since it involves points of view in terms of the definitions of what is being questioned in a controversy. These properties are shown in information records pertaining to the entities that are displayed on a map in Vesta Cosy.

As an example, we have defined the following properties, which we consider pertinent for characterizing a human actor entity in the context of the controversy over shale gas:

– status: social status or socio-professional category;

– category: category of the actor defined theoretically in terms of debate participation, for example expert, local witness, industrialist, etc.;

– general objectives: objectives concerning the participation of the actor in the debate, for example citizen participation, or the exercise of democratic power, or the collective building of expertise;

– belonging to an organization: belonging to collective social groups, such as the "No to shale gas" organization;

– definition of the general and individual interest for the actor: this property may possibly be deduced from verbatim debate records, or from information received in the form of interviews;

– epistemic culture: for example militantism or unionism;

– values: this property is a corollary of the above;

– area of concern: this has to do with the way in which an actor is concerned by the debate, and in what capacity he is invested in this participation, for example, because he has borne witness to a fact or been victim of an event;

– emotional register: this is correlated with the previous property; it is a way of describing the overall emotional register of an actor during his involvements in the debate, for example the level of horror, depression or accusation.

In the definition of the properties of subjects of debate (subjects of arguments), we recommend attempting to define them by taking them out of the context of the debate and trying to describe their fundamental nature in a neutral manner, beginning with their intrinsic characteristics. Pollution, for example, could be seen alternatively as either a cause or a consequence of other events; thus, we need to focus on the general characteristics of a "pollution" phenomenon, which may, for example, have a duration, cause an impact on elements of the environment, involve substances, be quantifiable or measurable, etc.

It is precisely this process of decontextualizing the subjects of a debate in order to model them that enables the user to put the proper distance between his own opinions and the debate. If the user is playing the role of mediator and seeking to have a global and exhaustive view of the positions in the debate, there is a high risk that he will insert his own opinions into the map to the detriment of the representation of the positions of other actors in the debate. We consider this decontextualization to aid in the objectivization of the elements and arguments of the debate.

With regard to the representation of arguments in debate, the figure below displays the potential difficulties that this procedure presents. The formulation of entities placed on a map has a great deal of influence on its structuring. Figure 1.6 shows two portrayals of an argument related to the controversy over whether living beings can be patented. We can see that on the left-hand side of the figure, this representation positions the arguments according to a binary axis that includes part of the formulation of the argument: "endangers" or "does not endanger". The subject of the argument in this case is biodiversity. This representation appears limited in its capacity to explain the positioning of the arguments, or to develop the range of the argument in terms of representation. This is linked to the formulation of what is entered into the nodes and links. The right-hand side representation in Figure 1.6 dedicates the function of the link to presenting the positioning of an actor on a subject of the reformulated debate, which includes in its title what is truly at issue in this argument: "endangering of biodiversity". Thus, the right-hand side representation in this figure seems more pertinent in order to represent the factual level of the argument.

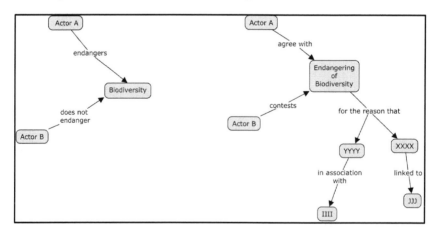

Figure 1.6. *Presentation of structuration in the representation of an argument*

Next, because Vesta Cosy offers an argument model based on the same model as the knowledge model, we will describe the argument itself in terms of properties, in the context of the analysis level described in section 5.3 of this chapter.

This part of the project is still in progress. It is oriented as follows: an argument may be described in terms of properties according to the following dimensions:

– type of argument or reasoning: inductive, deductive, argument by authority and value-based argumentation;

– function: affirm, justify, explain, demonstrate and incite;

– subject: it corresponds to what is placed on the map to link the argument to the mapping; the "subject of argument" entity can thus be described in the knowledge model and can be listed as a property of an argument;

– form of expression of the argument: it may include a verbatim record of the verbal formulation of an argument;

– register: this property is an adaptation of the approach used by the engagement systems of Thévenot [THÉ 06], and is used to describe the reference universe of the argument (for example, economic register, legal register, ethical register, geostrategic register, etc.) by grouping arguments according to a predefined set of registers;

– declaring actor: this human actor is described using the properties discussed earlier in this section.

1.7. New digital writings with hypermedia

Now that we have introduced Vesta Cosy in detail, we will turn to the nature of the digital writing that can be implemented with this new type of hypermedia.

1.7.1. *Extension of reasoning and paradigm shift*

It is not our intention here to analyze the types of texts extant in digital writings, that is, we will not revisit the differences and commonalities present among writings for the Web, from journalistic press writings to blog posts. Rather, we will take an ethnological perspective inspired by the work of Jack Goody, who studied the role of changes in modes of communication on the development of structures and cognitive processes, the growth of knowledge, and the capacities of men to store and enrich this knowledge. Thus, "writing , especially alphabetical writing, made a new way of examining speech possible thanks to the semi-permanent form to which it gave a verbal message. This means of speech inspection broadened the field of critical activity and encouraged rationality, skepticism, and logical thought" [GOO 79, p. 86].

The shift to writing in societies whose traditions are based on oral transmission had an effect of separation and objectivization on content. According to Goody [GOO 79, p. 96]: "When a statement is put in writing it can be examined in much more detail, taken as a whole or broken down into elements, manipulated in any direction, and taken out of its context or not. In other words, it can be subjected to a whole other type of analysis and criticism than a purely verbal statement. Speech no longer depends on circumstance; it becomes timeless". We suggest that the same type of paradigm shift is potentially at work in the development of hypermedia such as with Vesta Cosy.

We believe that if this type of hypermedia is considered to be capable of supplying a new digital writing syntax, along with a visual grammar [MIL 04], it becomes pertinent to ask ourselves about the emergence of new forms of reasoning that might be supported by this type of tool, and whether the cognitive capacities of users are aided or augmented by the algorithmic processes used to carry out classic reasoning. Applications such as Vesta Cosy could also contribute to the democratization of access to these new types of reasoning that are neither linear nor arborescent, but rather function in reference to a multifactorial network that is representative of the complexity of the questions being addressed.

1.7.2. *Hyperlinked content according to diversified details*

In another sense, it is worth looking at the process of meaning construction. On the one hand, it should be noted that, since the development of computer science and then of the Web, content has become more and more inseparable from its container. This is true of web pages into which tags are inserted to code the process of reading by a navigator, as well as of the inventor of the typographical policy used in publishing a text.

Souchier [SOU 98] and Cotte [COT 04] urge us to think of "onscreen text" as a "technological co-declaration". In fact, it is possible to the authors of artifacts produced by the medium (in the sense given by MacLuhan), such as the computer programmer who makes available icons created by designers, for example, as co-deliverers of the message. This is a new way of thinking about the concept of an author, widely evoked by Doueihi [DOU 11], with regard to digital artifacts.

Another dimension of hypermedia, first observed by Alexandra Saemmer, consists of focusing on the discursive aspect of production and circulation in hyperlinks. She defines the form of a hyperlink as "the fact of linking a word or phrase to another textual segment" [SAE 15] and studies the dialogic potential of the latter, particularly in the field of journalism. This absence of "signage", which would guide the reader in his journey and describe the nature of the hyperlinked content, is also evoked by Clément [CLÉ 95], who uses stylistic appearances to describe the phenomenon: synecdochic, asyndetic and metaphorical. Here, the classic technical form of hypertext does not contribute to building the connection of the meaning of the linked content.

In an item of hypermedia, the principle of hyperlinking is applicable to all types of content and representation available in the application; it is possible to link one entity to another in the map, as well as to create a classic hypertext link in information records about entities in order to document an entity. It is also possible to interact with the knowledge model, or with predefined links for an entity placed on a map. We can also explore categories of objects present on a map and made material by polymorphic icons developed by the project's designers. Generally, information, which has meaning for a user, is hyperlinked according to several details: graphic, textual, symbolic and modeled. Thus, we can say that the form and meaning mingle and contribute together to the construction of meaning: the message becomes part of the medium.

What is specific to hypermedia such as Vesta Cosy in terms of meaning construction is that this graphic digital writing/reading is based on a journey freed from the only possible interaction, that is, to follow or not to follow a hypertext link. This type of writing stimulates different modes of perception for the user, enabling him to enter into a question via the part that has meaning for him. This is a process of appropriation based on preexisting knowledge and on the user's preferred perceptive modes. The entry points into the exploration of an issue are thus multiplied, and are not only textual or narrative. This leaves him with the ability to exercise his expertise without perceptual constraints. He can then search for the details that interest him, which is generally more difficult in textual writings and requires visual exploration of a text and rapid reading, a practice that may seem cognitively costly or difficult to acquire. This type of digital writing thus makes it possible to call on the visual prehension of the subject and paves the way for other types of reading. The user may begin by detecting recurring visual forms in a map, or note the organization of a map by groups of entities, before focusing on the labels of these entities. This reading can be seen as intuitive and non-restrictive, enabling the user to concentrate on certain aspects of an issue or on other related tasks.

1.7.3. *Disorientation, hypernarrativity and interactions*

Finding the direction of a reading has also traditionally contributed to meaning construction, particularly in an argumentative context. The direction of reading is profoundly shaken up in this case, since the concepts of beginning and end are transformed into sequences (duration or period) and into axes of graphic and interactive exploration, in favor of the idea of hypernarrativity. This may consist of being able to reconstruct the progression and reasoning of the user, possibly by using the digital traces of his navigation and his interactions within the tool.

The potential disorientation of the user, often evoked in the literature with regard to hypertext and early hypermedia, is not necessarily seen in this context as a flaw in the device, but rather as a means of causing the emergence of new conceptions and explorations or unforeseen scenarios. Each person constructs his own reading path depending on what he is looking for, and his objectives, as well as the dimensions of information of interest to the user, are partially symbolized and graphically represented.

Finally, the details of interaction with mapping make it possible to manage any potential disorientation related to the loss of the markers that are normally used to situate relationships between a whole and its parts. The organization and reorganization of the map, deformations such as semantic zoom, and functionalities such as filtering or selective display provide support in this area. Interactions with models encompassing the content of issues being addressed consist of being able to enrich the model or, in other words, being able to annotate it in order to test potential enrichment hypotheses from a perspective of the iterative improvement of knowledge models.

All of the elements discussed here, we believe, contribute to the creation of a new definition of digital writing in which information is hyperlinked according to several details: graphic, textual, symbolic, categorical and modeled.

1.8. Conclusion

In this chapter, we have introduced the Vesta Cosy project, which is still in the process of being developed, and the questions that have emerged as part of the interactions between two testing grounds. Vesta Cosy, which is a symbolic information mapping tool, is part of a complex system of interaction between theoretical knowledge models, their instantiations representing real phenomena, the role of algorithms, products of the human mind and their possible limits or developments, the display of different points of view, and, finally, the contextual use of data in the evaluation of a scenario. The testing ground based on controversy representation has enabled us to advance the process of reflection on models, particularly the argument model, in this project. Future experimentation should extend and enable the evaluation of the methodology of the controversy analysis that goes along with this area, as well as the continuation of work in progress on interactions with knowledge models.

1.9. Bibliography

[BAY 14] BAYA-LAFFITE N., COINTET J.F., "Cartographier la trajectoire de l'adaptation dans l'espace des négociations sur le climat. Changer d'échelle, red(u)ire la complexité", *Réseaux,* vol. 6, no. 188, pp. 159–198, 2014.

[BUC 08] BUCKINGHAM SHUM S., OKADA, A., "Knowledge cartography for controversies: the Iraq debate", in OKADA D.A., BUCKINGHAM SHUM S.J., SHERBORNE T., (eds), *Knowledge Cartography: Software Tools and Mapping Techniques. Advanced Information and Knowledge Processing*, vol. 1, Springer, London, 2008.

[CAL 06] CALLON M., FERRARY M., "Les réseaux sociaux à l'aune de la théorie de l'acteur-réseau", *Sociologies pratiques*, vol. 2, no. 13, pp. 37–44, 2006.

[CLE 95] CLEMENT, J., "Du texte à l'hypertexte: vers une épistémologie de la discursivité hypertextuelle", *Hypertextes et hypermédias: réalisations, outils, methods, Acheronta*, available at: http://www.acheronta.org/acheronta2/dutextel.htm, no. 2, 1995.

[CHA 07] CHATEAURAYNAUD, F., "La contrainte argumentative. Les formes de l'argumentation entre cadres délibératifs et puissances d'expression politiques", *Revue européenne des sciences sociales*, vol. XLV-136, pp. 129–148, 2007.

[COT 04] COTTE, D., "Écrits de réseaux, écrits en strates", *Hermès, La Revue*, vol. 2, pp. 109–115, 2004.

[DAV 11] DAVIES, M., "Concept mapping, mind mapping and argument mapping: what are the differences and do they matter?", *Higher Education*, vol. 62, no. 3, pp. 279–301, 2011.

[DOU 11] DOUEIHI M., *La grande conversion numérique: suivi de Rêveries d'un promeneur numérique*, Le Seuil, Paris, 2011.

[DES 16] DESFRICHES DORIA O., FAGOT C., LAVENIR C., "Vers un environnement d'interaction symbolique avec les modèles, Des cartographies sémantiques à la prise de décision", *Revue Technique et Science Informatiques*, vol. 35, no. 2, pp. 203–236, 2016.

[ELS 05] ELSTER J., "L'usage stratégique de l'argumentation", *Négociations*, vol. 2, pp. 59–82, 2005.

[FRE 15] FREDRIKSSON, S., "Du design d'information à la visualisation de données: un enjeu de transmission de sens auprès de la société civile", *I2D–Information, données & documents*, vol. 52, no. 2, p. 36, 2015.

[GEN 08] GENARD J.L., "À propos de pragmatique…", in VRANCKEN D.D., DUBOIS C., SCHOENAERS F., *Penser la négociation,* De Boeck, Brussels, 2008.

[GOO 79] GOODY, J., *La raison graphique. La domestication de la pensée sauvage*, Editions De Minuit, Paris, 1979.

[KLE 91] KLEIN G., KLINGER D., "Naturalistic decision making", *Human Systems IAC GATEWAY*, vol. XI, no. 3, 1991.

[KLE 93] KLEIN, G., *Naturalistic Decision Making: Implications for Design*, Klein Associate Inc., Fairborn, 1993.

[LEG 96] LEGRENZI P., GIROTTO V., "Mental models in reasoning and decision making processes", OAKHILL J., GARNHAM A., *Mental Models in Cognitive Science: Essays in Honour of Phil Johnson-Laird*, Psychology Press, 1996.

[LEM 07] LEMIEUX C., "À quoi sert l'analyse des controverses?", *Mil neuf cent. Revue d'histoire intellectuelle*, vol. 25, no. 1, pp. 191–212, 2007.

[LIP 97] LIPSHITZ R., STRAUSS O., "Coping with uncertainty: a naturalistic decision-making analysis", *Organizational Behavior and Human Decision Processes*, vol. 69, no. 2, pp. 149–163, 1997.

[MER 11] MERCIER H., SPERBER D., "Why do humans reason? Arguments for an argumentative theory", *Behavioral and Brain Sciences*, vol. 34, no. 2, pp. 57–74, 2011.

[MAR 12] MARCHAND P., RATINAUD P., *Être français aujourd'hui. Les mots du "grand débat" sur l'identité nationale*, Les Liens qui Libèrent, Paris, 2012.

[MIL 04] MILON, A., "Hyperdocuments et hypercartes, vers une modélisation d'écriture...", *Hermès, La Revue*, vol. 2, pp. 77–83, 2004.

[OKA 08] OKADA A.; BUCKINGHAM SHUM S., SHERBORNE T., *Knowledge Cartography: Software Tools and Mapping Techniques. Advanced Information and Knowledge Processing*, vol. 1, Springer, London, 2008.

[POI 14] POIBEAU T., "Le traitement automatique des langues pour les sciences sociales. Quelques éléments de réflexion à partir d'expériences récentes", *Réseaux,* vol. 6, no. 188, pp. 25–51, 2014.

[RAC 97] RACCAH P. Y., "L'argumentation sans la preuve: prendre son biais dans la langue", *Cognition et Interaction*, vol. 2, nos 1–2, 1997.

[RAC 05] RACCAH P.Y., "Une sémantique du point de vue: de l'intersubjectivité à l'adhésion", *L'énonciation identitaire: entre l'individuel et le collectif. Discours Social*, vol. 21, pp. 205–242, 2005.

[RAC 90] RACCAH P.Y., "Signification, sens et connaissance: une approche topique", *Cahiers de linguistique française*, vol. 11, pp. 179–198, 1990.

[RHE 93] RHEAUME J., "Les hypertextes et les hypermédias", *Revue EducaTechnologie*, available at: http://www.sites.fse.ulaval.ca/reveduc/html/vol1/no2/heth.html, vol. 1, no. 2, 1993.

[SAE 15] SAEMMER A., "Hypertexte et narrativité", *Critique*, vol. 8, pp. 637–652, 2015.

[SOU 98] SOUCHIER E., "L'image du texte pour une théorie de l'énonciation éditoriale", *Les Cahiers de médiologie*, vol. 2, pp. 137–145, 1998.

[THE 09] THEVENOT C., PERRET P., "Le développement du raisonnement dans la résolution de problèmes: l'apport de la théorie des modèles mentaux", *Développements*, vol. 2, no. 2, pp. 49–56, 2009.

[THE 06] THEVENOT L., *L'action au pluriel*, La Découverte, Paris, 2006.

[TRI 98] TRICOT A., NANARD J., "Un point sur la modélisation des tâches de recherche d'informations dans le domaine des hypermédias", in *Les hypermédias, approches cognitives et ergonomiques*, Hermès, Paris, 1998.

[VEN 12] VENTURINI T., "Building on faults", *Public Understanding of Science*, vol. 21, no. 7, pp. 796–812, 2012.

[VEN 10] VENTURINI T., "Diving in magma", *Public Understanding of Science*, vol. 19, no. 3, pp. 258–273, 2010.

[WEI 79] WEICK K.E., *The Social Psychology of Organizing*, Addison Wesley, Reading, 1979.

2

Training in Digital Writing Through the Prism of Tropisms: Case Studies and Propositions

2.1. Abstract

The objective of this chapter is to present six digital technology tropisms that constitute a formalization, which helps in characterizing and thinking about digital writing: abstraction, addressing, connection, duplication, transformation and universality. These tropisms are defined based on the observation that digital writing responds to a logical sequence of mechanization of intellectual activity, and that these activities are transformed by this mechanization and the manipulation of content it involves. This formalization has a heuristic value in that it aids in the understanding and comprehension of digital objects. It is currently mobilized in theoretical training in digital writing in the university and professional contexts. We will pay special attention to the digital writing training deployed at the University of Crédit Agricole (IFCAM). On the basis of this experiment, we will propose a general scenario for training in digital writing.

2.2. Introduction

This chapter follows on the heels of previous publications introducing the principle of digital technology tropisms in the context of digital writing [CRO 12, CRO 15]. It is both a generalization beyond the context of

---

Chapter written by Stéphane CROZAT.

writing and an update, mainly in terms of exploitation for training in digital information literacy.

The objective is to present six key concepts – tropisms of digital technology – which aid in thinking about and characterizing digital technology. These are abstraction, addressing, connection, duplication, transformation and universality. These tropisms are defined based on the observation that digital writing responds to a logical sequence of mechanization of intellectual activity, and that these activities are transformed by this mechanization. Learning to read, research and write in the digital era means understanding how digital technology is changing the world in which we are evolving. The reading grid constituted by these tropisms can contribute to this understanding.

2.3. Issue: theoretical approach to digital technology

2.3.1. *The possibility of mechanizing intellectual labor*

Intellectual labor is not only composed of creative acts of thought, but also characterized by repetitive acts of thought such as the manipulation of texts (looking through them, comparing them, following references, archiving them, etc.). Bush [BUS 45] suggested that these repetitive (or repeatable) acts of thought could be mechanized: "For the [repetitive thought] there are, and may be, powerful mechanical aids" [BUS 45] and proposed Memex, a mechanized library that would enable users to manipulate, read, annotate and link texts [DAL 09]. In this, it was an instrument mechanizing intellectual labor. Reading does not simply mean interpreting a text, and writing means more than just inscribing a text; in both cases, it is necessary to carry out manipulations in order to make these texts available for reading and writing. Opening a book or picking up a pen are acts that have become so trivial as to seem unnoticeable today, but when we manipulate thousands of texts or produce as many annotations, the intellectual effort spent on text manipulation far exceeds what is necessary for reading or writing *per se*:

> "In fact, every time one combines and records facts in accordance with established logical processes, the creative aspect of thinking is concerned only with the selection of the data and the process to be employed and the manipulation thereafter is repetitive in nature and hence a matter fit to be relegated to the machine." [BUS 45]

The mechanization of intellectual activity is therefore possible, in the sense of assisting with tasks that precede and prolong purely interpretative and creative acts.

The principle of the mechanization of reasoning was initially explored mainly in the field of mathematics through the concept of the calculating machine. Bush's main contribution consisted of giving form to the idea of the mechanization of acts of reading and writing: "The repetitive processes of thought are not confined however, to matters of arithmetic and statistics" [BUS 45]. In this, he anticipated the versatility that future machines would develop thanks to the technological and industrial advances already in progress: "[The advanced arithmetical machines of the future] will be far more versatile than present commercial machines, so that they may readily be adapted for a wide variety of operations" [BUS 45].

Nelson [NEL 82] would later use the term "literary machines" to designate the programs he helped invent, which made it possible to effectively manipulate (record, link, copy, cite, archive, search, etc.) digitized texts. It is worth noting, however, that this was a mechanization of the means of thinking, and not of thinking itself. The questions of whether human thought can be fully mechanized, or if machines can think – questions central to the artificial intelligence movement, which began in the 1950s – are not part of this discussion; suffice to observe, as Bush did, that at least part of the activity of thought can be mechanized, and to agree with Goody [GOO 77] that thought cannot be independent of the means of thinking in the study of the implications of the mechanization of the means of thinking on thought.

The role universally occupied by computers in our intellectual activities shows that it is indeed our process of thought itself that is concerned by this mechanization. After all, what act of reading or writing these days is not preceded, extended or included in a process carried out by a machine?

2.3.2. Digitization of content

Bush's vision had a great deal to do with the work of Kurt Gödel. In 1931, in order to demonstrate his theory of incompleteness, Gödel created a system that enabled any statement to be coded in the form of numbers. The conversion into numbers of textual statements made it possible to generalize the principles of mechanization by calculation: "Ever since then, we have been able to mechanize meaningful expressions" [BAC 07, p. 26]. Gödel's particular needs placed the use of his coding system within the realm of mathematics, but he also digitized expressions which no longer had meaning as numbers. The procedure is applicable to any type of content; in this sense, it is an example of the systematic digitization of a text.

(	∃	x	)	(	x	=	s	y	)
8	4	11	9	8	11	5	7	13	9

Table 2.1. *Coding of "an x exists such that x is the immediate successor of y" (which means that every number has an immediate successor) [NAG 89, p. 73]*

Any code can be processed mechanically, and any statement can be coded; therefore, the means and products of intellectual work can be mechanized. Digital data is homogeneous; "the same principles are applicable to all digital objects" [BAC 04], and it is universal: "all content and all knowledge can be given digital expression" [BAC 04].

Digital data and computers are the constituents of a general technical procedure that can be used to mechanize any intellectual work. This does not mean that these processes are equivalent to thought, or that thinking can be reduced to these processes, but it does mean that our acts of thought fit into this mechanized environment and are profoundly affected by it.

2.3.3. *"It has been manipulated": manipulation as a source of digital content*

Bachimont [BAC 07] characterizes the noema of digital data – that is, what we must understand and think with regard to digital data – as "it has been manipulated". Interpreting the semiotic manifestation of digital content means, above all, becoming aware that this is a manifestation of a digital encryption that cannot be accessed directly (because it is recorded in digital memory), and that this manifestation is the result of a set of manipulations that have enabled it to be created via the peripheral devices of writing (mouse, keyboard, etc.), its storage in a digital memory (magnetic, optic) and finally its reproduction by a reading device (screen, printer, etc.). The term "content" in this case harks back to the idea of information inscribed on a material support. The support makes it possible to fix content in a format while materially influencing this formatting. An item of digital content is thus a fragment of inscription on a digital support [BAC 08].

For example, to read an e-mail is to read an item of digital content that has been extensively manipulated:

– characters have been encoded using a keyboard into binary form according to a certain format (ASCII, Unicode, etc.);

– these binary sequences (which we will call S) have been stored in the memory of the computer used to write the e-mail (which we will call the Sender);

– S has had other binary sequences added to it, such as metadata pertaining to the e-mail: sender, recipient, date sent, etc.;

– the Sender computer has sent S to another computer responsible for managing the sending of its e-mail (we will call it Server1). In order to do this S, has had to comply with a communication protocol and to be associated with new digital information (the address used to locate Server1 for example);

– the Server1 computer has transmitted S to a new computer (we will call it Server2) associated with the recipient;

– the recipient's computer (called Recipient) has communicated with Server2 to be notified of the existence of the e-mail and then to obtain a copy of S;

– Recipient has stored S in its memory and then transformed it in order to illuminate pixels on a screen to enable its reading.

2.3.4. *"And it will be again": manipulation as the future of digital content*

I suggest that "it will be" should be added to "it has been". All digital content becomes part of a manipulation that recurs every time the content is accessed or used.

Although we have seen the process of manipulation at work in the simple exchange of an e-mail, we must always remember that this process has not been completed, and in fact it never really will be. When I "close" the e-mail, I request a manipulation that causes the e-mail to disappear from my screen. When I open it again to reread it, I request a new manipulation and then of course when I want to answer it, move it, print it, delete it or restore it, each of my operations including those that seem the most trivial and "direct" (i.e. which do not seem to trigger a calculation, such as scrolling through the text or highlighting it with the mouse) places the digital content back into the dynamic of calculation.

It is important not only to interpret digital content as the result of a past process, but also to see it as an intermediate state in an ongoing process of construction, deconstruction and reconstruction: as a future, as a set of potential manipulations to come.

It is this manipulatory future of digital content that I suggest should be designated by the "it will be".

2.4. Proposition: tropisms of digital content

2.4.1. *The concept of tropism*

Digital objects, constructed in this or that context to fulfill this or that objective, are singular, fashioned by the environment in which they are created and evolve. However, these objects incorporate functions that are identified systematically: interaction with user, parametrability of presentation, multiplicity of semiotic forms, diffusion to others, multiplication of copies, conservation of archives, etc. The theory of technical tendencies, proposed by André Leroi-Gourhan [LER 45], helps us to think about the physical dynamic that imposes itself on technical objects and confers universal characteristics upon them. We propose characterizing this tendency in the form of six tropisms: addressing, abstraction, connection, duplication, transformation and universality.

A tropism is defined in biology as the directional reaction of an organism to the stimuli produced by its environment. We propose transposing this term to characterize the forces that naturally orientate the functions of digital objects. The term "naturally" here should be taken with the double meaning of:

– according to nature, based on what digital technology is, that is, a mechanical process of manipulation of discretized components of information;

– and by default, if things are left to develop without specifically constraining them.

Our approach is neither essentialist nor determinist, in the sense that it reduces a technical object to its nature, or that this technical object is completely determined by its nature. Rather, we believe that there is an essence or nature proper to the technical object, determined by its physical properties and its relationship with its associated environment, and that it is not possible to think of the technical object correctly without also considering this nature:

> "The greatest cause of alienation in the modern world lies in this misreading of the machine, which is not alienation caused by the machine, but by the misunderstanding of its nature and its essence, by its absence from the world of meanings, and its omission from the table of values and concepts that make up culture." [SIM 58]

We also believe that technology is autonomous; technical objects are no longer defined as utensils in slavery to humans, but rather as technical entities [SIM 58]. Objects are not constructed according to a schema defined theoretically by a designer; they are formed within an environment, within which the humans who construct and use them, the natural elements and other machines form a network of interactions. The study of the technical entities constituted by digital objects, software platforms for writing or reading, for example, requires us to consider this autonomy. The idea is therefore to integrate into our process of interpretation of digital phenomena, the awareness of concepts, which will allow us to grasp this autonomy in order to endow ourselves with a critical apparatus that takes it into account.

2.4.2. *Modeling of functional tendencies of digital objects*

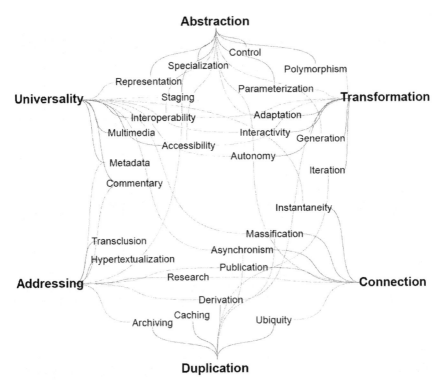

Figure 2.1. *Summary representation of digital tropisms*

2.5. Detailed description of tropisms

2.5.1. *Abstraction: it has been coded and will be recoded*

All numeric content has been coded according to a given model, and will be coded again according to other models within each system that exploits it.

All digitization is a representation of reality through digital modeling. This modeling is based on an abstraction in the sense that it is a separation from reality, is a construction intended for manipulation (algorithmic in this case) and is a simplification of reality.

The main functions are:

– Polymorphism: digital technology makes it possible to calculate multiple forms of presentation from identical resources.

– Control: digital technology can be used to guide the creation of content and to ensure compliance with previously set rules.

– Staging: digital technology makes it possible to break down content into units, which are then organized to recommend a path of consultation.

– Representation: digital technology allows information to be made available for viewing in graphic form.

– Specialization: digital technology makes it possible to create models proper to each type of problem or need encountered.

– Parameter-setting: digital technology enables the creation of reproducible content according to previously set parameters.

2.5.2. *Addressing: it has been found and will be found again*

All digital content has an address that has been used to identify and find this content, and will enable it to be found again later. Digital entities are independent and unequivocally dissociable; it is always possible to assign them a unique address – that is, a means of designating them specifically. This address makes it possible to access any piece of content directly.

The main functions are:

– Hypertextualization: digital technology enables us to represent content such as the nodes of a graph linked by explicit references.

– Transclusion: digital technology is used to integrate third-party content into a piece of content in order to display this third-party content as if it were an integral constituent of the whole.

– Searching: digital technology allows us to conduct a search within a piece of content and its metadata.

2.5.3. *Connection: it has been transmitted and will be retransmitted*

All digital code belongs within a logical transmission sequence. On networked computers, this code is often transmitted throughout the process of its production, and in any case this occurs regularly throughout its life cycle, via a network or an external storage medium. Any digital code can be transported by any medium over any network; digital machines are built to be connectable, in the sense that what they manipulate is communicable. The connection of computers within the global Internet network leads to the permanent transmission and retransmission of the information possessed by each of these computers.

The main functions are:

– Publication: digital technology can make a piece of content available for reading worldwide.

– Instantaneity: digital technology enables multiple individuals to access and modify the same object at the same time.

– Asynchronism: digital technology enables multiple individuals to work successively on the same object, in order to build it jointly.

– Massification: digital technology makes it possible to extend the volume and range of any digital system significantly, up to the global level.

2.5.4. *Duplication: it has been copied and will be recopied*

All digital content has been duplicated, both within the various components of the computer and within the network to which it belongs, and it will be duplicated again during most of its uses; using a piece of digital information first means making a copy of it. For example, saving of a document to a hard disk means copying what is in the RAM (and not actually of moving it) and sending of a message via a network means duplicating it from server to server, in a manner that resembles a telegraph more than it does the postal service (which transports a message that is only present in one place at a time).

The main functions are:

– Archiving: digital technology tracks the evolution of a piece of content by saving its different versions.

– Ubiquity: digital technology makes it possible for the same piece of content to be theoretically present in multiple places at the same time.

– Derivation: digital technology allows new content to be developed from a copy of previously existing content.

– Caching: digital technology can be used to create copies of an item of content in order to simplify subsequent access by machines or human users.

2.5.5. *Transformation: it has been changed and will be changed again*

All digital content has always already been transformed when it is accessed, and will be transformed again each time we manipulate it. Information saved in the memory of a digital medium is coded in the form of binary sequences. The principle of any computer application consists of transforming this information via algorithms executed by the machine in order to store the information, reproduce it or process it according to user requests. The intrinsic functioning of digital technology by necessity involves the systematic transformation of information.

The main functions are:

– Iteration: digital technology makes it possible to cause content to evolve progressively in successive stages.

– Interactivity: digital technology is used to program interactions between users and machines.

– Generation: digital writing makes it possible to create content automatically from both new and previously existing content.

– Adaptation: digital technology enables us to act on an existing item of content in order to adapt it for a particular use.

– Autonomy: digital technology enables an item of digital content to modify itself according to the information collected from outside of the system.

2.5.6. *Universality: it has been integrated and will be reintegrated*

All digital content has been integrated into a digital set, and will be integrated again into the digital sets that require it; any information can and will eventually be integrated. Digital representation has no theoretical meaning; any information can be encoded using the appropriate format, which can always be established. Digital support is thus a universal medium that makes it possible to incorporate any information once it has been encoded into numbers.

The main functions are:

– Multimedia: digital technology can be used to compose a piece of content from various semiotic forms (text, images, sound, video, etc.).

– Metadata: digital content enables the addition of metadata to content.

– Annotation: digital technology makes it possible to integrate text and paratext.

– Accessibility: digital technology can be used to integrate and configure multiple alternative formats for a single item of content so that it will remain accessible regardless of the context of reading.

– Interoperability: digital technology enables programs to exchange items of data in order to share their functions.

2.6. Application: training in digital technology with tropisms

2.6.1. *Training in ordinary digital writing at the University of Technology of Compiègne (UTC)*

The UTC course "Ordinary Digital Writing Studies" includes an introduction to tropisms and allows students to experiment through exercises. One exercise consists of producing a text in 20 min, as a group, using synchronous writing software such as Framapad (http://framapad.org), and then breaking down the process using functions (instantaneity) and tropisms (connections). Another exercise consists of studying traceability (archiving, caching, generation) through the examination on the Web of deliberate (written) and involuntary (automatic) traces. Students are also assigned projects that include identifying the tropisms involved in the writing tools they use. These exercises have been the subject of a detailed study [CAI 15].

Figure 2.2. *Example of the educational use of Etherpad at UTC [CAI 15]*

2.6.2. *BABA strings (abstraction and polymorphism)*

We have also designed several prototypes of editorial strings that act as demonstrators of tropisms [CRO 14], with the objective of using rapid (less than 1 h) writing experiments to underline typical manifestations of tropisms.

The BABA1 string can be an entry point into a series of exercises with these tools, as it can also be used to quickly demonstrate the principle of an editorial string and to familiarize users with the manipulation of the writing environment. Scenari (http://scenari-platform.org) is used to set up these strings. The BABA1 string is used to write a text according to four possible models: the first is very free and highly graphic, reproducing a classic WYSIWYG text-processing procedure, while the second is a relatively generic procedural model. The last two are highly specific, with one devoted to recipes and the other to protocols in experimental science. The educational scenario envisaged is based on the capture of a recipe according to these four models. The concern here is to make users aware of the abstraction proper to digital technology by emphasizing the model underlying each writing environment (although this is generally implicit).

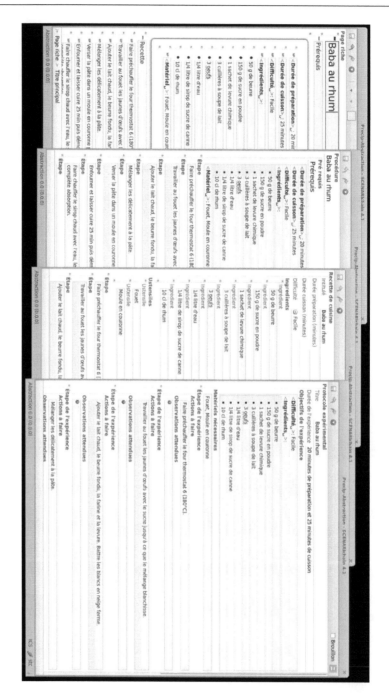

Figure 2.3. *Example of the educational editorial string for "Abstraction"*

---

1. Create a "rich page" and reproduce the recipe in the file **baba.pdf**

Expected observations: something close is achieved, but not exact; the writing software enables a certain field of possibility

2. Create a "Procedure" and recreate the recipe

Expected observations: field-specific language should be used (that of the procedure) but the graphic language is simplified; the most typical model shows adjustment problems

3. Create a "Recipe" and recreate the recipe

Expected observations: a highly adapted field model simplifies the work (adjusted field-specific language, more graphic language understood) and to check the results (fewer errors); loss of graphic freedom

4. Create a "Protocol" and recreate the recipe

Expected observations: this field model is not well adapted (it is a procedure, not a recipe) and is therefore difficult to use. Workarounds are necessary (duration); errors are encountered (red crosses), and the publication shows flaws

Conclusions sought:

- There is always a model in a writing software platform; we cannot do everything (**Abstraction** tropism)

- A model can be more graphic or more field-specific; it may be more or less adapted to the context (**Specialization** functions)

- The underlying model must be appropriate; a well-adapted field-specific model optimizes and controls writing (**Control** function)

Figure 2.4. *Example of "Abstraction" educational scenario*

This same string can also be used for publication according to four formats (Web, mobile device, paper and slide show) in order to work on "Abstraction/Polymorphism" in a second exercise.

2.6.3. SolSys string (staging, hypertextualization)

Other strings can be used to study other tropisms and functions. For example, one of these focuses on "Abstraction/Staging" and "Addressing/Hypertextualization" (Figure 2.5). It consists of staging several routes within a set of pages describing the stars in the solar system, in order to experiment with multiple forms of organization (linear, multilinear, arborescent, reticular, random, combinatorial, on-demand) and several types of linking (navigation, interpolation, augmentation).

Figure 2.5. *Example of the educational editorial strings for "Staging" and "Hypertextualization" (reverse engineering to the left, publication to the right)*

Figure 2.6. *Example of the educational editorial chain for "Transclusion" and "Interactivity"*

2.6.4. *BD string (transclusion, interactivity)*

Another string focuses on "Addressing/Transclusion" and "Transformation/ Interactivity" by making it possible to rearrange the fragments of a teaching support containing expository parts and quizzes (Figure 2.6). Another string is planned for "Universality/Multimedia, based on a simplified version of the free Webmédia model in Scenari (http://scenari-platform.org/webmedia). Our goal is to be able to illustrate each tropism with at least one educational string and an associated scenario.

2.7. Case study: training in digital writing at IFCAM

2.7.1. *Introduction to training*

IFCAM is the university of the Crédit Agricole group. It offers training in various formats (e-learning, custom, leading to a qualification, school and work experience alternating, etc.). Qualifications include a Bachelor's degree in Individual Client Consultation (BAC+3). This degree is intended for employees who already hold a BAC+2 degree; it is studied alongside professional activity, usually remotely, which takes 2–3 years. A total of 5,000 to 10,000 Crédit Agricole employees take the program each year.

IFCAM's newest version of this Bachelor's degree program includes a 24 credit module entitled "MOOC digital writing ". The first session of this training program began on 8 March 2016, with 588 employees enrolled for the 8-week course.

This module provides theoretical and practical training in digital writing, based in particular on an introduction to the concepts of digital technology such as computational reasoning, tropisms of digital technology and the relationship between digital writing, programming and encoding.

The class is offered as a fully remote MOOC, with the pace of instruction tailored and the possible number of participants reaching several thousands. The training program is open to all employees of the group, including those who are not enrolled in a Bachelor's degree program (although most of the participants in the first session are Bachelor's degree candidates). It is anticipated that the course will be eventually offered even more widely to Crédit Agricole clients and even to the general public. The training includes an initial synchronized remote stage.

2.7.2. *Training scenario*

The training program is designed to equip learners with concepts that will allow them to understand the functioning of digital technology and to develop a reflective stance with regard to the practice of these concepts.

The scenario begins in week 1 with a remote, collaborative, synchronized writing experience using Etherpad, intended to increase learner awareness and to introduce concepts. Weeks 2 and 3 are devoted to the consultation of resources introducing theoretical concepts in the form of audiovisual presentations by experts and multimedia content to be studied independently with formative self-evaluations. This first 4-week section concludes with an assignment for learners to analyze three individual writing samples using the concepts they have learned. The second section of the scenario, which also lasts 4 weeks, is made up of new resources focusing on the evolution of reading and writing in the context of digital technology, and of a second assignment involving an overnight observation exercise (reading) and the duplication of this observation (writing).

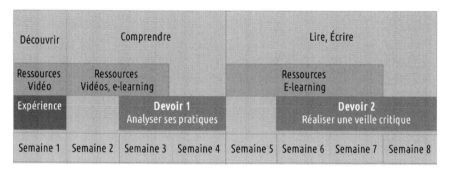

Figure 2.7. *IFCAM scenario for the first session of the MOOC on digital writing. For a color version of this figure, see www.iste.co.uk/reyes/hypermedia.zip*

2.7.3. *An experience to increase awareness using Etherpad*

The first sequence is a remote, synchronized learning experience conducted in groups of 10 learners with one or two group leaders in a virtual classroom. Sessions lasting 21 h are conducted for 100 students. The current sequence used at IFCAM has been strongly inspired by the teaching practices of Isabelle Cailleau at UTC in her course "Ordinary Digital Writing Studies", whose objective is to develop digital literacy among student engineers.

Students connect with one another on a synchronized public writing tool (a publicly hosted Etherpad such as Framapad) to write a joint text focusing on a discussion pertaining to their profession. After 20 min, the session is jointly debriefed and the group's observations illuminated by explanations using tropisms. Certain particularly salient practices or functions emphasize the major issues in digital technology. For example, Etherpad's system of archiving and replay makes it possible to record several thousand versions and to replay the whole writing process from the beginning of the experience, letter by letter; learners are asked about the concerns of this function and the tropism of duplication. Another discussion is opened on addressing, since content has been produced on a public site that is accessible to everyone, without the question of publication having been previously posed.

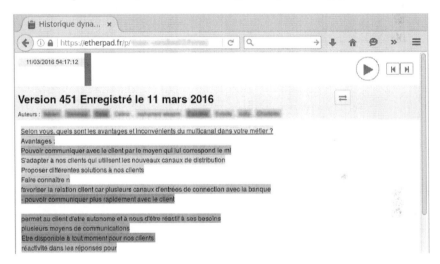

Figure 2.8. *Etherpad archiving interface as used at IFCAM. For a color version of this figure, see www.iste.co.uk/reyes/hypermedia.zip*

This sequence causes a cognitive impact by involving an exercise that justifies why it is necessary to study the question of writing, and why the study of theory is useful as well. It increases students' awareness of the issues inherent in digital writing; they realize that our intuitive practices (what we do without thinking) can be problematic, which helps with our subsequent acceptance of the reflective attitude (I force myself to think about what I am doing when I do it). In addition, the sequence is enjoyable and enables most students to discover a new way of writing through synchronized collaboration. Finally, it creates a group effect which can be put to use during subsequent activities (and which compensates in part for the remote and solitary learning involved in the course).

The device has worked perfectly, the ideal being to have between 5 and 10 participants. If there are less than three students, the group leader must play the role of a student, and if there are more than 10, work on the pad starts to become too muddled. One route that has not yet been explored consists of distributing the participants over two pads and then conducting a joint debriefing.

2.7.4. *Understanding the properties of digital technology and theoretical content*

After this learning experience, students are left to independently consult theoretical resources: graphic reasoning and computational reasoning; tropisms of digital technology; computer functions; principles of coding. One resource in particular has been designed specifically to present professional situations typical of the context of Crédit Agricole, for which learners must identify the tropisms and functions in play using an interactive map.

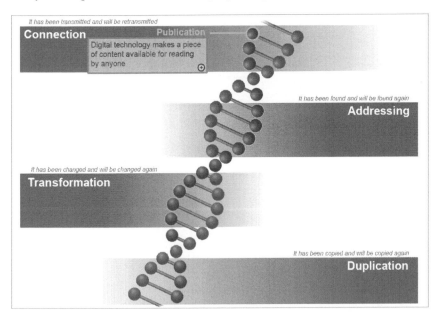

Figure 2.9. *Interactive map of the properties of digital technologies established using tropisms and functions. For a color version of this figure, see www.iste.co.uk/reyes/hypermedia.zip*

2.7.5. *Assignment 1: analysis of practices*

Next, learners are given a mandatory assignment to analyze writing situations. They are first instructed on the concept of reflective practice, that is, the act of forcing ourselves to think about what we are doing at the same time as we are doing it; with the objective of analyzing the way in which they do this, in order to modify the way they do it.

The assignment consists of describing three professional and personal writing situations, criticizing them and putting them in perspective using the theoretical concepts previously studied. The challenge is to discover how these concepts operate in daily professional life and to internalize the reflective approach that is one of the objectives of the training. These assignments were in the process of being corrected as of April 2016.

2.7.6. *Part two: reading and writing, second assignment (critical observation)*

The second part of the training course is organized much like the first: the independent study of resources followed by an assignment. Learning resources address the effect of digital technology and the Web on our reading practices, the most classic elements of written expression adapted to digital writing (such as e-mail), and information on publication practices (code, e-reputation, intellectual property, etc.).

The second assignment consists of conducting an observation on a freely chosen subject and then exploiting this observation as part of a set of exchanges with a colleague or client. As with the first assignment, a work of reflective analysis and engagement with concepts is required. The challenge of this assignment lies less in the work of writing itself than in the reflective attitude associated with it, and the opportunity to work with theoretical concepts.

2.8. Perspective: a MOOC "digital literacy" project

These cases of training in digital literacy in action at UTC and IFCAM have led us to propose a massive, open training project in digital literacy. The objectives of this training would be for students to know how to find their way in the world of digital objects by mobilizing concepts that will allow them to understand the functioning of these objects, and to know how to adapt their reading and production of digital writings to any context by developing a reflective attitude toward their own practices. The training would require no specific prerequisites and could be aimed at high school students (all years) and university students (Bachelor's and Master's degree levels), as well as professionals (business training) and the public at large (personal enrichment). A second version could be developed targeting a younger segment of the public (high school and primary school).

2.8.1. *Defining information literacy*

Information literacy encompasses all of the *"human activities which involve the use of writing, in reception and production. It places a set of basic linguistic and graphic skills at the service of practices, whether they be technical, cognitive, social, or cultural"* [JAF 04].

"All of the knowledge in reading and writing needed for a person to be functional in society (GDT)."

> According to the Organization for Economic Cooperation and Development (OECD), information literacy is "the ability to understand use written information in everyday life, at home, at work, and in the community, in order to achieve personal goals and broaden one's knowledge and abilities" (in the report published on 14 June 2000, *Information literacy in the Information Era*) (Wikipedia).

Information literacy, unlike the simple terms *literacy* and *illiteracy*, is defined more broadly than the simple ability to read and write, which is necessary but not enough for information literacy. It enables us to see writing not only as a technique of inscription or a simple channel of communication [REU 06], but as a relationship with the world, or even a condition of access to the world, which it itself produced particularly by writing:

> "Entering into the written word means, on both the societal and ontogenetic levels, entering another universe, a culture of the written word, which modifies—or is liable to modify [...]—the relationship to words and language, and thus to the world." [REU 06]

Information literacy is thus a skill set that requires technical mastery of writing and reading as well as the knowledge of codes of communication, but is not limited to these. It is also based on more fundamental knowledge that enables us not only to belong to a culture and a tradition, but also to participate in creating and inventing them. Information literacy is a necessity and challenge [REU 06] – a game of knowledge and power [GOO 07] – the alternative to which is proletarianization as defined by Stiegler [STI 06], that is, the loss of the ability to affect the world around us:

> "Concerns over educational failure are a reflection of the new requirements of a world which, since electronic and digital technologies have replaced the mechanical [...], and since we are witnessing the incredibly rapid emergence of new knowledge, demands the mastery of abstract models which are separate from the empiricism of daily life and from mimetic trial and error. At every level of the professional and social hierarchy, the person who has not received a solid initial education risks being quickly left behind to grope blindly in a universe whose workings he does not understand." [CHU 13, p. 8]

2.8.2. *Defining digital technology*

In the context of digital technology, one hypothesis we are working under is that it is necessary to acquire an understanding of the technological principles that govern the digital world. Digital technology can be defined according to the following four layers:

– It is a representation of information in the form of numbers, which occurs via the construction of a discretization and a manipulation (Bachimont). The idea of a systematic codification of the world in the form of symbols goes back to the 18th Century (Leibniz) and took firm root in the early 20th Century (Gödel).

– It is a representation that enables the representation of its own manipulations. While a loom is an automatic machine that is externally programmed, a computer is a universal Turing machine, that is, a machine that can be used to represent any automatic process (the program is a given and is thus calculable itself; therefore, the machine can develop its own program).

– It is a specific technology of representation, which is currently based largely on the binary principles and architecture of von Neumann.

– It is communication technology in the form of a network of representations, which relies on a structure of machines, standards and protocols (TCP/IP, etc.).

2.8.3. *Issue: teaching information literacy*

Information literacy is thus the sum of knowledge and skills necessary to mobilize digital technology as a technique for the coding and manipulation of information with computers within networks. However, there are three specific characteristics of information literacy, in particular which make its teaching problematic.

First, information literacy calls for new practices of reading and writing, which are inherent in the transformation of the medium; therefore, writing and reading correctly with a computer involves mastering tools with multiple functions that are constantly changing. This problem might be considered the easiest one to address, with procedural training available for the tools. *However, technological development is significant and rapid, and tool-oriented skills are quickly rendered obsolete,* so they must be regularly updated (which is complicated by a tool-based approach).

Second, digital technology does not belong to an established tradition in which codes have been theoretically established that are subsequently valid; these codes are still in the process of being invented and compiled. Thus, we are in a state of limited information literacy, as posited by Goody, that is, a state of partial and imperfect mastery of this new kind of writing [GOO 07]. We might ask ourselves, although this is a hypothesis that it is not necessary to address for now, whether digital technology is not intrinsically a vector of constant evolution for which it will be difficult, if not impossible, to stabilize the codes, in which case we would be in a sort of permanent state of limited information literacy.

Finally, digital writing implies a wider world in comparison to graphic writing, in the sense that there is a shift from written text to digital objects. Digital writing can have a direct effect on the physical world. It is the particular nature of all technology to be both technology for thought and technology for action at the same time, but text and the hammer fall into categories that are relatively distinct, whereas the computer represents a complete fusion (even though there are still many specialized software programs, the dividing lines are becoming thinner and thinner). The universality of the computer is contained in the very technical principle of the universal Turing machine: the computer manipulates symbols with symbols, and can thus write its own program. The evolution of input–output interfaces does the rest. Digital writing thus produces digital objects that enable writing. *Digital technology is an environment in its own right*, whose laws have to do with its specific technical characteristics.

The issue inherent in the teaching of information literacy is the mastery of an emerging and continually changing technological – and therefore cultural and technical – environment.

2.8.4. *Components of teaching information literacy*

How can information literacy be taught in a context like this? We believe that, rather than training people to use ephemeral and debatable tools and codes, it is a matter of equipping them with the means of adapting to multiple new codes and of participating in the establishment of their own codes.

We do not therefore plan to linger – or even spend any time at all – on the teaching of procedural knowledge, whether technical (tools) or communicational (good practices). We will use these only as examples and illustrations of the current reality.

Rather, we propose working on a more fundamental kind of teaching, one based on "abstract models", which will provide access to the "universe" of digital technology and enable learners to understand its "workings", in the sense proposed by P. Meirieu [CHU 13]. We believe a reflective approach should be developed, that is, a method enabling the learner to decide how he or she will exist in the digital world.

This fundamental basis can, however, be paired with more localized training concerning the proper use of social networks, openness to self-publication or the integration of business procedures and tools.

2.8.5. *Format: challenges of MOOCs*

Why have we envisioned this training as an MOOC and not in a more classic, university-type, in-class learning form? We believe there is a great deal of merit in training people quickly (in a few years) and in large numbers (tens of thousands). MOOCs are a potential vehicle for achieving these kinds of results. In addition, the development of quality teaching in MOOC mode – that is, firmly based on independence and personal engagement – is more demanding than in-class, compulsory teaching in terms of finalization of supports, scenario sequencing, educational tools, etc. Thus, in a sense, "he who can do more can also do less", and training designed in the MOOC format could easily be adapted to more traditional settings.

MOOCs are also an interesting manner of taking teaching outside the walls of the university, thus making it able to reach a population that is not exclusively composed of students enrolled in an institution of higher learning. This means that it can be a bridge between different groups, with students, the professional training sector and the public education sector. In this way, teaching becomes exoteric in the Greek sense of opening learning up to the public and the world.

Finally, MOOCs are a way of becoming part of the digital environment, to explore its laws (read it) and its potential (write it). Training in information literacy thus becomes an area for research and experimentation in information literacy. Beyond serving as an example and encouraging reflectiveness, according to the same reflective logic on which our concept is based – we believe the only way to implement this training using the hypotheses we have posed is to construct a system that participates in its own construction.

Here, we can draw a parallel with the idea of technological research as it is thought of and practiced at UTC: in order to study new technological objects, we must build them, and it is by constructing them that we learn about them and that we can understand them. Technology is anthropologically constitutive (the "TAC" thesis); it shapes humans as much as humans shape it:

> "On the negative side, this thesis goes against an image of technology as anthropologically constituted. Anthropologically constituted technology is technology as the simple product of

human work or intelligence, as posterior to a humanity that is anterior to it and independent from it. On the positive side, it encourages a program of research intended to understand concretely how technology modifies our sense of place in the world." [STE 10]

In concrete terms, this attitude will lead us to explore various technological and educational methods, based in particular on independent learning, peer-to-peer learning and/or remote experience – not in order to fulfill needs (which are already there), but to explore possibilities (which remain to be created). We propose, therefore, that the MOOC is the most logical format in terms of its size and openness with regard to its target public, and not as a given method, since this may be specified by a specific publisher (FUN, Khan Academy or Coursera). Indeed, it is by detaching ourselves from these details that we can maintain diversity, which Boullier [BOU 13] makes a condition for the principle of openness of MOOCs, in the face of the potential standardization that mass learning systems intrinsically possess. Stiegler [LAC 13] reminds us that in order to adapt content to suit themselves, readers must make themselves into writers, and that in order for parity to exist, tools of contribution must enable real digital writing. Learners must be able to have the same abilities to write as teachers, rather than being limited to the production of textual statements that are barely structured or not structured at all and posted on forums or blogs, confining their possibilities of contribution to formats of restricted expression.

The challenge here is to maintain a high degree of technical agility in order to retain our capacity to explore, invent tools and shape the environment.

Finally, we maintain that it is necessary to preserve, within the conditions of mass-learning and openness of the MOOC, the requirements of a classic training program, specifically the monitoring of learners by teachers and tutors (for which peer-to-peer learning is no substitute, despite its merits), and certification via a valid assessment (of which at least half must be based on individual work that can be checked).

2.8.6. *Proposition: content and scenario for an information literacy MOOC*

In this final section, we will propose a general training scenario based on around 150 h of learning work (or 6 ECTS according to the university standard). The training is broken down into six sequences of 24 h, with each sequence being further divided into three blocs of 8 h. The complete training program may be taken over a short period (12 weeks, or 1 university semester) or a longer period (1 or 2 years of continuing training, typically). Enabling multiple learning timelines to coexist is a significant challenge, a point beginning to be raised by MOOC organizers in 2016.

Training will be structured around groups of 20–50 learners, with one tutor per group. These groups will particularly help with the organization of peer-to-peer work. Tutors will be responsible for individualized monitoring, moderation and assessment for certification. Peer-to-peer reviews will be based on the involvement of one learner with the contribution of another learner. These reviews are composed of a peer-to-peer assessment with a grade and a commentary and a set of suggestions for improvement in the form of tickets. Tickets can also be assessed (moderated, ranked) by the group. They act as a list of tasks to do for the learner concerned (improvement of his/her work) or, in the case of recurring contributions, for a learner continuing with an editorial project (see below). Tutors' interventions occur by the same method as peers, with greater power of expression (typically a higher assessment weight) and a more systematic role of comment moderation.

Learners are equipped with Scenari editorial strings in order to experiment with tropisms and for real production in the context of educational synopsis reading exercises (ESR) and digital work (DW). An ESR exercise consists of creating a remote training support around a text having to do with the field. A DW exercise consists of creating a work of literature or a game around a freely chosen theme, but using advanced tropes in digital writing (multimedia, hypertextualization, etc.). In both cases, learners produce an original document or improve an existing document.

Sequence 1: Introduction to the digital environment through tropisms
Bloc 1.1: Digital tropisms
Bloc 1.2: Experimenting with tropisms
Bloc 1.3: Introduction to reflective practices
Sequence 2: Digital writing and media theory
Bloc 2.1: Theoretical contributions
Bloc 2.2: Educational synopsis reading (ESR)
Bloc 2.3: Reading and peer-to-peer reviews of ESR
Sequence 3: Introduction to information technology
Bloc 3.1: Algorithms and programming
Bloc 3.2: Principles of coding and computer operation
Bloc 3.3: Networks and the Internet
Sequence 4: Digital literature and "boundary" studies
Bloc 4.1: Analysis of works of digital literature
Bloc 4.2: Production of literary and/or entertaining digital works (DW)
Bloc 4.3: Peer-to-peer review of DW
Sequence 5: Reading, writing and broadcasting digital content
Bloc 5.1: Reading and writing in the Babel library
Bloc 5.2: Publishing its content
Bloc 5.3: Authors' rights and open licenses
Sequence 6: Project
Assessment for certification

Table 2.2. *Proposed training program*

2.9. Conclusion and perspectives

The tropisms we have proposed and their definitions and characterizations should not be taken as established truths, but rather as heuristic, that is, provisory, uncertain and debatable formulations, the advantage of which is that they help with learning and understanding. Tropisms and the functions that characterize them can emerge and vanish and their definitions evolve along with the uses that are made of them, the observations they enable to be made and the comments they provoke. We must consider them both as a snapshot of a given moment and a point of view, as well as a tool of exchange.

Our current projects have led us to the incorporation of tropisms into training programs at UTC and IFCAM, and directed us toward the creation or mobilization of writing tools dedicated to the learning of these tropisms through experience . An open mass learning project in information literacy, as presented in the last part of this chapter, could be implemented rapidly (6–12 months) and progressively (based initially on a partial scenario). The implementation of such a project could be managed by an institution of higher education or a group of organizations for internal use (students on certain courses in these schools) as well as external use (continuing education, public education); by a state or region, in an academic (information literacy in high school) and civil context, by companies internally (business MOOCs); and/or as a transparency measure for clients (commercial approach) and/or citizens (corporate responsibility approach). Depending on the context of delivery and the initial financing, this openness can be progressively extended, bearing in mind that the ultimate objective is openness to all citizens in the medium term (2–5 years after the launch of the project).

2.10. Acknowledgments

I would like to thank Serge Bouchardon, Isabelle Cailleau and the other members of the PRECIP project (http://precip.fr) who have assisted me with the formulation of tropisms; the members of the EPIN research group at the Costech laboratory for their comments and Sylvain Spinelli and Bruno Bachimont for our exchanges and their contributions. I am also grateful to IFCAM for its confidence in me and for having authorized me to present their work.

2.11. Further reading

My work has been presented throughout its development on the website: http://aswemay.fr, which serves as a public forum for my research notes. We invite readers interested in the evolution of our research to visit the site for further reading.

2.12. Bibliography

[BAC 04] BACHIMONT B., Arts et Sciences Du Numérique: Ingénierie Des Connaissances et Critique de La Raison Computationnelle, Thesis, Université de Technologie de Compiègne, 2004.

[BAC 07] BACHIMONT B., *Ingénierie Des Connaissances et Des Contenus: Le Numérique Entre Ontologies et Documents*, Hermès Science-Lavoisier, 2007.

[BAC 08] BACHIMONT B., "Audiovisuel et numérique: la reconstruction éditoriale des contenus", in CALDERAN L., HIDOINE B., MILLET J. (eds), *Métadonnées: mutations et perspectives*, ADBS Editions, 2008.

[BOU 13] BOULLIER D., *Mooc: la standardisation ou l'innovation?*, in InternetActu.net, available at: http://www.internetactu.net/2013/02/20/mooc-la-standardisation-ou-linnovation, 2013.

[BUS 45] BUSH V., "As we may think", *The Atlantic Monthly*, vol. 176, no. 1, pp. 101–108, 1945.

[CAI 15] CAILLEAU I., Récit d'une enquête sur l'écriture numérique collaborative synchrone, Thesis, Université de Technologie de Compiègne, 2015.

[CHU 13] CHUPIN, *Échec scolaire: La grande peur*, Éditions Autrement, 2013.

[CRO 12] CROZAT S., BACHIMONT B., CAILLEAU I. *et al.*, "Éléments pour une théorie opérationnelle de l'écriture numérique", *Document numérique*, vol. 14, no. 3, pp. 9–33, 2012.

[CRO 14] CROZAT S., "Precip: Formation à l'écriture numérique via des chaînes éditoriales ayant fonction de démonstrateurs pédagogiques", *Journées Scenari*, Paris, France, 2014.

[CRO 15] CROZAT S., "Les tropismes du numérique", in *H2PTM'1 5* ISTE Editions, London, 2015.

[DAL 09] DALL'ARMELLINA L. "Le MEMEX de Vannevar Bush", available at: http://www.hypertexte.org/blog/?p=125, 2009.

[GOO 77] GOODY J., *The Domestication of the Savage Mind*, Cambridge University Press, 1977.

[JAF 04] JAFFRÉ J.-P., "La litéracie: histoire d'un mot, effets d'un concept", in BARRÉ-DE MINIAC C., BRISSAUD C., RISPAIL M. (eds), *La littéracie: conceptions théoriques et pratiques d'enseignement de la lecture-écriture*, L'Harmattan, Paris, 2004.

[LAC 13] Lacroix D., Réinventer un rapport au temps, par Bernard Stiegler, available at: http://reseaux.blog.lemonde.fr/2013/10/03/reinventer-rapport-temps-bernard-stiegler, 2013.

[LER 45] Leroi-Gourhan A., *Milieu et Techniques*, Albin Michel, 1945.

[NAG 89] Nagel E., Newman J., Gödel K. *et al.*, *Le Théorème de Gödel*, Editions du Seuil, 1989.

[NEL 82] Nelson T., *Literary Machines*, Mindful Press, 1982.

[REU 06] Reuter Y., "À propos des usages de Goody en didactique: éléments d'analyse et de discussion", *Pratiques*, vol. 131, available at: www.pratiques-cresef.com/p131_re1.pdf, pp.131–154, no. 132, 2006.

[SIM 58] Simondon G., *Du mode d'existence des objets techniques*, Éditions Aubier, Paris, 1958.

[STE 10] Steiner P., "Philosophie, technologie et cognition: état des lieux et perspectives", *Intellectica*, vol. 53, no. 54, pp. 7–40, 2010.

[STI 06] Stiegler B., *Réenchanter le monde: La valeur esprit contre le populisme industriel*, Flammarion, Paris, 2006.

3

Assessing the Design of Hypermedia Interfaces: Differing Perspectives

With their relatively short history – the appearance of the first graphic interface dates back only to 1963 [BEA 01] – digital interfaces have become a subject of study in numerous disciplines, with each of these disciplines possesing its own perspective and theoretical tradition regarding them. This chapter is intended to be less an exhaustive listing of all the authors who have studied interfaces than an acknowledgment of the conceptual foundations and implications for design of some approaches that have been recognized – but never compared – in the field of information technology, ergonomics and semiotics. We have grouped these approaches according to the type of mediation conducted by the interface in each approach, which has yielded three different categories: man–machine interaction, mediated human activity and systems of meaning.

It is interesting to note that these three perspectives have never been in competition, remaining incontestable in their disciplinary context, although they have a common objective: to judge whether an interface is suitable or not. It is with this ultimate goal in mind that we have put them side by side in order to compare the theoretical suppositions upon which they are based, as well as their methodological consequences during the assessment of the design of hypermedia interfaces. Comparisons such as these are essential, we believe, in order to design hypermedia interfaces that take into account the complexity of human communication.

Chapter written by María Inés LAITANO.

3.1. Man–machine interaction

A first grouping can be made of the authors who see the interface as a means of interaction between humans and machines. The fundamental supposition of these approaches is that humans are on the same level as machines. In other words, in order for humans and machines to communicate, they have to "speak" the same language and "function" in a similar way. This has led Jakob Nielsen, in particular, to draw on a standard of communication among computer networks (Open Systems Interconnection) to develop a model with seven levels of communication between humans and machines. Likewise, Donald Norman explains the interaction as a translation of physical variables – the state of a machine – into psychological variables – mental representations of a human.

A second idea underlies man–machine interaction-based approaches: the human has an objective that will be achieved through the execution of a task, that is, by a series of actions carried out on the machine. The task will be broken down into linguistic levels of decreasing complexity for Nielsen and into successive cognitive stages for Norman.

3.1.1. *Fundamental principles of usability*

The first theoretical interface model designed in information technology circles was created in the 1980s by Jakob Nielsen – still a leading light in the field of usability – who posited the existence of a dialogue between humans and machines. In his early writing, Nielsen [NIE 86] proposed a Virtual Protocol Model for Computer-Human Interaction that contained seven levels of abstraction (Figure 3.1). The model postulated that a human has an objective to achieve in the real world, for example, deleting the last part of a letter he is writing to a friend. Level 7 of the model represents the real-world concepts associated with the human's objective; in this case, "deleting the last part of a letter". Levels 6 to 2 deal with the different levels of representation of these concepts in the interface. Again using our example level 6 would be expressed by "delete the last six lines of an editable text"; level 5 by the operation "deleting a line" with the object "line number" and level 4 by "DELETE 27", which responds to verb/noun syntax. A unit of level 3 would be the word "DELETE" and a unit of level 2 would be the letter D. Finally, level 1 would be the equivalent of the material interface.

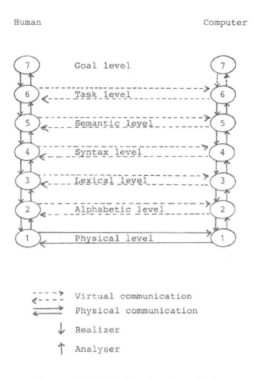

Figure 3.1. *Virtual protocol model for Computer-Human Interaction [NIE 86]*

For Nielsen, the quality of an interface can be evaluated by its usability, that is, its ease of use. Usability is defined by five components of quality: ease of learning, effectiveness at executing tasks, ease of interface memorization, error management and user satisfaction. Accordingly, he has established a usability evaluation method – Heuristic Evaluation [MOL 90, NIE 94] – which has been extremely successful in technical training programs and the world of Web development. The method calls for a small group of evaluators to examine an interface in order to judge its degree of compliance with the following 10 usability heuristics [NIE 95]:

1) The IT system should always keep users informed about what is going on, through appropriate feedback within reasonable time.

2) The IT system must "speak" the user's language and use concepts familiar to the user rather than terms proper to the system.

3) The IT system must provide functions to cancel and redo an action.

4) The IT system's language must be consistent and standardized and must adhere to the conventions of interface design.

5) The IT system must prevent errors, either by eliminating the conditions liable to produce these errors or by giving users the option to confirm an action before taking it.

6) The IT system must minimize the user's cognitive overload by rendering objects, actions and options visible.

7) The IT system must be as effective for novice users as it is for experienced ones.

8) The design of the IT system must be aesthetic and minimalist.

9) Error messages must be expressed clearly, indicate the problem precisely and propose a solution.

10) Although it is preferable for the IT system to be able to be used without referring to documentation, it may be necessary to provide instructions for use. These must be easy to find and focused on the user's task and must include concrete steps that are not overwhelmingly detailed.

Of course, Heuristic Evaluation is based on the concepts of the Virtual Protocol Model for Computer-Human Interaction. For heuristic number 2, in particular, Nielsen suggests minimizing computer-oriented representations in favor of real-world representations. For Nielsen, a transparent   interface designates an immediate correspondence between what we want to do and what we can do; in other words, an immediate correspondence between level 7 and level 5 of the Virtual Protocol Model. The user should not have to translate objects and operations from the real world into computer-oriented objects and actions. "The term [transparency] itself suggests the 'disappearance' of the computer oriented concepts in the dialogue" [NIE 92, sect. 4, Direct Mappings].

3.1.2. *Cognitive engineering*

Donald Norman is a researcher in Cognitive Sciences who is also widely recognized in the field of interface design. In one of his first articles, entitled "Cognitive Engineering" [NOR 86], he postulated that a person who wishes to carry out a task on a technical system has objectives and intentions, which he calls psychological variables. These variables exist in the mind of the person and differ from the physical variables that describe the material system with which the task will be executed. The person himself must make the link between these two types of variables. Thus, the task is accomplished in seven stages, which are depicted in Figure 3.2. First, the person perceives and interprets the current state of the system. The, he assesses it with regard to his objectives, which involves a translation of the physical state of the system into a form compatible with his psychological objectives. The difference between the objective desired by the person and the current state of the system thus gives rise to a psychological intention. This intention is finally translated into a sequence of actions executed by the mechanisms of the material system.

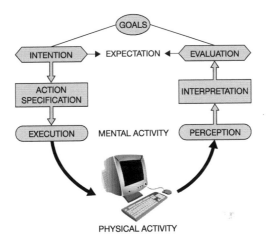

Figure 3.2. *Seven stages in the execution of a task [NOR 86]*

When expert users or simple situations are involved, the psychological effort made by the person to associate the physical variables with the psychological ones is negligible. However, in the case of complex situations or novice users, Norman maintains that it is necessary to develop a conceptual model of the physical system [NOR 86, pp. 45–47]. Accordingly, he has introduced the notions of *designer's model, system image* and *user model* to designate the three conceptual models to be considered. Designer's and user's models are mental models, meaning the internal models that people form of themselves, others and the things with which they interact. The designer's model is the model created by a designer of a technical system to be built, ideally based on the needs of the user and considering his task and capabilities. The system image is "[…] the image produced from the physical structure built (including documentation and instructions) [...]"[1] [NOR 86, p. 47]. Finally, the user's model is the model that the user constructs based on his interpretation of the system image. Thus, the final objective of a design is to construct an adequate system image, so that the user model will be compatible with the designer's model: "If the designer wants the user to understand his technical system, to use it correctly and to enjoy using it, he must construct a system image that is explicit, intelligible, and consistent"[2] [NOR 86, p. 47].

Norman [NOR 15] uses the idea of affordances to assess a design. This is a concept borrowed from James Gibson [GIB 77] and redefined as the perceived and actual properties of an object, which determine how this object can be used[3]. These are the leads that indicate how the object should be manipulated. The classic example is that a chair "affords" the opportunity to sit down. In an interface, a change of pointer indicates the possibility of clicking. Norman explains that affordances result from our interpretation of the world, an interpretation that results from the influence of our knowledge and experiences on our perception.

3.2. Mediated human activity

New theoretical models emerged in the early 1990s, based on Activity Theory (henceforth AT) as proposed by the Soviet psychologists Vygotsky, Rubinstein and Leontiev. AT-based approaches are critical of the technocentric aspect of previous approaches, and argue that man cannot be put on the same level as machines, that they must be thought of in different terms from one another. Likewise, laboratory experimentation concerning cognitivism is questioned:

> [...] analyses concerning individuals without reference to their culture, history, and problems are defined and evaluated by the experimenter and posed in an unfamiliar environment; the true nature of the task and the behavior expected are often unclear

---

1 Original citation: "The third concept is the image resulting from the physical structure that has been built (including the documentation and instructions): I call that the System Image".
2 Original citation: "If one hopes for the user to understand a system, to use it properly and to enjoy using it, then it is up to the designer to make the System Image explicit, intelligible and consistent".
3 For a discussion of the acceptations taken on by the concept of affordances in the field of interface design, we refer readers to [KAP 14].

for subjects, and the question of meaning for the subject is only rarely explored. Performance is evaluated in relation to norms of rationality external to the subject and characterized in terms of its difference from these norms[4] [BAN 89, p. 4].

In the same article, Bannon and Bødker emphasize the fact that even an exhaustive description of a task is always an incomplete description of the use the user will make, since it does not take into account the tacit knowledge required in a skilled activity, or the knowledge brought into play during use. They insist on the limited applicability of the methods thus constructed, as much for the design as for the evaluation of interfaces.

Finally, Pierre Rabardel underlines the importance of "[...] developmental aspects pertaining to both tools and user skills" [RAB 95, p. 41]. Laboratory experiments can only evaluate the user's initial contacts with an interface, and are incapable of taking into account the long-term development of the relationship between the user and the machine.

The category of instrumented activity evolves from the idea of a task to that of an activity, thus causing the machine to change from a partner in communication to a means of this communication. The evolution of the idea of a task to that of an activity implies an amplification of the scope of analysis. The user's objective is no longer oriented toward the machine, but toward an object in the world. In other words, it is not the deletion of a line of text that interests the user, but rather the creation of a poem. In brief, the activity becomes the *raison d'être* of the task.

Because this second category is confined to man's interaction with objects in the world, the idea of sociocultural context becomes fundamental. The user's knowledge, acquired individually or through his belonging to a certain social group, influences his interpretations, particularly

---

4 Full original citation: "However, these studies tend to analyze the individual without reference to their community, or their history, performing on a task designed by the experimenter in an unfamiliar environment. The 'problem' is defined and valued by the experimenter, not by the subject, who is then expected to perform in certain ways. In some experimental manipulations, even the very nature of the task, or the required behavior, may not be clear to the subject. The question of how 'subjects' make sense of the game in which they are playing, trying to discover the 'rules of the game', i.e. what the experimenter is after, is often not explicitly discussed in these studies. Performance is measured relative to a certain 'ideal', rational model of problem-solving, and the deviations of subjects from this abstract logic is noted".

communication via the interface. This is what Bødker refers to as praxis, and Rabardel calls utilization schemes.

3.2.1. *The Danish school*

Susanne Bødker recognized very early that applying AT to interface design was of interest, and began to study activity mediated by computerized artifacts. Figure 3.3 shows her interpretation of AT.

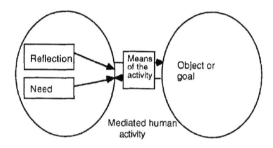

Figure 3.3. *Mediated human activity [BØD 87]*

According to Bødker [BØD 87, pp. 25–26], a *need* mobilizes humans to take actions with certain intentions that will come up in the physical and social world. This action is based on a *mental reflection* of the world that is not the reflected image or mental representation of cognitivism, but a construction made by man based on his activity. On the other side, all activity is linked to an *objective* and/or an *object*: man can aim to achieve an objective and/or direct his activity toward an object. The object is a physical object or another subject that will be affected by the activity. Finally, the activity will be mediated by *means* which can be artifacts, cultural techniques or languages.

Computerized artifacts are a specific type of artifact, and thus a specific type of thing that mediates human activity. In most cases, they do not allow direct contact with the object of the activity, as a traditional artifact such as a hammer would. The object of the activity is merely represented in a computer application.

For Bødker, computerized artifacts take charge of the intentional and operational dimensions of the activity, that is, what can be done via the artifact and how it can be done. The interface itself is composed of all of the aspects of the computerized artifact that indicate how to make use of the artifact. There are three types of aspects to consider [BØD 87, pp. 42–43]:

1) The physical aspects indicate how to make use of the computerized artifact as a physical object, and correspond to material interfaces.

2) The handling aspects indicate how to make use of the computerized artifact as an artifact, that is, as an instrument. For example, in a text editor, the handling aspects are those that indicate how the user can edit the document scrolling mechanisms, text manipulation (selecting, copying, pasting), etc.

3) The subject/object directed aspects indicate how to act on the object or subject. For example, in the text editor I am using to write this chapter, one of the object directed aspects is the type of display of a document. The type of display in pages enables me to reflect on the final form that the printed document will have, forgetting the computer artifact.

Consequently, in a "good" interface, the physical and handling aspects must remain transparent for the user, while the subject/object directed aspects must foster the development of operations [BØD 87, pp. 152–153].

In a later article, Bødker and Klokmose [BØD 15] emphasize the importance of collective skills in determining whether an interface is suitable or not. For these authors, the praxis is the knowledge associated with an activity, anchored in tradition and shared by a group of people. Thus, the design process of an interface must begin with a study of the praxis of future users. This makes it possible to design an interface that will be suitable for this group of people.

For the authors, the design process creates the artifact: "Design […] can be viewed as a process in which we determine and create the conditions which turn an object into an artifact of use" [BAN 89, p. 22]. They also insist that it is impossible to conceive an artifact design that will be perfectly adapted to future usage; however, this usage may be anticipated by careful study of praxis and the area of activity (artifacts currently used, context of their use). The use of prototypes and mock-ups by future users is useful in predicting usage. Finally, they draw attention to the learning support that must be provided with the artifact; because the artifact will modify the praxis of its users, these users must be trained during use.

3.2.2. *Instrumental psychology*

Pierre Rabardel [RAB 95] studied the particular case of human activities mediated by technology. The means used for mediation is referred to by Rabardel as the *instrument*, and thus the name *instrumental psychology* has been given to his approach. For him the instrument is a mixed entity made up of two inseparable dimensions. One of these is the artifact, which is defined as "a thing liable to be used, developed to be part of finalized activities", which "realizes a solution to a socially posed problem or set of problems" [RAB 95, p. 49]. The concept of artifact includes both material and symbolic things. The other dimension is the associated usage scheme(s) which for Rabardel are modes of use, anticipated by the designers of the artifact but constructed by the subjects who use these artifacts. The production of usages can be a private development by the subject or "[...] an appropriation of social usage schemes already formed externally to the subject" [RAB 95, p. 95]. These schemes are cognitive entities.

Rabardel proposes the model in Figure 3.4, which shows the three poles of his approach, the subject, the object and the instrument, in a certain environment. He confirms that, in addition to the direct relationships existing between all the poles in the model, there are two instrument-mediated relationships represented on the diagram by the two-directional arrow S-O m:

1) Epistemic mediation, which takes place from the object toward the subject and enables knowledge of the object.

2) Pragmatic mediation from the subject toward the object: "[...] the instrument is the means of a transformative action (in a broad sense including control and regulation) directed toward the object" [RAB 95, p. 72].

The environment is composed of conditions that influence the subject in its activity and can enter into interaction with the other poles or with the relationships in the model.

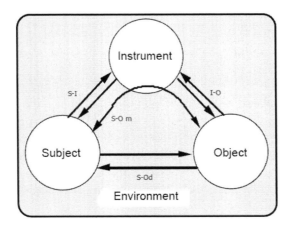

Figure 3.4. *Instrumented activity situations [RAB 95]*

Rabardel also posits that instruments crystallize accumulated experience. An instrument is the means implemented in a particular action by a subject, but it is also reused in similar actions by the same subject, enabling him to gain experience. The capitalization of knowledge occurs not only at the individual level, but also at the collective level. When the instrument is used by a group of people, it has a meaning shared by this community and it reflects the knowledge of this group.

Toward the end of his book, Rabardel focuses on artifact transparency. He differentiates between the metaphor of the black box and that of the glass box. The first, which coincides with Bødker's conception, refers to the invisible character of the artifact: "the artifact is a mediator whose presence must not pose any kind of obstacle to the relationship between the subject and the object of its activity" [RAB 95, p. 184]. Conversely, the conception of transparency as a glass box means that "[...] the artifact, or a part of the artifact, must be visible so that the subject can take it into account in his activity" [RAB 95, p. 186]. It is this latter metaphor that encompasses *operative transparency*, introduced by the author to designate "[...] the characteristic properties of the instrument that are relevant to the action of the user, as well as the way in which the instrument makes them accessible, understandable, or even perceptible for the user" [RAB 95, p. 189].

3.3. Meaningful systems

Finally, the third category, which we call the *meaningful system*, represents a widening of the scope of analysis toward the design situation. Considering the design situation transforms the phenomenon of communication into a deferred phenomenon, meaning that the designer and the user do not share the same space-time. This is why the designer "will make himself present" inside the interface in de Souza's metacommunicational message, in Scolari's implicit designer and in Stockinger's semiolinguistic policy. Although these notions stem from relatively dissimilar theoretical presuppositions, they are all attempting to show that the designer, whether deliberately or not, "leaves traces" in the design phase.

The authors for whom the interface mediates a meaningful system are in agreement with the fact that, in a usage situation, the user interprets the interface. De Souza explains that the user decodes the designer's message; Scolari affirms that this user accepts or rejects the designer's proposition, and Stockinger claims that the user conducts a personal reading of the *editing regions*. Nevertheless, there is a fundamental difference between authors who believe that the designer can exactly predict the user's interpretation and authors for whom this is impossible due to the unique and individual interpretation made by each user. For de Souza, the algorithmic nature of the medium mechanizes human semiosis, and the designer is in a position to anticipate the user's interpretations. For Scolari and Stockinger, on the contrary, the designer can only hypothesize with regard to the user, and make presumptions about his expectations, skills and position in the communication situation. These hypotheses are what Scolari refers to as the implicit user, and what Stockinger means when discussing the interpretive field.

3.3.1. *Semiotic engineering*

In his initial proposition concerning Semiotic Engineering, de Souza [DES 93] proposes a model in which the interface mediates the communication between the designer and the user (Figure 3.5). The message sent by the designer to the user via the interface is a performing message; it performs an act of communication in itself, in which it acts simultaneously as the sender and the receiver of other messages. Note that the use of the terms "message", "receiver", "coder" and "decoder" place this model within the mathematical approach to communication. The author himself admits that Semiotic Engineering makes broad use of Jakobson's communicational model, which is ultimately a semiotic re-reading of the model proposed by Shannon and Weaver [DE 05, pp. 65–66]. This approach to communication leads de Souza to say, in a recent explanation of his theory, that there are a limited number of possible interpretations of the interface, and that these are influenced by the algorithmic nature of the computerized medium:

> Systems designers must create representations that by necessity have a single definitive encoded meaning – no matter if the designers (and the users) can easily produce evolved meanings for these representations in natural sign-exchange situations. The algorithmic nature of the medium in which metacommunication takes place mechanizes human semiosis [...][DES 13]

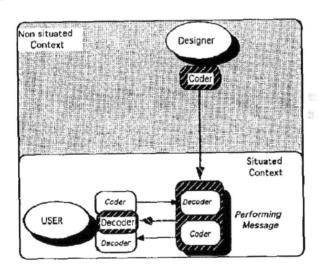

Figure 3.5. *Semiotic engineering communication model [DES 93]*

De Souza's communication model includes the designer of the interface as a partner in the communication mediated by the interface, a communication that is otherwise deferred. In view of the fact that the designer cannot be present in person when the user interacts with the interface, de Souza [DES 13] maintain that this designer must represent himself in the interface. To do this, he uses a system of meaning (a code) that is specially designed to tell users what the application can do, how it can be used and for what objective. In this sense, the designer's message is a *metacommunicational* message, meaning that it speaks of how, when, where and why to communicate with a computer application. De Souza describes the designer's metacommunicational message (with the first person representing the designer and "you" representing the user) as follows:

> Here is my understanding of who you are, what I've learned you want or need to do, in which preferred ways, and why. This is the system that I have therefore designed for you, and this is the way you can or should use it in order to fulfill a range of purposes that fall within this vision [DES 13].

De Souza agrees with Shannon's model that the user must learn the language of the interface in order to respond to the designer's message. The language of the interface is the code in which the designer's message has been completely encoded. If the user encounters problems during this learning process, it is because the designer has not anticipated the user's interpretation strategies [DES 13].

The methods proposed by Semiotic Engineering to evaluate the design of an interface are Semiotic Inspection and Communicability Evaluation [DES 09]. These are qualitative methods aimed at assessing communicability, that is, "[...]a system's ability to signify and communicate the designers' intent (which is ultimately to satisfy the users" [DES 13]. Communicability is assessed on the message transmission side (Semiotic Inspection) as well as the reception side (Communicability Evaluation).

Semiotic Inspection evaluates the way in which the message is composed and sent by the designer. The method suggests examining a sample of screenshots and instructions in order to identify the metacommunicational signs used by the designer in his message, according to the following three categories [DES 06]:

1) Static signs: do not vary with time and can therefore be correctly interpreted in a screen capture.

2) Dynamic signs: are dependent on time and causal relationships, specifically interactivity. These signs can be correctly interpreted in a series of screen captures.

3) Metalinguistic signs[5]: static or dynamic signs that differ from the above because they constitute an explanation, description, illustration, manifestation or indication regarding other signs in the interface. They are typically composed of textual or video material (e.g. help and documentation), which refers to the meaning of another static or dynamic sign.

These signs must then be gathered and compared and their coherence verified in order to gain a general estimation of their communicability.

Semiotic Inspection goes along with Communicability Evaluation. Communicability Evaluation is intended "[...] to identify, by means of user observation, empirical evidence of the effects of the designer's messages as they are encountered at interaction time" [DES 09, p. 25]. Users interact with the interface in order to achieve the objective set by the analyst. The method proceeds in three stages [DES 09, pp. 37–48]:

1) Tagging, which identifies the problems encountered by the user during interaction and tags them with specific utterances. Tags are preset in statements that express breakdowns in communication, for example "I can't do it this way", "Where is it?" and "What now?" [DES 09, p. 38].

2) Interpretation, which organizes evidence according to four dimensions in order to arrive at a more abstract interpretation: the frequency and context of occurrence of each type of tag; the existence of repetitive sequences of types of tag; the level of problems indicated by the types of tag and the communicability problems that caused the observed incidents.

3) Semiotic profile, which interprets the results in terms of the designer's metacommunicational message in an attempt to recover the original

---

5 The term "metalinguistic signs" has nothing to do with the nature of signs, but with their function. De Souza borrows Jakobson's concept of "metalinguistic function", which indicates that signs serve to give information about other signs.

intention. By revealing to its designers the implicit intention stemming from their interface, these designers can then modify or confirm their choices.

De Souza emphasizes the necessity of validating the results obtained in both methods using the technique of validation by *triangulation* [DES 09, pp. 33, 48], particularly by comparing the results of the two methods with one another, or by comparing them with the results of other methods.

3.3.2. *The sociocognitive model*

Carlos Scolari [SCO 01, SCO 04] has adopted a semiocognitive approach to the interface by incorporating Verón's concept of the reading contract [VER 85] – which is drawn in turn from both the theory of textual cooperation postulated by Eco [ECO 84] and the ideas of the designer's model and user's model in Cognitive Engineering [NOR 86]. Scolari maintains that communication establishes a contract:

> To initiate this exchange [communication], every text contains within itself a *simulacrum of the recipient*. The survival of the discourse depends on the precision of this imaginary construction or, in other words, on the correspondence between this virtual recipient and the *empirical* recipient of the communication. Thanks to this virtual figure or "decoy", the real recipient is invited to participate in an exchange, a proposition which may be accepted or rejected. Communication is established only after the establishment of a contract that regulates the exchange[6] [SCO 04, p. 80]

Scolari thus maintains that the interface includes a simulacrum of a virtual user, or an *implied user* who will or will not be accepted by the *empirical user*, thus becoming a *proposal of interaction*. Unlike the printed press for which Verón initially proposed the reading contract model, the proposal of interaction incorporates the interactive dimension.

---

6 Original citation: "Para iniciar ese intercambio todo texto incluye un *simulacro del destinatario* en su interior. La supervivencia del discurso depende de la exactitud de esta construcción imaginaria o, en otras palabras, de la correspondencia entre ese destinatario virtual y su destinatario *empírico* de la comunicación. A través de esta figura o "señuelo" virtual el destinatario real es invitado a participar en un intercambio; la propuesta podrá ser aceptada o rechazada. La comunicación se establece solo después de la institución de un *contrato* que regula el intercambio [...]".

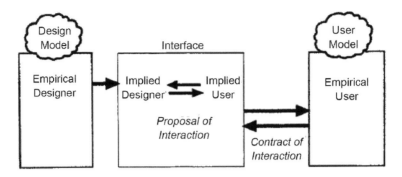

Figure 3.6. *Semiocognitive interaction model [SCO 01]*

Because communication between the designer and the user occurs by means of the interface and in a deferred manner, the proposal of interaction also includes a simulacrum of the designer, or an *implied designer*. "The *empirical designer* [our emphasis] delegates his functions to this virtual figure who is manifested at the surface of the interface in the form of *traces* and *marks* [author's emphasis] of an instructive action"[7] [SCO 04, p. 82]. For Scolari, the implicit traces of the designer are what determine the rhythm of interaction, the data to be presented, possible navigation routes, etc. The *implied* user is the hypothetical behavior of the empirical user, a presumption of his experience, skills and interactive expectations. If the empirical user recognizes himself in this virtual user, the interaction proposition will be accepted and interaction will take place. The designer can never predict the exact way in which the user will use the interface. He can only propose a range of possible interactions within which the user moves independently. The user will often find himself in unforeseen situations, and can even divert expected forms of interaction [SCO 04, p. 82]. The mental models of Cognitive Engineering correspond clearly to the empirical entities of the designer and the user.

In terms of methodology, the author proposes a method for analyzing the design of graphic interfaces. The method differentiates between four levels of analysis, which correspond to the four stages of the activity of interpretation. The *plastic* level analyzes the basic elements of the interface (shapes, colors, positions of elements, spatial oppositions, contrasts, etc.) and

---

7 Original citation: "El proyectista empírico delega sus funciones a esta figura virtual, la cual se manifiesta en la superficie de la interfaz bajo forma de *huellas* y *marcas* de una acción ordenadora".

identifies the basic structures of the production of meaning. The *figurative* level analyzes the elements represented (icons, photographs, videos, etc.) and any type of changes (animations, statuses, trajectories, actions, etc.). The *communicational* level analyzes the virtual communication strategies within the interface (implied designer vs. implied user). Finally, the *metacommunicational* level analyzes the user's relationship to the overall communication situation. This last level appears only in certain interfaces, such as those of videoconferencing software, which reproduces the user's face on a screen [SCO 09, pp. 9–10].

3.3.3. *Semiotic scenario*

In France, Peter Stockinger [STO 05] has developed a theoretical and methodological framework for the semiotic description of websites, which addresses the concept of interface. The framework is based on an institutional metaphor: the website is an institution, a social place where services are provided for a group of visitors/users. In this institution, the interface mediates both communication between the institution and its visitors and communication among the visitors themselves:

> [...] the interface is the place which gathers and organizes in space or time all the elements required to make a Web service communicable or to establish and manage communication between the website and its visitors/users, as well as among the visitors/users of the website who form [...] its "virtual" community. [STO 05, p. 175]

One concept that is fundamental to Stockinger's approach is the *semiotic scenario*, a conceptual model of the website defining: (1) the organization of the content of all services; (2) the forms of services appropriation by its visitors and (3) the logical (textual) organization of services, their expression and the staging necessary to make them communicable to visitors. The interface is concerned with this third aspect above all.

The semiotic scenario is composed of a set of *scenes* that take place in the interface through *editing regions*. A scene describes the content of a web service, the strategies for making it available and the strategies for appropriating it, while the editing region explains how the content and methods regulating its availability and appropriation can become communicable and establish themselves as objects in a semiotic system (linguistic, visual, etc.) [STO 05, p. 178]. Thus, the editing region not only has a physical and perceptive identity (eidetic, chromatic [color], topographical, etc.) but a specific functionality: to make a service and its appropriation communicable as well as enabling communication about the service between the site and its visitors.

The editing region is made concrete in various forms: as a static and permanent part of an HTML page, or as a dynamic or interactive part, or as part of the background, or even as an HTML page itself; it may also be a pop-up window, among other things. It can also be found on other pages, or even on all the pages of a website [STO 05, p. 176]. It is for this reason that the author speaks of a tripartite relationship between the concepts of scene, editing region and web page. While the scene and the region belong to the semiotic scenario of the website, the web page is part of its technological production.

The approach also proposes a principle of composition:

> a [editing] region is a meaningful unit that can be separated into more limited regions but which can also combine with other regions to form larger meaningful configurations, which we call *zones* [STO 05, p. 180].

The degree of granularity to choose in order to evaluate a design remains dependent, of course, on the degree of precision desired in each situation. However, Stockinger provides description criteria that can be used to identify the editing region or regions of an interface beyond the degree of granularity. These criteria are shown in Table 3.1.

The semiotic scenario remains a reference model for both the creation and the evaluation of a website. From a production perspective, the identity and specificity of an editing region is normally stipulated and imposed. Conversely, from an assessment perspective, the region acts as a perceptive and semantic unit, but its identification, comprehension and classification can vary from one reader to another [STO 05, p. 185]. Consequently, the editing region does not correspond to a specific interpretation of the web page, but to a *meaningful configuration* [STO 05, 179], that is, to a certain order of the elements on the page intended to open up a certain *interpretive field* to its visitors [STO 05, 186].

Criterion	Question
Logical structure	What is/are the editing region(s) chosen to communicate the web service(s) of a website?
Elements of expression	What are the signs (textual, visual, audiovisual, sound, animated, etc.) used in an editing region to express the content of a service?
Eidetic form	What is the perceptive configuration (surface area, edges, etc.) of the editing region communicating a service?
Chromatic (color) structure	What is the color structure that characterizes the editing region expressing and staging a service?
Topographical structure	What is the spatial structure that organizes the expressive elements of an editing region in relation to one another and defines the place of the editing region within a broader zone or within the interface of which it is a part?

Table 3.1. *Criteria for describing editing regions [STO 05, p. 178]*

When discussing the designer, Stockinger speaks of the *proprietors* of the site, having communication objectives that are expressed in a *semiolinguistic policy*:

> [...] whether deliberately or not, each site implements a [...] semiolinguistic policy, the objective of which is to enable communication that is effective as possible and a coordination of activities between the site and its users. [STO 05, p. 188].

3.4. Three mediations: three ways of evaluating a design?

Man–machine interaction, mediated human activity and meaningful systems constitute three ways of envisioning the intermediary role of hypermedia interfaces, with each having theoretical and methodological bases as we have just discussed. What are the points of agreement and divergence in terms of criteria for evaluating the design of interfaces? We will now identify them, and illustrate them thoroughly using the design decisions made for the hypermedia interface of the website New Impressions of Africa (*Nouvelles Impressions d'Afrique*[8]), hereafter referred to by the acronym NIA. This hypermedia system is a new digital

---

8 http://rousselnia.fr/

mediatization of the original printed work by Raymond Roussel, a masterpiece of constraining literature [LAI 13].

Authors anchored in man–machine interaction seem to be mainly preoccupied by the user's performance relative to the machine. The ease of use of the design – its usability – is the quality criterion evaluated. The interface design will be usable if it is *explicit*: there must be a large number of affordances (Norman), that is, objects, actions and options must be visible (heuristic no. 6 as posited by Nielsen). Likewise, a usable interface will be *intelligible* and *coherent* (Norman): it will speak the user's language (heuristic no. 2) and follow the conventions of design interface (heuristic no. 4). Nielsen's other heuristics also support the idea of explicit design, particularly constant feedback, the option to confirm an action, precisely worded error messages, instructions for use, etc.

The topographical view of our example interface contains several elements intended to make its use easier. In particular, the tabs on the left-hand side of the screen indicate the existence of menus. Anchor highlighting and changing the shape of the pointer when anchors are moused over, as well as the X enabling closure of pop-ups comply with the conventions of interface design. The highlighting in orange of a text fragment when a user mouses over a textual pop-up makes the location of this text clear in the overall structure (Figure 3.7).

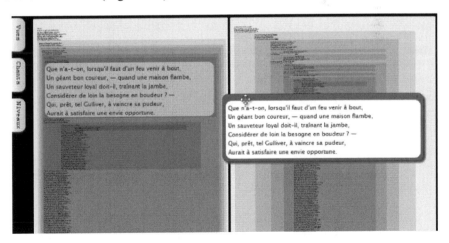

Figure 3.7. *Design facilitates use*

While man–machine interaction approaches favor a manifest design, authors attached to mediated human activity tend to speak of a transparent and invisible interface. For these approaches, the user's attention must remain focused on human activity, which is the *raison d'être* of the task on the machine, and in order for this to be the case, the design of the interface must not disrupt the relationship between the user and the object of his activity. For this reason, according to Bødker, the physical aspects (material interface) and the handling aspects (scroll, copy, etc.) must remain transparent so that the object directed aspects are foremost in the interface. Likewise, Rabardel introduces the metaphor of the glass box and the concept of *operative transparency* in his argument that the operative plan should not negatively affect the properties of the interface that are relevant to the user's activity.

A second dimension raised by the authors of mediated human activity that is not insignificant for interface design is the *praxis* of future users. The design cannot be culturally neutral, but must be adapted to the knowledge of the community that will use it. This recommendation has proven for the most part to be more precise than the minimalist design proposed in the first category by Nielsen.

NIA principally targets a public that is literary and interested in the activities of reading and analyzing the work of Roussel. Therefore, it is preferable to use the label *Songs* for the topographical view menu, rather than the label *Clusters* or *Columns*. While songs belong to the literary semantic field, clusters fall within the domain of hypertext and columns merely to the idea of verticality. In addition, when an illustration is moused over, an info-bubble displays the instructions given by Roussel to the illustrator for this image, and the background of the lines of verse semantically associated with this image changes color (Figure 3.8). These interactive behaviors are not intended to make it easier to manipulate the interface as in the previous case, but rather to provide the literary readership with new tools to analyze the work.

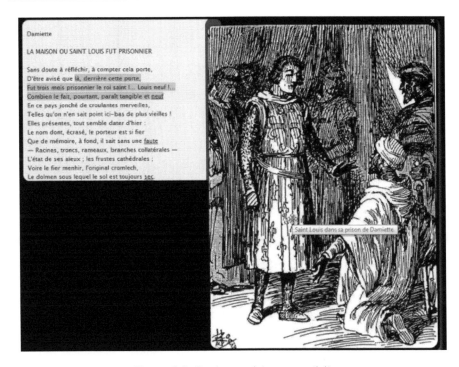

Figure 3.8. *Design assists user activity*

The essential difference between the authors we have placed in the third category – meaningful systems – and the authors already discussed is that the design of the interface is evaluated from the viewpoint of the designer rather than the user. Thus, de Souza assesses communicability, which is the ability of the interface to communicate the *intention of the designer*. Likewise, the communicational level in the method proposed by Scolari analyzes virtual communication strategies within the interface, which goes back to the *relationship between the implied designer and the implied user* (recalling that the implied user is, when all is said and done, a construction of the designer). Finally, Stockinger's first criterion for describing an editing region is the logical structure, that is, the region chosen by the designer to communicate his *service*.

For the authors in the third group, the designer's intention, strategy or service is expressed in the form of a system of (semiotic) *signs*. The rules of description range from the most concise – variation in time and linguistic function for de Souza – to the most customized – elements of expression, eidetic form and topographical and chromatic structure for Stockinger.

The designer of NIA offers two different views of the work, adapted to two different implied users or profiles of reader. The linear view sets up a sequential pathway, closer to a classic book, for an occasional or beginner reader who is not familiar with the work or has never read it. The topographical view, on the contrary, gives an overall and complete view so that readers can begin to read where they wish and can move around freely. This view is designed for a researcher–reader profile that is familiar with the work in its printed edition and will explore new reading possibilities in this digital edition. Finally, in the third view, the designer proposes a pictorial pathway by presenting a slideshow of 59 illustrations from the book.

An element that is secondary to the design of interfaces but deserves to be examined nevertheless is the set of *user instructions*. These instructions play a major role in Semiotic Inspection, because they contain metalinguistic signs that explain and describe the signs in the interface. Thus, in Semiotic Engineering, the user instructions also serve to evaluate the communicability of the design. For Bannon and Bødker, the instructions for use are a learning support that accompanies the user in the transformation of his praxis produced by the interface. This is why the user instructions, like the interface design, must be part of the user's sociocultural context. Finally, the user instructions are optional for heuristics of usability but, if they exist, they must comply with certain criteria that are again aimed at good user performance. The welcome video that plays the first time the topographical view of NIA is opened shows the possible usages that the designer has imagined for this view. The objective of representing the mouse and various manipulations is, above all, to ensure ease of use.

To sum up, three forms of evaluating the design of hypermedia interfaces stem from the three types of mediation. Because each of them concerns a different dimension – user performance, user activity and design strategy – all three of them can be applied to a single design, as we have shown in the case of NIA. However, it is clear that the most applicable method of evaluation will always depend on the objective of the interface and that, in this vein, meaningful systems seem to include and subsume the other two forms of mediation.

3.5. Bibliography

[BAN 89] BANNON L.J., BØDKER S., "Beyond the interface: encountering artifacts in use", *DAIMI Report Series*, vol. 18, no. 288, pp. 1–35, 1989.

[BEA 01] BEAUDOUIN-LAFON M., "40 ans d'interaction homme-machine: points de repère et perspectives", *Actes de la Conférence ASTI'2001*, available at: http:// www-ihm.lri.fr/~mbl/ASTI2001/40ansIHM-papier.pdf, 2001.

[BØD 87] BØDKER S., "Through the interface – a human activity approach to user interface design", *DAIMI Report Series*, no. 224, available at: http://ojs. statsbiblioteket.dk/index.php/daimipb/article/view/7586, 1987.

[BØD 15] BØDKER S., KLOKMOSE C.N., "A dialectical take on artifact ecologies and the physical-digital divide", *Proceedings of the 33rd Annual ACM Conference Extended Abstracts on Human Factors in Computing Systems, ACM*, pp. 2401–2404, 2015.

[DES 93] DE SOUZA C.S., "The semiotic engineering of user interface languages", *International Journal of Man-Machine Studies*, vol. 39, no. 5, pp. 753–773, 1993.

[DES 05] DE SOUZA C.S., *The Semiotic Engineering of Human-Computer Interaction*, MIT Press, Cambridge, 2005.

[DES 06] DE SOUZA C.S., LEITÃO C.F., PRATES R.O. *et al.*, "The semiotic inspection method", *Proceedings of VII Brazilian Symposium on Human Factors in Computing Systems*, available at: http://dx.doi.org/10.1145/1298023.1298044, 2006.

[DES 09] DE SOUZA C.S., LEITÃO C.F., *Semiotic Engineering Methods for Scientific Research in HCI*, Morgan & Claypool Publishers, San Rafael, 2009.

[DES 13] DE SOUZA C.S., "Semiotics", in SOEGAARD M., DAM R.F. (eds), *The Encyclopedia of Human-Computer Interaction*, The Interaction Design Foundation, Aarhus, Denmark, 2013.

[ECO 84] ECO U., *Semiotica e filosofia del linguaggio*, Einaudi, Turin, 1984.

[GIB 77] GIBSON J., "The theory of affordances", in SHAW R., BRANSFORD J. (eds), *Perceiving, Acting, and Knowing*, Erlbaum Associates, Hillsdale, 1977.

[KAP 14] KAPTELININ V., "Affordances", in *The Encyclopedia of Human-Computer Interaction*, 2nd ed., available at: encyclopedia/affordances_and_design.html (consulted on March 9, 2015), 2014.

[LAI 13] LAITANO M.I., BOOTZ P., SALCEDA H., "Re-hypertextualisation d'œuvres littéraires: Nouvelles Impressions d'Afrique de Raymond Roussel", *Pratiques et usages numériques H2PTM'13*, Paris, France, pp. 135–147, 2013.

[MOL 90] MOLICH R., NIELSEN J., "Improving a human-computer dialogue", *Communications of the ACM*, vol. 33, no. 3, pp. 338–348, 1990.

[NIE 86] NIELSEN J., "A virtual protocol model for computer-human interaction", *International Journal of Man-Machine Studies*, vol. 24, no. 3, pp. 301–312, March 1986.

[NIE 92] NIELSEN J., "Layered interaction analysis of direct manipulation", available at: http://www.nngroup.com/articles/direct-manipulation, 1992.

[NIE 94] NIELSEN J., "Heuristic evaluation", *Usability Inspection Methods*, John Wiley & Sons, Inc., New York, 1994.

[NIE 95] NIELSEN J., "10 heuristics for user interface design", available at: http://www.nngroup.com/articles/ten-usability-heuristics, 1995.

[NOR 86] NORMAN D.A., "Cognitive engineering", in NORMAN D.A., DRAPER S.W. (eds), *User Centered System Design*, Lawrence Erlbaum Associates, Hillsdale, 1986.

[NOR 15] NORMAN D.A., "Affordances: commentary on the special issue of AI EDAM", *Artificial Intelligence for Engineering Design, Analysis and Manufacturing*, vol. 29, no. 3, pp. 235–238, 2015.

[RAB 95] RABARDEL P., *Les hommes et les technologies: approche cognitive des instruments contemporains*, Armand Colin, Paris, 1995.

[SCO 01] SCOLARI C.A., "Towards a semio-cognitive theory of human-computer interaction", *CHI '01 Extended Abstracts on Human Factors in Computing Systems*, available at: http://dx.doi.org/10.1145/634067.634120, 2001.

[SCO 04] SCOLARI C.A., "Hacer clic. Hacia una sociosemiótica de las interacciones digitales", *deSignis*, vol. 5, pp. 73–84, 2004.

[SCO 09] SCOLARI C., "The sense of the interface: applying semiotics to HCI research", *Semiotica*, vol. 2009, no. 177, pp. 1–27, 2009.

[STO 05] STOCKINGER P., *Les Sites Web: Conception, Description et évaluation*, Hermès-Lavoisier, Paris, 2005.

[VER 85] VERÓN E., "L'analyse du contrat de lecture: une nouvelle méthode pour les études de positionnement des supports presse", in *Les médias, expériences, recherches actuelles, applications*, IREP, Paris, 1985.

4

Experience Design: Explanation and Best Practices

For far too long now, products and services have not been designed with us in mind. They are merely designed, which is simply not enough. Buying a television with a hard-to-find "delete program" function hidden in the "modify program" menu, or using software with obscurely titled functions whose real purpose continually eludes us, or using a tablet that reacts by itself and closes the web page found after 20 min of careful navigating. It is likely that you have all experienced this!

The products and services related to information and communication technologies (ICT) have greatly evolved since the 1960s [PRO 01] and they are still expanding. However, consideration for the user is still disappointing in this area. Too many projects still result in a failure: rejected by the public, avoided by employees, etc. Thinking like a designer can change the way we develop projects, services, processes and even strategies. This can open the door to innovation, which is key to reaching a superior level of customer service.

However, companies have started to realize the importance of focusing their products and interactive medias around the user. They are increasingly investing in professionals who can provide a memorable client experience

Chapter written by Leslie MATTÉ GANET.

and redefine their business approach, but the attempts are awkward and the implementation of an efficient methodology remains difficult. It must be said that we can quickly become lost. A large number of concepts have appeared: *user experience, UX Design, visual designer, Interaction Designer, User Interaction Designer*, etc. This list is far from exhaustive and what a wealth of terms! Each new actor's role adds further confusion to the difficult implementation of the user experience. Additionally, today, the service provided by media extends beyond the framework of the interface; broadly, designing a user experience has expanded to the process of life before and after the interface. The experience beyond the media must be taken into consideration. The term "user" has become restrictive for representing the human for whom we are designing a product, service or platform. In the Information and Communication Sciences, the concept of using is widely preferred. In the end, it can represent a customer, employee, apprentice, consumer, prospective client, objector, etc. In the context of the need for clarity and bringing a vision beyond design to the ICT, we have chosen to discuss Experience Design (XD) for 2 years now [MAT 14].

But what exactly is user experience? Good question. There are theoretical and academic explanations that vary depending on the area in question: marketing, business, digital technologies, etc. The commonly accepted idea is to design for the user, and not for clients, the ideas of an agency or any other reason. An Experience Designer's work consists of making sure usage problems do not occur and, moreover, to create user-friendliness.

This chapter was designed for those of you who have heard Experience Design discussed without really knowing what it is or why it is important. For everyone else, you will acquire some good frames of reference and reflections. This chapter focuses on:

– Perspectives on the favorable conditions of Experience Design in order to establish good work conditions for XD;

– Means to convince clients, colleagues and superiors about the Experience Design approach;

– Good reflections that make it possible to use XD to produce the best-quality screens.

4.1. Several problems identified with interface creation

4.1.1. *Users have difficulty too often*

In the struggle between individuals and machines, user success rates are still, and continue to be, very low: e-commerce sites record five sales per 1,000 visits, 20% of Internet users do their shopping online, 12% manage to fill in forms, 0.5% choose online assessment services, etc.

During 16 years of practice and 70 interface ergonomics projects, we have only observed once, on a touch screen, a 100% success rate on a user test! After some research, this touch screen was indeed developed by ergonomists.

The difficulties that users have with ICT also stems from the fact that these technologies evolve very quickly. Household equipment rates have not seen such an increase since 1960. Internet users have grown from 150,000 in 1995 to 26 million in 2005 in France. The number of subscribers quadrupled between the beginning of 2000 (3.1 million) and the end of 2005 (13.1 million), with high-speed access growing from 50,000 to 9.5 million subscribers during this time. This uninterrupted growth has no equal (Sources: national records, base 2000, Insee).

In the space of only a few years, users have had to discover, understand and learn how to use first the Internet, then mobile telephones and now touch technologies. Predictions currently point to using two screens at once or connected objects. The consequence is that the practices and expectations of users are evolving very quickly! Their standards, skills and needs are changing at the same speed.

4.1.2. *An awkward practice of Experience Design*

Even when ICT manufacturers are open to XD, their practice of it remains awkward and the results are not very qualitative or lack ambition. For example, a major bank may wish to implement a user-centered process without ever consulting a single user. This is UXD without the "U". The most astonishing part was their surprised reaction when we brought this to their attention.

Another bad practice observed is the design of personas by anyone, at any time, in any way. We call this practice "back-of-the-envelope personas". A persona is a tool describing a group of users that summarizes field observations (targets, practices, needs) for any project team. This tool has suffered the reverse of its success, because anyone and everyone thinks they are capable of creating these personas, without empathy or knowledge of cognitive functioning and social factors. These "back-of-the-envelope personas" either describe super-powered human beings or simply one archetypal social class, etc. very far from the human beings that we really are.

We must also mention this bad practice provides the Experience Designer with the opportunity to implement one tool, or sometimes two, but never the entire process. Imagine a gardener being asked to transform an abandoned garden into a beautiful living space using only a spade and three seeds! Yes, manufacturers, still very poorly versed in this discipline, think that one drop of XD will produce a miracle.

4.1.3. *A difficult beginning for Experience Design in France*

In 2011, companies finally began to invest in XD significantly in order to design products that were more than simply usable. However, the momentum is still modest where, as we just mentioned, there are fragile internal practices. A hint at an explanation of this can be found by looking at the history of the introduction of Experience Design in France.

Ergonomics has been the science of design centered on users since 1970. However, because the first 30 years of ergonomics only focused on the subjects of optimizing work conditions, ICT merely gathered momentum. Between 1980 and 1990, the first powerful and mass-produced ICT arrived on the market, but realizing that an ergonomist could adapt ICT for humans was particularly difficult in a domain where very operational methods were in place. Human resources directors in ICT industries knew absolutely nothing about this work. Upon leaving university, these ergonomists even had to convince themselves, as they had only been trained in work ergonomics! Furthermore, ergonomics had long been accompanied by a deeply rooted preconceived idea that "an ergonomist is expensive". The turning point was in 2011, when for the first time a manufacturer said, "It will cost us more to not consult an ergonomist".

Another movement advocating a user-centered approach has been widespread in France since 2005: UX design (User eXperience Design), –

the term commonly used in the US. This American movement, which appeared in the 1990s, proposed a very influential methodology for the creation of Experience Design. The trans-Atlantic UX is embedded in the DNA of manufacturers.

However, UX design arrived in France marketed in a diluted form, ergonomics light, but it was notable for finally leading ICT manufacturers to open up to User Design. The French UX movement was a fast-growing movement on unstable ground; there was little existing training for the disoriented manufacturers. This was the "UX wave". The roles, responsibilities and skills were not clearly defined. Sylvie Daumal [DAU 12] explains it very well in her book: "With time, experience, and often by necessity, the professionals acquired skills in fields that were not their primary focus". The consequences were substantial: awkward experience design certainly, as well as exhausted Experience Designers heaped with responsibilities, working in difficult conditions with few means to complete responsibilities that exceeded their skill set, etc.

In 2008, the ergonomics market was essentially dominated by computer services companies who hired or set up "Ergonomics" centers. These companies sold their skills like the others, which is to say without real distinction in terms of knowledge. Aside from these, some agencies which specialized in UX design took over large parts of the market by offering services specific to UX, notably in e-commerce. There are still experts in interface ergonomics who "pursue their paths", fighting for the expert, and quality services.

To date, the roles and intervention of ergonomists and Experience Designers have considerably evolved. In the early 2000s, they were involved at the end of a project to implement a unique tool: the user test. Today, they intervene earlier and earlier in the project to implement three to five tools, but their roles still seem obscure.

4.1.4. Ill-defined jobs

Simply looking at job postings of profiles for "five-legged sheep" that require taking on the entire process of a digital media design is enough to scare any prospective job seeker – or choke them with laughter. In 2005, a UX designer had to understand the users, structure the entire interface, develop a visual design and integrate html pages!

The last 10 years have been full of discussions, exchanges and debates around this issue: should I hire a UX designer or an ergonomist? The article by Gilles Démarty, "I am not an ergonomist" [DEM 13] outlined the problem of boundaries and notable differences between a UX Designer and an ergonomist.

Therefore, what is the difference between these two professions? A very interesting exchange on the Ergo HMI list occurred in April 2015 entitled "Survey: Is the Name UX Designer Detrimental to HMI Ergonomists?" Some excellent comments and contributions were made. Here are a few examples:

> "In France, I sometimes get the feeling that we hire an Ergonomist to fill the job of a UX researcher + UX designer (at least). A French ergonomist finds themselves caught in the middle. Once they have completed their training, they must learn a whole new trade if they want to be a UX Designer." Johan Antonin, ErgoIHM list, 2015

> "In France, generally, we have an Ergonomist + Artistic Director (if I'm not mistaken). The English have UX Researcher + UX Designer + Visual Designer. And then the UI Designer." Anonymous, ErgoIHM list, 2015

It has become imperative to clarify the roles and the limits of the responsibilities for each function and align them in relation to their training.

4.1.5. *Manufacturers at various XD maturity levels*

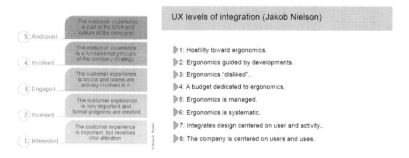

Figure 4.1. *The five possible levels in Experience Design for a company according to Sylvie Daumal [DAU 12] (left). Jakob Nielsen's 10 levels of integration in the UX approach [NIE 01] (right)*

Jacob Nielsen [NIE 01] was one of the first to propose a tool to gauge a company's XD maturity, which makes it possible to determine the probability that an organization will implement a user-centered approach for the development of ICT. Sylvie Daumal [DAU 12] later proposed a classification system simplified into five levels.

We will simply use the four levels of a company proposed by Timothy Embretson [EMB 16].

Barrier company

This company does not open any conversation around the implementation of a user-centered approach. Any efforts in this sense are not welcome. The arguments put forward to block this approach are:

– no time in the project calendar to allow for extra work;

– no adequate financing to allow for investment in extra resources;

– clients that are not interested or in favor of an XD approach.

Behind this is a struggle against change. These companies often say that they have always proceeded like this, that it works and that they do not need to change. The internal technicians, not trained in XD, put an end to all proposals for the benefit of the final user because of a lack of sensitivity and putting their own interests first.

Apprehensive company

The conversations around XD have been initiated, but the implementation is sporadic. There is probably a small number of individuals supporting the approach but there are still many obstacles. The unfamiliarity and reticence to implement the XD approach is generally located at the level of leadership.

The contributions of XD have begun to demonstrate their utility and occasionally a partner on the project has been required to carry out research about users and develop usage scenarios and screen mock-ups. However, there are still many cases of rejection claiming a lack of financing and an unsuitable timeline. The ICT sold remains not very profitable or ambitious.

Supportive company

In these kinds of companies, XD is in place and working well. The adoption of the process extends beyond a small percentage to all projects.

Every person in the company has contributed and now it is time to focus on the managers of the company. In general, the top-down hierarchy in place must be revised to become an advocate company, the final level of maturity. The managers are probably informed about the XD process, but they are not yet enthusiastic champions, ready to change up the entire company. The most common situation in a support company is that a large number of collaborators are aware of XD, but they probably do not make it a priority. While the added value has been demonstrated in the general process of a project, a user-centered approach is not always the business strategy of the company.

Advocate company

This is the ideal company environment. The road maps for every product or service, the project strategy and the business decisions are the result of XD thinking where the user-focused approach is the heart and soul. The managers are not only familiar with the XD basics, but understand the XD lifecycle in detail and advocate it at almost every step.

4.2. What is good Experience Design?

The answer to the question "What is good Experience Design?" is expressed on different levels. Different levels of usability are possible, depending on the XD effort put into a project.

Level 0: a system without bugs

This was the level sought after by companies from the 1980s to the 2000s and still today by barrier companies. No experience or success of a product is ensured.

Level 1: an easy-to-use interface

This basic level is concerned with making sure all interactions are fluid, the information is clear and the interface offers proper guidance. All of the screens respond to the original requirements of usability listed by Bastien and Scapin and to the ISO norms for human–machine interaction. The screens are standard and designed for a very large public, without understanding the specific target of the product. Therefore, the interface is:

– easy to learn;

– effective: avoids as many errors as possible and facilitates the correction of errors;

– efficient: allows the user to reach objectives in the minimum amount of time;

– pleasant to use.

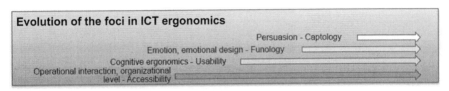

Figure 4.2. *Evolution of foci in ICT ergonomics according to their level of usability [SER 16]*

Level 2: a useful and practical interface

The second level that arises in the user experience of a system is the level of satisfaction. Obviously, this supposes that the first level has been reached and then offers to answer the essential needs of the target user. This level can only be reached by meeting the users and giving them a chance to speak. This level consists of going to discover and understand the ICT user: their professional needs, usage needs and service needs. This Experience Design is becoming personalized and adapts to the target user. A level of comfort is available to the user and innovative functionalities appear.

Level 3: an interface that fades away in favor of the original activity

Finally, there is emotional design [WAL 11], the level currently almost never reached, that proposes a real user experience: an experience where the screen disappears, the steps of interactions are forgotten and mental effort is no longer necessary to understand the system. The technology makes it possible to live an experience, benefit from the moment and create positive emotions, or play in such a way that the moment spontaneously inspires loyalty or even addiction in the user.

4.3. How does Experience Design work?

Experience Design is not simply the visual part of a product. It is the entire product design process. It is a process in which we must take into account the technical data of the product to design as well as the marketing approach and even the culture of the company. It is a process that hinges on observing and listening to users. Indeed, it relies on usage in real situations and on the study of user processes to imagine an effective user experience.

4.3.1. *A method, more than a result*

Experience Design is a "design-oriented" principle that leads to innovation and allows the co-creation of value with all parties involved in a project. The creation cycle of digital projects is totally redesigned, starting from a scientific approach while stimulating creativity and with the goal of giving priority to people. We must turn from a *product-oriented* project management style to a *client-oriented* project management style.

The design of experience is presented as a revolution for the process of digital production by Antoine Monchecourt [MON 15], a postdoctoral researcher in Information and Communication Sciences.

4.3.2. *Focused on humans*

Experience Design is a *human-centered method*, based on an intimate knowledge of the public and its cultural practices rather than on technology and marketing fundamentals. Experience Design is the search for the voice of the end user.

Different movements subscribe to this vision. Whether it is UX Design, Design Thinking [BRO 14] or ergonomics, each of these disciplines has exactly the same aims to design for and by the user.

4.3.3. *A transformed project management*

Experience Design makes it possible to explore more ideas and must be present from the start of the creation and innovation processes for interactive media. Instead of starting with technology, this method begins with humans and their environments, leaving behind a product/sale focused vision and moving toward a vision centered on service and humans, reinforcing the capacity of the company to innovate. Today, Design Thinking can be applied in several domains: health, education, security, etc. not only in ICT.

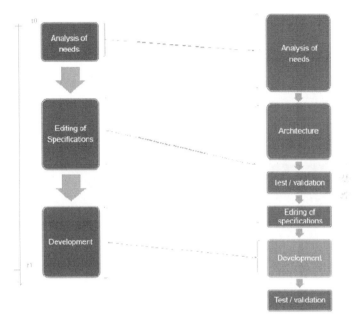

Figure 4.3. *Traditional ICT project management (left). XD project management: a reorganization of the phases around the user in the same time constraints (right). For a color version of this figure, see www.iste.co.uk/reyes/hypermedia.zip*

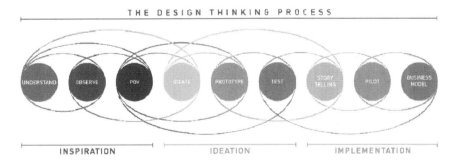

Figure 4.4. *A representation of the process of design in three steps and nine sub-steps (source: Paris-est D. School). For a color version of this figure, see www.iste.co.uk/reyes/hypermedia.zip*

Iteration and prototypes

A second notable point: project management is usually thought of as a linear process moving through stages such as planning, design, production and evaluation. On the contrary, Experience Design is a cyclical, iterative method, based on trial and error and back and forth (between observation and design, abstract and concrete, generating ideas and eliminating them, etc.). As in a traditional project, it is about reaching a final objective by a fixed timeline, but the progress is more fluid, experimental and open. The main support of these different exploration cycles is the prototype.

Figure 4.5. *Three examples of very simple prototypes: foam blocks to rethink a space, a post-it mock-up of a smart phone interface and role-play (source: Design thinking in a day, IDEO, 2014). For a color version of this figure, see www.iste.co.uk/reyes/hypermedia.zip*

Creative organizations and work spaces

Design requires an environment that is stimulating for creation, which translates not only into how the objectives are distributed but also into the workspaces themselves. At an organizational level, it consists of making up multidisciplinary and non-hierarchical teams as well as encouraging interconnections between professional activities and individual interest in order to foster creativity and multiply perspectives. This does not mean that anarchy reigns, but on the contrary, the project is driven by "a general direction so that the organization knows which objective it should move towards and so that the employees responsible for innovating do not feel the need to constantly refer to their superiors" [BRO 14].

4.3.4. *New professions*

We stated earlier that there is some confusion between the different professions involved in XD. This field is still young in France and is progressing very quickly. The job description of a *Web ergonomist* only appeared on the government Website in October 2012. Today, the job *web designer* is disappearing and being refined by the discipline.

ROLE	BRAND PRESENCE	MARKETING CAMPAIGN	CONTENT SOURCE	TASK-BASED APPLICATION
Information Architect	Medium involvement. The greater the content challenge, the more like a content source the project will become.	Low involvement for smaller sites (like a single landing page). Medium involvement if working with larger microsites.	Very high involvement. Content sources require an information architecture that has an appropriate balance of structure and flexibility, to give users a solid base to stand on and allow for planned growth.	Medium to high involvement, mainly focused on creating the navigational framework, unless there are larger content areas that need to be referenced during some workflows.
Interaction Designer	Medium involvement. The greater the number of tasks, the more like a task-based application the project will become.	Low involvement for smaller sites. Medium to high involvement for larger microsites or *advergames* (sponsored online games meant to generate play and buzz).	Medium to high involvement. Search, tagging and filtering features cross the line between information architecture and interaction design. Content sources may also have workflows involving content creation and management.	Very high involvement. This kind of project often requires the heaviest lifting, as interaction design deliverables (such as user process flows and wireframes) are key to communicating requirements visually.
User Researcher *Involvement will vary based on budget and access to users. Listed here are common techniques for each project type. For more on each of these techniques, see Chapter 6.*	Research efforts may focus on understanding needs of priority user groups (through surveys or interviews) or design research testing the effectiveness of a particular visual design in conveying the right brand message.	Due to the often temporary nature of campaigns, user involvement is often light. More permanent solutions may use research similar to brand presence sites. It's also common to use analytics tools to present two or more variations of a particular page to see which one leads to the most conversions. This is called *A/B testing*.	Field research such as contextual inquiry can help the team understand how different users currently work with information. Card sorting is an excellent way to understand how your users may group information and common patterns and mental models. Once a framework has been set, usability testing can validate the structure.	Field research such as contextual inquiry can be done to understand tasks as users are currently completing them. The most frequently used and best understood technique for involving users in the design of a task-based application, however, is usability testing.

Table 4.1. *Jobs in UX Design [UNG 12]*

In Experience Design, the vocabulary is very rich and it can be difficult to see differences clearly: *User eXperience, UX, UX design , design for users, "designed for you", Experience Design, User-centric, User-centered, digital design, interaction design, interactive design, ergonomic design, interface designer, interactive designer, interactive interface, user-centered design, user-centered process, user satisfaction, human factor, information technology ergonomics, software ergonomics, digital ergonomics, interface ergonomics, good design, digital design, intuitive software, software architect, etc.*

New professions are appearing, such as *UX Designer, narrative designer, digital designer, interface designer, interaction designer, ergonomist, information architect and app designer, game designer, level designer, quest designer, game ergonomist, game platform designer, toy designer, gamification expert, game monetization designer and transmedia experiences designer.* You can even meet hybrid professionals who wear many hats.

The training must adapt, but so far has not been able to keep up with industry needs. New courses dedicated to human–machine interactions are still being developed today, such as the Masters of Cognitive Sciences at the Université Lyon 2 in 2015.

Unger and Chandler [UNG 12] describe an XD very clearly inherited from the American perspective and propose a nomenclature of professions (Table 4.1) that could be introduced to French manufacturers. There are three distinct skills that must be disassociated on the project manager's side:

– the specialist of human factors who is similar to the ergonomist;

– the graphics specialist who is similar to the graphic designer who is also called a UI Designer (User Interaction Designer) in France;

– the technical specialist who will be the developer.

A fourth skill, unique to our culture, is missing from our story: the French UX Designer. Our universities currently train these creatives, who are very sensitive to the XD approach and trained in a large number of XD tools, but – while aware of them – lack proficiency in human factors.

	Business Context Analysis	Usability Engineering	User Experience Planning	Content Publishing	Information Architecture	Interaction Design	Visual & Information Design	Computer Science
User Experience Design	Context Map	Synthesis	UX Brief	Content	Navigation	Wireframe	Graphics	Front-end Code
	Performance Measures	Primary Research	Personas	Editing	Information Organization	Interaction	Layout	Database Design
	Product / Service Definitions	Testing	Engagement Definitions	Governance	Information Relationship	Patterns	Style Guide	Server Code
	Business Intent	Logistics	UXD Management	Content Management	IA Management	Conventions	Art Direction	Infrastructure
	Mission / Vision	Research Design	UX Strategy	Content Strategy	IA Strategy	Device Strategy	Creative Strategy	System Architecture
	Business Model	Analytics	Research	Research / Analytics	Research / Analytics	Research / Analytics	Research / Analytics	Research / Analytics

Figure 4.6. *"UX Design practice Verticals" official illustration produced by DSIA Research Initiative UX Design Practice Verticals v1.3.0, © 2011–2013 Nathaniel Davis | DSIA Research Initiative*

Raphael Yharrassarry [YHA 15] reflected on the skills that make a "good UX designer" by relying on the model in T[1] (see Figure 4.6). In his very interesting article, he lists a set of skills (in columns) by area of expertise (in rows): the principle of the T model indicates that you must have more or less advanced knowledge on all of the horizontal fields and be an expert in one to three of the vertical fields (the shape of a T). This situates the French UX Designer between the professions of ergonomist and UI Designer.

French UX Designers are excellent screen architects, with an ergonomist ensuring the cognitive ergonomics of the digital service.

---

1 A model that lists the skills of a person with expertise in an area and good general knowledge about connected activities.

4.3.5. *Tools in DX*

Many tools are used in Experience Design. So far, we have referenced nearly 70 of them. We will not detail all of them here, as there are several specific works that do this very well (*IDEO methods cards* [BRO 14], [LAL 15]). Here are the most recent as an example:

– heuristic analysis;

– user research;

– audit;

– contextual inquiry;

– personas, mentioned above;

– mock-ups and prototypes;

– design guides.

These tools make it possible to understand the user, build creatively and validate an ICT project. For the most part, these tools come from UX Design. Other current movements, such as Design Thinking, also propose very interesting tools. We will detail two here, known for their originality and potential: the WAD Book and the Six Thinking Hats.

Bono's Thinking Hats

The Six Thinking Hats is a well-known tool of business coaching. Proposed by Edward De Bono [DE 13], the use of this tool allows a company to benefit from all possible resources in a team of collaborators. Indeed, De Bono explains the originality and the power of lateral thinking, a way to approach questions from a new angle and easily generate new ideas.

MATTE integrated this tool into the XD approach for the first time in 2011 in a method called Design Pensé® in order to respond to issues about creativity fatigue brought on by a still-irregular implementation of XD. The method was tested in the ICT domain and it transfers perfectly without any other adjustments.

Wide Angle Design Book

Tabs of the WAD Book	Professional Interests
The main questions direct the field survey	Guide the survey and the interview
Ontologies	Understanding the studied domain through the categorization of identified items and their modalities
Vocabulary	Capture phrases verbatim
The empathy card	Capture emotions
Screen templates	Capture the creative thinking of the premises of interface elements
Documentation in relation to the project	Facilitate the understanding of the subject to be treated
Breakdown of activity in the first-identified action sequences	Start a case by case review of the activity analysis
If the context allows, A3 pages can be used for the participant to draw on	Capture solutions based on the user

Table 4.2. *Content of the WAD Book: the tabs and their respective roles*

Two years ago, at the intersection of several approaches, there appeared the Wide Angle Design Book or "the WAD method". Developed by Leslie Matté Ganet [MAT 13], this tool aims to adapt field observations to suit the restrictions on gathering data imposed by manufacturers (very short observation times, limited number of interactions, off-limits digital tools such as the camcorders and Dictaphones) and the *level* 3 objective of creating emotional design (see section 4.2 Level 3 of this chapter).

This tool is above all based on paper thinking, which is more rich, more analytic and more creative. Paper thinking frees up cognitive resources to allow for a maximum mental load in order to "be present in your actions" in the observation phase. The different parts of the WAD Book as well as their roles are detailed in Table 4.2. In Figure 4.7, the WAD Book is elaborated with a few sheets of color and a clip to bind them.

Paper thinking is certainly more effective, but this WAD book offers many other professional and intellectual contributions. Creative thinking is directly captured and analytic thinking is directly translated. The work of data recovery, interpreting and modeling, generally put off until later, is completed immediately. The time gain is clearly significant and carries over to the quality of the work that follows. It makes it possible to categorize directly from observations through the quick manipulation of the tabs on the sheets. Each part can be quickly identified by a color scheme.

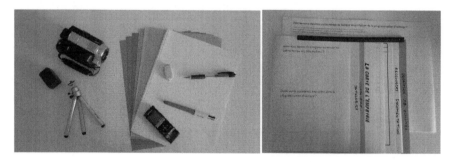

Figure 4.7. *The Wide Angle Design Book [MAT 13]. For a color version of this figure, see www.iste.co.uk/reyes/hypermedia.zip*

Comparing, adding and removing observations is made possible by deletions and short timeframes, when a capture tool such as a tablet or laptop absolutely does not allow for it. Usually on a tablet, a data file would be prepared beforehand using PowerPoint, Excel or another program. This method causes us to lose precious time relocating where the data can be found! In general, we end up saving everything in the same space and saying that we will sort it out later.

The WAD Book also allows for a multimodal collection in the form of texts, drawings, folding, etc. It also offers a considerable time gain, especially post-treatment, as well as in the field to translate, make models at the same time as gathering data, pose more detailed questions and progress further through the reasoning.

4.4. A powerful approach

XD offers a framework for all actors in a project to solve design issues in a short time and a creative atmosphere.

4.4.1. *XD protects from rejection*

Historically, the very first objective of XD was to protect a company from the substantial costs of ill-adapted interfaces (interface rejections, complexity, inefficiency, inadequacy, etc.) and so, at the same time, increase the company revenue and profits.

An excellent understanding of final users and iterative processes make it possible to specify the project even more each time. Usage cases are reviewed and so any usage problems, if they exist, are identified earlier.

4.4.2. *XD allows for an important gain in time*

There are still "extended" projects that can stretch out over 2 years, but this is no longer the case with Experience Design, because the screens are developed before the technical phase. The media is formatted into a well thought out form, validated and completed before being implemented. This process makes it possible to progress much more quickly because the decisions are settled.

It is true that the field phase can appear to be a huge task to a team starting directly with the functional specifications. For this stage, 20–30 days should be set aside. It is key to the success of the method and the accelerations that follow. The gain in time during the development phase and project management is substantial.

If time is a strong limitation, there are fast tools that rely on Experience Design and make it possible to create some leverage in a very short time. For example, you could skip the design brief and make a Design Sprint, a tool inspired by Design Thinking and the agile approach.

Day 1: Understand –pose the problem to be resolved;

Day 2: Diverge –find the maximum amount of solutions to answer the problem;

Day 3: Decide –select a solution;

Day 4: Prototype –complete the POC (i.e. *Proof of concept*) of the solution;

Day 5: Test –validate the solution by submitting it to the users.

4.4.3. *The XD facilitator*

Other considerations have also been demonstrated and warmly welcomed by ICT manufacturers, such as:

– obtaining an excellent understanding of their own clients, who provide depth and material for marketing strategies;

– optimizing the ICT design process, making it more agile, custom and profitable;

– reducing the effect of the changing opinions of participants and integrating them;

– stimulating creativity and tending toward innovation;

– facilitating the support of customers and participants in the project and making team coordination more fluid;

– accelerating decision-making;

– producing high-quality work.

4.5. Example of XD contribution to an industrial project

Here, we will present a project that was first completed using traditional project management and then revised using Experience Design project management. By doing so, we hope to demonstrate the differences between these two project management approaches in terms of results, procedure and facilitation.

The project consists of a Website destined for the public, an audience with a wide diversity and a large variability in terms of use skills, level of needs, experience with digital tools and several other use problems.

The role of this Website, without unveiling its identity, is to guide the individual through the creation of an administrative file addressed to the state, who in return contributes a financial incentive.

Throughout the creation of this file, the site will determine the amount of the bonus expected, take into account all of the relevant supporting documents and the necessary conditions to qualify for the incentive and progressively submit documents for validity checks, all within the personal space. The Website checks the quality of the file at every step in order to ensure that the user receives the bonus.

This Website project is interesting because it has a public part whose main goal is *to explain* its purpose and convince the visitor to register. The underlying usability objectives for these parts include offering quick reading times, clearly presenting all services and ultimately leading the visitor to create their own account, because that is how the company generates its profit.

This site also has a private section accessible by logging in: a personal space for the user. This space is closely tied to software issues, because it must allow the user *to succeed* in creating their administrative file. The underlying usability objectives for this second part must allow the user to understand how to create their administrative folder. Here, the ergonomic challenges are linked to guidance issues for actions, adapting vocabulary, protecting against errors and bringing a sense of lightness to unappealing administrative tasks.

4.5.1. *Creating the Website with classic project management*

Project sequence

The company responsible for the project can be described as an apprehensive company (see section 4.1.5) in terms of its XD maturity. Indeed, it is a company that does not have good knowledge of the XD sequence or an awareness of its importance and the risks of creating an interface without the user's input.

This type of project is often conducted quickly, even hastily. The team overseeing the project was a very technical team with a communication person, a technical person, a developer and a company manager, who provided the commercial objectives.

This team did its best to iron out the proposal and the service, produce content for the site, solve the technical component and develop dedicated functional specifications. However, the team did not have enough knowledge about web use to put themselves in the user's shoes and make choices that benefit them. The team made choices that prioritized function rather than use.

Figure 4.8. *Public part of the site before classic project management. For a color version of this figure, see www.iste.co.uk/reyes/hypermedia.zip*

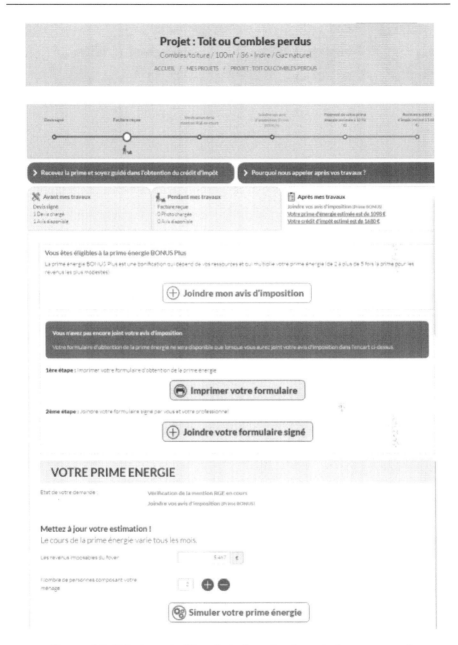

Figure 4.9. *Private part of the site before classic project management. For a color version of this figure, see www.iste.co.uk/reyes/hypermedia.zip*

Project length

This project took 5 months, which is relatively fast for creating an HMI web project of this size using classic methods. On the contrary, the team commented that this project was indeed difficult to bring to fruition.

Screen quality

The result revealed very complex and technical screens:

– the services are presented with a lack of coherence between the access flow (steps 1, 2 and 3) and the description of content contradicts this temporality;

– the vocabulary used corresponds more to the vocabulary of the company than that of the public;

– the service is not clearly explained in one sentence in the 500 px at the top of the page;

– the quality of the screens, as you can see in Figures 4.8 and 4.9, is low: not very readable, welcoming or understandable.

Cost-effectiveness

The cost-effectiveness of this project is very disappointing. The indicators reveal truly catastrophic numbers (see Table 4.3). The conversion rate, which is the number of users who created an account compared to the total number of visitors, should be close to 100%. In this case, it was 0.5%, while the usual conversion rate for free account registration is generally between 20 and 40%.

The bounce rate, which is the number of visitors who leave a page compared to the total number of visitors, is an indicator that should be close to 0%. In this case, it was 66%, while the rate for a healthy Website is between 30 and 50%.

Therefore, the company had to recognize its failure: the results do not measure up. The company needed help if it wanted the Website to generate the expected profits. Realizing that visitors were poorly understanding its services and not knowing how to proceed otherwise, the company called upon an Experience Design ergonomist.

	Cost-effectiveness of the site with classic project management	Cost-effectiveness of the site with XD project management after 30 days online	Norm
Conversion rate	0.5%	10%	Between 20 and 40%
Bounce rate	66%	30%	Between 30 and 50%

Table 4.3. *Cost-effectiveness of the project with and without Experience Design*

4.5.2. *Revising the Website with XD project management*

Project sequence

The ergonomist introduced the point of use into this very technical-centered project. The XD does not have a very large-scale service, and only one single tool is implemented: the user test. This test makes it possible to consider the user and their needs, expectations and practices in the project.

Project length

The project took place over 1.5 months. The reflections were carried out, verified and validated by producing about 20 screen mock-ups that developed the entire Website and suggested several use scenarios.

Screen quality

Figures 4.10 and 4.11 present the new screens created using the XD approach. They reveal a higher quality of usability with much more guidance and clearer content. The quality of the screens is significantly increased. The "personal space" part takes the user by the hand to build the administrative file step by step.

Cost-effectiveness

Thirty days after the new version went online, the rates had changed significantly (see Table 4.3):

– the bounce rate was considerably reduced to become very good;

– the conversion rate multiplied by 20 and more progress is expected in the coming term;

– the turnover corresponds more to the business manager's objectives.

Figure 4.10. *Public part of the site after XD project management. For a color version of this figure, see www.iste.co.uk/reyes/hypermedia.zip*

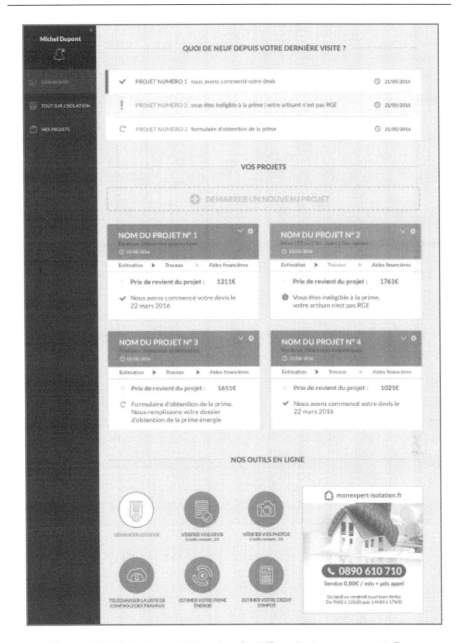

Figure 4.11. *Private part of the site after XD project management. For a color version of this figure, see www.iste.co.uk/reyes/hypermedia.zip*

4.6. How can we improve the quality of Experience Design in the ICT industries?

The problem is less about studying uses than converting them into real potential to design media where the tool fades away in favor of the action and experience. Three factors directly affect the humanity of these technologies:

1) the user's level of knowledge being the excellent understanding of a consumer, user, collaborator, etc.;

2) the industry, its agility and its awareness of the user's experience and the means implemented;

3) the technology.

These three factors are valuable for all kinds of ICT projects, in planning or objectives, and for all sizes and structures of different companies.

4.6.1. *A team with an open mind and empathy*

The most effective approach to improve XD maturity in *barrier companies* is to introduce the value added by XD incrementally, without disturbing the timeframe of the project. Consider building and launching a questionnaire remotely during the start of the project. Integrating the user progressively as a function of their traditional business needs to demonstrate the time gain, support, decrease in problems, etc.

Every person involved must remain positive and observe gradually how the approach of user-centered projects produces positive results. If even one collaborator does not adhere to this approach, it will reduce the XD-oriented efforts, such as a graphic designer who "is used to" creating menus in their screens or a developer who simply wishes to replicate their technical solution identically.

4.6.2. *Co-design, creativity, ideation and respiration*

Weekly collaboration sessions are indispensable for all parties involved in order to share progress and discuss status updates at each stage of the project's development. This ensures that all of the actors are regularly given a chance to speak and the project benefits from the experience and skills of everyone.

Until recently, in the field of creation, a project that was deemed a "work in progress" tended to have a negative connotation. It was much more professional to present a completed project that demonstrated high-quality work and professionalism. There was a fanatical desire to unveil a solution that was completely finalized like the opening night of a show on Broadway. However, if criticism is expressed at that stage of a project, it can be very painful to the authors, who must gather their courage to revise their work.

Today, the tide is turning and "works in progress" are supported. Instead, the idea is that a project is born, grows, expands and corrects itself. We can present unfinished ideas and functional pieces and validate the direction of the project step by step. Actors can challenge the project, in whole or in part, in a less attached way. It is no longer about undoing steps in order to redo them, but continuing to build.

To generate innovation, tools that stimulate creativity, such as Bono's Six Thinking Hats [DE 13], are obviously essential. However, an element that is even more rarely observed in these projects, and which is also very valuable for generating ideas, is *respiration*. This does not consist of working "just-in-time" with as little space as possible between each step. It consists of scheduling time to air out ideas between key steps and giving the project time to breathe. The parties involved should also have the possibility of stepping back, taking time to reflect when the pressure of deadlines that cruelly stifle creativity are eliminated.

4.6.3. *Good skills for appropriate responsibilities*

In a good XD project, an ergonomist is needed: someone who has knowledge of human factors and cognitive sciences, to understand attentional processes and memorization in order to determine cognitive limits, explain them and solve them. Only a UX designer has the primarily creative training to touch on these dimensions exclusively.

The ergonomist considers the human through the following three angles:

– cognitive: knowledge (to make understand);

– affective: sensitivity, preference (to make like);

– conative: behavior, action (to make react).

4.6.4. *The systematic presence of the user and going into the field*

After all, how can we create products centered on the user without meeting the user? We repeat, the user must be *systematically* involved from the *beginning* of the project. To do this, the best method is to go out into the field, commonly referred to as the "point of contact".

This means no longer observing the fish in its tank (through the perspective of the project team, technician, sales inquiries, etc.), but diving into the open sea. It is imperative to observe and understand users, gather their vocabulary, collect the ontologies of the domain and register their emotions. A good field makes it possible to gather enough observations about a group of users that are sufficiently representative of the target audience and gather the other elements cited earlier in the chapter too (see the WAD Book).

To give the reader an indication, a field is sufficiently rich when we learn all of the different user profiles, which can be represented by a very heterogeneous sample of 15–40 people. Observing them for an hour also makes it possible to collect a lot of information. We are referring to the tool called *shadowing* [BRO 14] which suggests observing without intruding, during which the observer remains discreet like a shadow. On the contrary, we also recommend systematically studying user interviews that last 1 or 1.5 h. These interviews are very useful for understanding and interpreting a large part of the profession.

4.6.5. *No longer using the term UX*

The term UX, which has an appropriate and refined meaning on the other side of the Atlantic, is more confusing in France. This has produced the misunderstandings listed in this chapter. This term allows each actor to define their rules arbitrarily.

The term limits the creation of design for the user, the "U", but design can go beyond an interface and an interaction. XD opens up the experience before and after the interaction. The "U" can be the consumer, the employer, the visitor, etc. Challenges increase each day as technologies, uses, needs and interactions become more ubiquitous and cross-media, where digital technology is no more than a link. In this context, the "U" becomes restrictive.

Matté Ganet [MAT 14] explained why UX design is dying at the 2014 FLUPA conference. Many discussions with professionals in this area demonstrate the exhaustion and the limits of these deteriorating practices. However, the user-centered approach remains essential to the values demonstrated for the past 50 years.

We should cast aside this term and promote the meaning and values advocated in this chapter to rebuild the bases of a healthy profession. Let us give the ICT manufacturers good comments and better direction with a method that is adapted to our culture, the maturity of our professions and our relatively small experience in this new era of digital project management. Today, Experience Design is a tried and tested method that provides convincing results and makes it possible to satisfy the final users as much as the actors in the project.

4.7. Conclusion

Forty-five years after the first ergonomists, 20 years after the arrival of the Internet in France, the user is still too infrequently considered in ICT projects.

There are many reasons for this:

– unfamiliarity with the interests of Experience Design;

– unfamiliarity with Experience Design project management;

– difficulties changing methods that are deeply rooted in companies;

– vague definitions of the new professions involved, professions recently taught in schools;

– confusion brought about by a clumsy adoption of American UX Design;

– low ambition of French companies who are stimulated merely by competition, performance and rivalry instead of innovation.

All the same, there is an excellent knowledge base in France. Experience Design combines the skills of ergonomics, user design and design thinking. The results are convincing and the cost-effectiveness has increased for companies. The projects are carried out in stimulating and innovative atmospheres with great success. Users are satisfied and even have good experiences.

Perspectives are starting to shift. Since 2011, it has been said that it is more expensive not to use Experience Design. More and more companies are implementing a user-centered approach earlier, but they still only represent 20% of the economy.

That is not enough. We must continue to advocate. We must teach our youth in school. We must introduce companies to these ideas every day and continue to give users a voice. We must design for and with users.

4.8. Bibliography

[BRO 14] BROWN T., *L'Esprit design: Comment le design thinking change l'entreprise et la stratégie*, Pearson Education, Montreuil, 2014.

[DAU 12] DAUMAL S., *Design d'expérience utilisateur : Principes et méthodes UX*, Eyrolles, Paris, 2012.

[DE 13] DE BONO E., NICOLAÏEFF L, *La boîte à outils de la créativité, Par l'inventeur de la pensée latérale*, Eyrolles, Paris, 2013.

[DEM 13] DÉMARTY G., "Je ne suis pas un ergonome", available at: http://dmrty.fr/blog/je-ne-suis-pas-un-ergonome, 2013.

[EMB 16] EMBRETSON T., "Principles of UX Design: What is user experience?", Blog INVision, available at: http://get.invisionapp.com/chapter-1-of-9-principles-of-ux-design, 2016.

[LAL 15] LALLEMAND C., GRONIER G., *Méthodes de design UX: 30 méthodes fondamentales pour concevoir et évaluer les systèmes interactifs*, Eyrolles, 2015.

[MAT 13] MATTÉ GANET L., "Notre méthode maison le Design Pensé® à 1 an déjà !", available at: https://intuitiveworld.wordpress.com/2013/12/06/notre-methode-maison-le-design-pense-a-1-an-deja/, 2013.

[MAT 14] MATTÉ GANET L., "Pourquoi l'UX Design va s'éteindre en France, heureusement pour nous", *Conférence FLUPA UX-Day 2014*, Paris, available at: http://tinyurl.com/matte-ganet-ux2014, 2014.

[MON 15] MONCHECOURT A., *UX Design: introduction a une pratique revolutionnaire*, Antoine Monchecourt, Le Teich, France, 2015.

[NIE 01] NIELSEN J., *Coordinating User Interfaces for Consistency*, Morgan Kaufmann Publishers, 2001.

[PRO 01] PROULX S., "Usages des technologies d'information et de communication: reconsidérer le champ d'étude, Emergences et continuité dans les recherches en information et communication", available at: http://www.er.uqam.ca/nobel/grmnob/drupal5.1/static/textes/proulx_SFSIC2001.pdf, 2001.

[SER 16] SERINDOU M., "Ergonomie? UX? Design thinking?", available at: http://www.ux-republic.com/ergonomie-ux-design-thinking/, 2016.

[UNG 12] UNGER R., CHANDLER C., *A Project Guide to UX Design: For User Experience Designers in the Field or in the Making*, 2nd ed., New Riders, 2012.

[WAL 11] WALTER A., ROBERT C., SPOOL J., *Design émotionnel*, Eyrolles, Paris, 2011.

[YHA 15] YHARRASSARRY R., "Compétences Ux Et Modèle En T", available at: http://Blocnotes.Iergo.Fr/Articles/Competences-Ux-Et-Modele-En-T/, 2015.

Designing Authoring Software Environments for the Interactive Arts: An Overview of *Mobilizing.js*

5.1. Research context: artistic practices of interactivity

The interactive arts that we are interested in and that we practice are rooted in the use of digital machines capable of interactivity. These can take the shape of a computer, a mobile screen, a video game console, a smartwatch or any other technological object that is capable of running programs and belongs to the set of digital technology that is typical of our era. We believe that the technological potential that these machines offer has a particularly important place in the development of our artistic practices, both individually as artists and, more broadly, as researchers. Our focus is on interactivity, a technical term that has gradually found its theoretical and aesthetic definitions[1], and we believe it is the cornerstone of contemporary practices linked to digital technologies in art and design. However, the relation between the technical potential of a certain material and its artistic applications is not *a priori* a novelty.

5.1.1. *Art and technique in the face of the digital*

At first glance, it seems as if the history of the arts working with digital technologies and the history of computer science intersect in the same way

---

Chapter written by Dominique CUNIN.
1 In particular, we are thinking of the work of Jean-Louis Boissier [BOI 09, p. 180].

that the history of art is tangled up with the history of techniques. For example, consider an obvious and famous example of this kind of entanglement. The invention of the tube of paint in the 19th Century[2] was a well-known technical development that consequently allowed painters to leave their studios in order to paint directly from the outdoors and use real life for models to complete their paintings. Impressionism resulted in part from this new technical possibility. Its potential, paired with the portable easel, was perfectly fitting for the artistic project of the Impressionist painters, located at the intersection of, on the one hand, the desire to capture fleeting and subjective "impressions" observed and felt by the painter when faced with the world, and, on the other hand, a profound questioning of the function of painted images after the invention of photography (another major technical artistic development). So, it could be said that the invention of the manufactured paint tube and the exterior easel produced "latent technical content" that artists could use in their practices, which they did, and which had the consequences that we know in the field of art and its history.

The situation may seem similar to the application of digital technologies by artists, but it is important not to be satisfied with this superficial resemblance. First of all, while the tube of paint had the potential to influence the artistic practices of painting (which may seem natural, because a painter was involved in the story of this invention), the computer has been a fundamental vector of change for all technology that regulates our daily lives for decades now, at the origin of the "all-digital" that we currently know. There is a difference in the scale and the scope of the two inventions: whereas the tube of paint solved a problem that was rather specific to painting in art, the digital has reached most of the actors that make up our technological, social and political milieu. There is also a difference in the type of invention. The tube of paint, as an evolution in the way to conserve the colored material used by painters, fell under the existing technological sequence of the refinement of tools. The computer, on the other hand, is a machine that automatically processes information using calculations, based on a long tradition of research in mathematics and logic. Programs that are written and represented in the form of encoded sequences in order to be "computed" by a physical processor are designed to be executed to produce

---

2 This invention is attributed to John Goffe Rand, an American painter, for filing a patent in 1841 describing soft metal tubes sealed with a clip and containing paint, and Alexandre Lefranc, in France, for the commercialization of similar tubes with a screw-on cap in 1859.

a result. This activity happens through the implementation of programming languages that facilitate the ability of humans to write programs.

As machines of language and writing, the computer and its avatars cannot be considered as simple tools. In a world and a time when most of human activity is regulated, restricted and supported by information systems, computer use can range from the production of personal text documents to an international-scale cyber attack on a bank security system. If a computer is a tool, it has multiple forms at once and it also produces an entire series of contexts: work support, entertainment, communication and managing infrastructures, and it is also the origin of certain thoughts about various fields (economic, political, social, intellectual, etc.). With this in mind, it is difficult to reduce the computer to an equivalent of the brushes, easels and tubes of paint of the Impressionist painters.

Because they are necessarily confronted with the machine that conditions their practice, digital interactivity practitioners (artists or designers) cannot limit themselves to considering it as only a tool whose use falls under common sense or daily banality. Indeed, it is indispensable to understand the computer in its fundamental language and operational dimensions to be able to define the attitude that we hope to adopt in relation to this technical object that is so particular. We support the fact that artists and designers working with interactivity should practice computer programming, whatever the form and level (in the computer science sense of the word), to reach the right understanding of the technical object that they use to create artworks and adopt a knowledgeable position toward it. But what are the software tools available to creators to take a computer "in hand"?

Starting from the observation that the languages used to write computer programs are borrowed from a logical-mathematical line of thought, does this mean that artistic practices are condemned to intrude into the computer sciences, adapting to their tools and school of thought in order to realize their projects? We would like to believe that no, this is not inevitable, and that the artistic practices can get involved in the wide field of software to produce their own tools of creation using programming. We believe that the history of these tools is divided into two main branches: tools that are intended for creative practices in general and tools produced by artists for themselves and their peers. Our research relies on the analysis and practice of software tools belonging to these two branches, because they are related to one another and have influenced each other throughout history. Also, in order to find a common denominator for the wide variety of tools that make up these two categories and their hybridization, we believe it is useful to come back to the notion of the authoring software environment, because this makes it possible to consider the different aspects that a software tool must have in order to be implemented by artists and designers.

5.1.2. *An idea: an authoring software environment*

After the appearance of personal micro-computers in the second half of the 1970s and a surge in the numbers of owners and users during the 1980s, questions about the use of these digital machines by non-computer specialists were raised. Beyond word processing software and other "office" software, software applications that could create interactive objects were gradually developed on domestic and personal computers. The first micro-computers were essentially terminals that required the use of command lines to execute programs in the machine. The writing of the programs themselves was thus indispensable each time we wanted to execute them. This situation continued until magnetic tapes for registering digital data became available. Cassettes, diskettes and other cartridges are media that made it possible to store programs that a computer could execute at any time once they were loaded into the memory. What were before only small internal programs allowing the computer to interpret and execute a particular program with an external support evolved to become more complex and complete, making it possible to operate the material capacities of the machine more efficiently: operating systems. With the introduction of hard drives, in which the data of the operating system were saved (or installed), micro-computers were equipped with a device that regulated their base functions while avoiding the systematic introduction of a program loaded from an external medium. This meant that the machine could be used as it was. Finally, the creation of graphic interfaces that allowed for data manipulation (through different layers of the software system) made it possible, in the mid-1980s, for a very large number of people to use computers by completely masking the complexity of lines of command and programming.

A new way to use computers was born, founded mainly on the use of software with interactive graphic interfaces that were often dedicated to a set of precise tasks: publishing text documents, creating and retouching images, audio and video editing, processing databases, etc. The sharp decrease in the need to implement programming on computers intended for the public, mainly brought about by the use of graphic interfaces and the appearance of peripheral controls like the mouse, was at the heart of the democratization of the personal computer around the world, but it also led to a kind of separation between the users and the designers of software: the computer became (and remains today) a black box, a technical and technological object whose workings are more or less opaque to most of its users. However, the computer never stopped being a machine that allows both the creation of software and its consultation, experimentation and use. This is why software for creating new programs and applications has been gradually developed in a logic similar to that of the graphic interfaces that attempt to make the computer accessible to non-specialists. Because these software tools are destined for *authoring*, we propose uniting them under the name of "authoring software environments", of which we will give a brief overview below[3]. The expression "authoring software environment" is derived from "development environment" which designates, in computer science, software that supports the creation of other software using programming language by proposing an environment that includes various tools of software engineering (automatic code formatting, compiler, debugger, etc.).

The two programs that we are using as examples to represent what a software environment is were chosen because they incorporate programming languages, which strikes us as the way in which these environments give access to programming and its use to different types of authors, whether novices or specialists.

5.1.2.1. *Layout and hyperlinks: HyperCard*

In 1987, the program *HyperCard* appeared on personal *Macintosh* computers, which at the time had black and white screens and used System 6. It was initially distributed free of charge as an application included in all Macintosh computers on the market, in accordance with the desire expressed by the designer and developer of the program, Bill Atkinson. The founding and guiding idea behind *HyperCard* was to allow non-computer specialists to create interactive and dynamic computer programs. Terry Winograd suggested describing this approach, which aimed to produce tools to design software applications for the greatest number of users, with the phrase

---

3 A much more extended version of this overview is available in my doctoral thesis: [CUN 14]

"*programming for the rest of us*"[4], borrowed from a slogan used by the Apple company starting in 1984, "*Macintosh: the computer for the rest of us*"[5].

As its name implies, *HyperCard* was built on the idea of cards whose digital content could be linked to allow for navigation between several cards. The *Rolodex*, a rotating cylindrical index that allowed for quick consultation of cards, was the "physical" office object that most resembled the model used by *HyperCard*. It consisted of a set of cards that contained different types of information, which could be gathered into a *stack*, which could potentially be linked to other stacks through the cards. Each card could contain different "media", images, text fields and buttons, whose layout was facilitated by a series of creation and modification tools, all united in a palette accessible from the menu bar. *HyperCard* 2.0, distributed at the end of 1989, introduced its own programming language: *HyperTalk*. In order to allow for a more complete and precise control of all of the elements making up a stack, a script could be attached to each of the objects used on a card, to the card itself, or to the stack. *HyperTalk* belongs to the category of "verbose" languages, which is to say that its writing is very close to human language (in this case, English). This greatly facilitated both writing the instructions that make up the scripts and learning of this language, but does not totally mask the fact that it is, after all, a kind of computer programming: the syntax must be strictly respected at the risk of causing errors, the events must be thought out so that they unfold in a logical fashion and certain functions that are not integrated in the language have to be built and written by the user, which implies that the basic ideas of programming must be known, etc.

While *HyperCard* was innovative in the way that it proposed organizing scripts and attached them to different elements of a project, the innovation that we wish to highlight concerns the "publishing" and "viewing" modes in *HyperCard*. Cards could be created and modified using the same software that allowed them to be read. The combination of the creation and viewing functions in a single program environment introduced a fundamental difference from traditional computer development tools and an unheard-of flexibility that was unfortunately lost over time[6]. At the same time as

---

4 Terry Winograd [WIN 96, p. 207].

5 Slogans noted by Terry Winograd [WIN 96].

6 But which tends to come back to the forefront, as we will see later with *Live Coding*.

HyperCard, another category of authoring software was developed, whose metaphor was not based on work done in an office, but rather on the figure of the film director and animator.

5.1.2.2. *Multimedia producer: Director*

In 1986, an animation creation program called *Videoworks* was marketed on Macintosh computers. This happened at the same time as the appearance of *HyperCard* and used the same computers with black and white screens, still incapable of showing any shades of gray. This program was developed by the company *MacroMind*, who would later change their name to *Macromedia* before being bought by the giant *Adobe*. In its first version, *Videoworks* laid the foundations of what would become one of the most important authoring software environments for artistic creation working with digital technologies in over a decade. The metaphor of the animation studio crossed with the film set is the base of the design of this program, which was originally exclusively dedicated to the production of animated films. The organization of the workspace in *Videoworks* is therefore familiar for animators and directors. The strong similarity to the situation of the movie director explains why this software itself was renamed *Director* in the end, and we will summarize its main technical principles here.

Different graphic elements (text, images, geometric forms, etc.) could be created using a drawing palette to become the independent *members* stored in a *cast*, which was a reserve of resources visually organized in the form of a table of vignettes that offered a preview of the actors. These different actors could be placed freely in a *stage*. In order to organize each temporal fragment that made up the animation film, each frame that composed it, there was a time line, referred to as the *score*. When it became *Director* in 1988, the program was equipped with a script language that increased its artistic creation potential exponentially: *lingo*. The very idea of a script language fits particularly well in the framework of the authoring environment of *Director*: in the logical sequence of the cinema metaphor, *scripts* refer to parts of the program that are attributed to certain "actors" present on the "stage" so that they can interpret them (in the computer science sense as well as the theatrical sense of the term). *Director* also became a program that allowed for the production of interactive animations, as access to standard peripheral devices such as the keyboard and the mouse became possible.

Script languages allowed for the automation of program functions that could also be accessed through the graphic interface. Several levels of access to the program could be planned and used concurrently during the production of a project. Also, because they were interpreted, these languages allowed for a kind of programming on the fly, as the instructions that were entered in a message zone had an immediate effect on the graphic stage. This is outside the classic event sequence of the development of computer science writing, compilation, execution and correction that imposes a spatial and temporal separation between the program and its result. Later, we will see that this ease of access was lost in a large number of software creation environments and that it would be beneficial to reintroduce it.

5.2. Computer graphics, game engine, art engine?

Authoring software environments all share a common characteristic: they are based on a set of functional components that can be reused as many times as necessary in the design of the project. This reusability, which creates an organization by functional blocks, is obviously not exclusive to authoring software environments. It is inherited from general computer science practices and examining it will prompt us about an idea that raises questions for us today: the notion of the engine.

5.2.1. Reusability

For many years, computer programming has implemented a certain number of strategies and methodologies to avoid rewriting function blocks that are equivalent to one another. Starting from a problem or a particular object that has been defined as precisely as possible, a program can be designed and specified in an abstract way and then implemented using a programming language, making it effective and able to be executed. The practice of programming reveals very quickly that similar problems can appear in very different creation contexts: if, for a work, there arises a need to display a cube in perspective that rotates in real time, we can assume that the program written for the occasion will contain elements that could serve another project (artistic or not) that may also need to display a cube, among other elements. In this situation, why write a new program when all of the elements are already present in another?

Facilitating the reuse of parcels of a program by bundling them or connecting them to others is one of the foundations of the object paradigm in programming. This paradigm leads to a modular thinking about the structure of programs, which are made up of independent elements (objects) that can interact with each other through messages according to a determined interface – entrances and exits, in the middle of which the data is processed. This is called encapsulation. Not all computer science relies on the object paradigm, which was established for the long term in the technical landscape after the 1970s. Many other programming paradigms exist (functional, logical, procedural, etc.) and hybrids between these paradigms are common. So, it would not be appropriate to reduce the field of computer programming to object-oriented[7]. What caught my attention here is that one of the metaphors frequently used to explain the object-oriented principle is that of a vehicle and its engine. The engine in a vehicle can only accomplish its task with the help of a set of smaller technical elements whose functions are clearly defined and registered in a "flow" of interactions with the functions of other pieces that surround it – which are themselves technical objects. The engine can be made up of elements with diverse internal functions, as long as they fulfill their function, and according to a different assembly logic, as long as the general function of the engine is accomplished. So, there is a particular effort required to make the constituent pieces of the engine as compatible as possible with the other pieces, so that they can be used in different assemblies, different technical devices, while respecting the pursuit of the same objective. The "engine" objective can be integrated into other elements that contribute to defining a certain type of vehicle (car, motorcycle, train, etc.)[8].

The idea of an engine raises questions and problems, because its use is particularly frequent in the design of environment and software libraries.

---

7 The vision that Casey Alt proposes about the influence of the object paradigm on all technical and social activities that made the computer a medium can appear too exclusive from other paradigms, and, in particular, the functional declarative paradigm derived from the lambda calculation whose influence on the field of creation in programming is far from negligible. See *Objects of Our Affection – How Object Orientation Made Computers a Medium*, in *Media Archaeology – Approaches, Applications, and Implications,* Erkki Huhtamo and Jussi Parikka [HUT 11].

8 While this frequent use of the engine as a pedagogical explanation support for the general principle of object-oriented programming arises essentially from my personal experiences, a few searches online for tutorials about learning languages like Java or C++ reveal the regular use of cars and engines as examples.

Intuitively, it seems to me that neither the metaphor of engine or vehicle, nor the discrete and diffuse adoption by the community of object paradigm programmers are the only reasons for the use of this term. Where does the idea of the engine come from and how should it be considered in the field of artistic practices of programming and interactivity? This is where we turn to the world of video games.

5.2.2. *Game engine: when the metaphor and the objective design the tool*

Henry Lowood, curator of the *History of Science & Technology Collections* and the *Film & Media Collections* at the Stanford University libraries, carried out research to identify the precise origin and date of appearance of the term "engine" in the definition of software with which video games were created[9]. His main clue was the online announcement, destined for a specialized press, at the launch of the game *DOOM* just before 1993, which detailed the technological innovations reached by the creation of the game and which mentions the "*DOOM* engine"[10]. The story that he wrote after an interview with the authors of the famous video game led him to make a strong distinction between pre- and post-*DOOM* in the technical design of video games, of which the pivotal point is the idea of a game engine. Indeed, the historian discovered that, before *DOOM*, video games were programs specific to each title, always written starting from zero. What John Carmack introduced was "separating execution of core functionality by the game engine from the creative assets that filled the play space and content of a specific game title"[11]. So, it is possible to use the same set of features, the same base technical sequence, to create different *DOOM* games, which can then be considered as a specific creation relying on a sequence of generic components.

To design this generic, functional and operational layer that is generally found in software engineering, John Carmack and John Romero, who were both passionate about cars, naturally used the term *engine*. Indeed, they

---

9 Henry Lowood [LOW 14].

10 "I've had some very good insights and optimizations that will make the DOOM engine perform at a great frame rate" (emphasis added). The original announcement is accessible through many URLs as well as a document created by Tom Hall, *DOOM Bible*: http://5years.doomworld.com/doombible/

11 Henry Lowood [LOW 14, p. 181].

explain that, just as the engine "is the heart of the car, this is the heart of the game; it's the thing that powers it ... and it kind of feels like it's the engine and all the art and stuff is the body of the car"[12]. The metaphor of the engine thus came to refer to a generic software structure, but we can assume that it influenced the design of this structure and participated in its design. As a consequence, the video game world was gradually reconfigured around engines, which became the location and inspiration for technical innovations not only in the field of graphic computer science, but also in the mechanics of the game (gameplay and interactivity), in the behavior of non-player characters (artificial intelligence), the application of communication networks (multi-user), and many other aspects.

Jason Gregory, in his reference work *Game Engine Architecture*, proposed an in-depth study of different technical aspects of game engines and introduced a taxonomy of engines in relation to the types of games that triggered their construction (or vice versa)[13]. Open-source and proprietary engines in 2D and 3D, from small to very large scale, were reviewed and compared to each other. This work, in principle destined for video game professionals who were already certified programmers, gives a complete view of all of the complex techniques required for the creation of a video game on the contemporary video gaming market. What astonishes me most when I consult this mass of technical information is the extent to which the majority of them are more or less familiar to me because I have already applied them to my own artistic creation activities. And with good reason, as some of my works have been completed using game engines.

A video game engine is considered to be a complex composite software element with a wide range which, as a technical object, falls mainly under the engineering sciences. What authoring software environments do artistic practices of interactivity implement? At the core, is there a difference between a game engine and an authoring software environment? Our hypothesis is that there is in reality almost no difference, from a technical point of view, and that authoring software environments are the equivalent of game engines, although their potential is more reduced without being more precise. In this case, what justifies the creation of art-oriented software libraries when a video game engine can perfectly fill the same role as a technical interface?

---

12 John Romero, cited by Henry Lowood [LOW 14, p. 186].
13 Jason Gregory [GRE 14].

We will see that the pedagogical dimension is one of the essential reasons for the existence of these authoring software environments because it facilitates access for non-specialists of computer science and, consequently, makes it possible to practice programming. Without an introduction to this practice, it is impossible to increase our knowledge of the machine and thus to adapt its potential with the critical distance that characterizes the contemporary arts and the relation that they propose with the world. These tools are thus the entry points toward a *critical technical practice* or an *artistic technical conduct* that we believe it is important to reproduce here.

5.2.3. *Programming for the interactive arts: toward complexity*

Creation programs that are explicitly declared as intended for artists and designers are few and far between. One of the most famous examples of this is probably the succession that started with *Design By Numbers*[14] (DBN), by John Maeda in 1999, followed by *Processing*[15], created by Ben Fry and Casey Reas in 2001, and then *OpenFrameworks*[16] (OF), created by Zachary Lieberman, Theodore Watson and Arturo Castro in 2005. Observed closely, these three projects do not exactly start from the same premise, but their respective positions concerning the practice of programming for the arts remain very similar. The observation, analysis and practice of these programming-oriented authoring environments inform their tendency to move increasingly toward the standard tools of software engineering. Indeed, one of the effects that I have observed in the development of these environments is that the introduction to programming that they hope to foster in new artists and designers is becoming more and more difficult to approach in reality. What is the cause of this and what are the consequences? We will examine how the sequence that started with DBN moved toward ever more complexity and less accessibility.

5.2.3.1. *Design By Numbers*

DBN explicitly states that it has a pedagogical objective. *Design By Numbers* (DBN) was created for visual designers and artists as an introduction to computational design. It is the result of a continuing endeavor by professor John Maeda to teach 'the idea' of computation to

---

14 http://dbn.media.mit.edu/whatisdbn.html

15 http://processing.org/

16 http://openframeworks.cc

designers and artists. It is his belief that the quality of media art and design can only improve through establishing educational infrastructure in arts and technology schools that create strong, cross-disciplinary individuals. DBN is both a programming environment and language. The environment provides a unified space for writing and running programs and the language introduces the basic ideas of computer programming within the context of drawing. Visual elements such as dot, line and field are combined with the computational ideas of variables and conditional statements to generate images"[17].

The features of DBN are thus voluntarily limited because it consists above all of familiarizing users with the fundamental ideas of procedural programming by making the creation of graphic compositions the main objective. The primary recipients of DBN are thus people involved *a priori* in the practices of art and graphic design who are curious enough to move toward the machine and its creation potential. This largely explains the syntactic and semantic choices that were made when building the programming language. The terms used are simple and directly related to the practices of paper drawing (*paper*, *pen*, *line*, etc.), which are also at the base of the general metaphor of the language: the main idea is that of a drawing area with a surface on which a pencil, whose color can be changed, can draw geometric figures that can be configured, layer after layer.

The language of DBN, which demonstrates a certain similarity with the *Logo*[18] language, had to be implemented so that a text, written by the user and respecting the specifications of the language, becomes operational and orders the execution of "effective" functions, located in a lower layer and written in a standard language (Java, in this case). So we find two large elements in DBN: a script system (which analyzes the text of the program to make it operational) and a set of generic functions (which are executed from the script when it is interpreted). We can say that the set of features constitutes an "engine" because, as in the case of video games, it allows for their implementation in the service of various creation projects, within the limits of the DBN framework.

---

17 http://dbn.media.mit.edu/whatisdbn.html

18 The expressions and keywords are short, the instructions are completed by a carriage return, the arguments of the functions occur with a space and not parentheses, etc. *Logo* is a programming language founded on the ability to draw using simple commands invented by Seymour Papert in the 1970s.

5.2.3.2. *Processing*

The primary goal of *Processing* is the same as that of *Design By Numbers*, "to teach the foundations of computational programming used in a visual context"[19], but also to help extend the range of the tool by allowing it to "serve as a sketchbook program and to be used as a production tool"[20]. *Processing* is without question the direct successor of DBN. The results of the research led through the creation and use of DBN were put to good use in *Processing* and allowed for the definition of a new type of tool geared toward artistic and visual creation. As John Maeda had stated before, Ben Fry and Casey Reas stated that learning programming required an involved, if not intensive, application. They insisted on the particular aspect that the practice of programming takes on in relation to other artistic practices, because its primary material, *software*, is itself so particular:

> "Software requires its own terminology and discourse and should not be evaluated in relation to prior media such as film, photography, and painting. History shows that technologies such as oil paint, cameras, and film have changed artistic practice and discourse, and while we do not claim that new technologies improve art, we do feel that they enable different forms of communication and expression. Software holds a unique position among artistic media because of its ability to produce dynamic forms, process gestures, simulate natural systems, and integrate other media including sound, image, and text"[21].

The idea of a sketch, of a preparatory drawing, is at the heart of the vision of these two artist-engineers, because according to them, "it is necessary to sketch in a medium that is related to the final medium so that the sketch can be similar to the final product. [...] To sketch with electronic media, it is important to work with electronic media"[22]. To summarize, the authors highlight the fact that computer programming is not reserved for computer science specialists, but requires an effective and supported application to become a true tool of creation with, potentially, the same function and fluidity of design as a sketchbook in which an artist or designer can create many sketches.

---

19 Ben Fry and Casey Reas [FRY 07, p. 1].
20 [FRY 07].
21 Ben Fry and Casey Reas [FRY 07, p. 1].
22 [FRY 07].

From a technical point of view, *Processing* left behind the script component that existed in DNB in order to concentrate on the graphic engine and its scalability. Indeed, *Processing* cannot be considered as being a language insofar as it is in reality a set of features written in a single language, Java, which provides a creation framework and aims to make an environment. The core of *Processing* is a graphic context in which the graphic shapes and various "media" (text, images, sounds, videos) can be drawn in two or three dimensions. Once again, the core can be considered as an engine in the sense of video game engines, because it consists of a set of functional components opening a creation potential that is *a priori* close to the concerns of artists.

However, although the potential is greater in *Processing* than in DBN, the impact on the accessibility of the language must also be taken into account. Indeed, *Java*, a programming language widely used in the software industry and which goes through a virtual machine to run programs after a kind of compilation, does not share many characteristics with the DBN language. Fundamentally object-oriented, designed to be multi-platform and allow for the creation of client-side applications like servers, Java requires several days to learn its basics and several weeks, even months, of practice to be implemented with ease. It is frequently used as the base language in advanced studies specialized in computer science and programming. In these conditions, although *Processing* attempts to limit difficulties by providing a minimal integrated development environment (a graphic interface that allows for writing, producing and launching programs) and a clean and coherent programming interface[23], novices who approach programming for the first time with *Processing* are confronted with a particular syntax that does not make their task easy: the use of "{" "}" and "[" "]", which most users do not even know where to find on their keyboard, closing instructions with a ";" which is most often forgotten and creates compilation errors, a tendency toward breakages that also provoke compilation errors following typing mistakes, not counting basic programming ideas like variables, functions, objects, control structures, etc.

The "inflexibility" of Java syntax is automatically imposed on every library completed in this language and necessarily on *Processing* as well. Incidentally, this is the case in all libraries written in a particular language

---

23 The API of *Processing* is accessible here: https://processing.org/reference/

that inherited *de facto* the characteristics of the language in question[24]. The dream of a simplicity and ease of access to computer programming is thus driven away[25]. For those who succeed in becoming accustomed to the language and the integration of its corresponding thought process, *Processing* can become a kind of Swiss army knife for the interactive arts[26], another kind of engine that takes on a more creative than technical meaning. For everyone else, another alternative must be found (in visual programming, for example), or they will abandon the idea of programming their own productions. However, things get a bit more complicated in the project that followed *Processing*.

5.2.3.3. *OpenFrameworks*

OpenFrameworks is intended to be an open-source *framework* destined for visual artists who want to develop their artistic practice with new technologies and interactivity. While the philosophy behind the project is roughly the same as the one behind *Processing*, OF is based on a different programming language, C++, in order to allow for the creation of applications that are robust, stable and as powerful as the material integrated into the computer used will allow. Essentially, OF is a program framework that allows concurrent use of a certain number of C++ open-source[27] libraries (processing images, sound, real-time 3D rendering, etc.) through a

---

24 There are a few rare exceptions, in particular when a language does not propose certain specificities that do exist in others. For example, people accustomed to the C++ or C# language know that it is possible to overload the binary operators (+, −, *, /, etc.) and bitterly regret their unavailability in a high-level script language like *JavaScript*. Depending on the flexibility of the language in question, it is possible, with the help of a true taste for hacking, to introduce the overloading operators where it is not usually standard. This is the case of *Paper.js*, a vector drawing library for the web created by Jürg Lehni and Jonathan Puckey, which integrates a kind of (complicated) hack allowing the overload of operators in *JavaScript*. A complete description is available here http://scratchdisk.com/posts/operator-overloading (consulted 31/03/2016).

25 To be specific, we should say that the *lingo* language of *Director* had already largely started this progression toward complexity before *Processing*. While the first version of *lingo* was verbose, the final was based on *JavaScript*, which presented many syntactical similarities with Java (although less at the paradigmatic level).

26 As proof, there are many artistic projects listed with the help of the *Processing* tag on creativeapplications.net: http://www.creativeapplications.net/category/processing/

27 *OpenGL, GLEW, GLUT, libtess2* and *cairo* for graphics, *rtAudio, PortAudio* or *FMOD* and *Kiss FFT* for the entrance/exit and audio analysis, *FreeType* for fonts, *FreeImage* for saving/loading images, *Quicktime* and *videoInput* for reading and capturing video, and *Poco* for various utilitarian functions.

programming interface that unifies access to their features. The users targeted by OF are thus not quite the same ones as those targeted by *Processing*, which is to say computer programming novices, but rather more advanced users who already have a certain amount of experience and who often turn out to be users of *Processing* looking for a more powerful tool. Because it is not aimed at beginners, but rather at qualified and experienced programmers, OF avoided a specific development environment, preferring the use of standard integrated development environments (IDE – *Integrated Development Environment*) used by computer science professionals. So, to use OF, you must not only become accustomed to a relatively difficult programming language, C++, which has certain characteristics that Java does not (manual memory management with pointers, among others), you must also track the practice of programs such as *Xcode*, Apple's previous IDE on its platform Mac OS X, *Visual Studio* on Windows or *Eclipse* (in its C++ version) on multiple platforms. OF shares many technical characteristics with game engines, in particular in its graphic library, of which the construction and naming conventions are similar to those of video game development tools.

According to the evolution of programming tools from DBN to OF, it would seem that artists and designers learning programming must necessarily follow a curve of knowledge acquisition in programming that allows them to go *in fine* toward languages that are usually reserved for industry professionals. By way of illustrating this phenomenon, we will observe how the same function is written in the three environments: the drawing of a line from the origin point of the drawing surface to the coordinates 100 on the *x*-axis and 200 on the *y*-axis.

DBN:

line 0 0 100 200

Processing:

line(0, 0, 100, 200);

OpenFrameworks:

drawLine(0,0,0, 100,200,0);

This demonstrates the differences of writing, with the syntactical elements of the languages being more numerous in Java and in C++ than in

DBN. But we also see an increase in the number of parameters passed to functions. This reveals a small change in the paradigm: 3D drawing was not planned for DBN; it was optional in *Processing* and imposed in OF.

The use of developed and common languages in the software industry is definitely beneficial for artists who end up mastering them, and this technical autonomy opens the door to a vast field of experimentation that their intimate knowledge of the machine allows. However, obviously, one of the solutions open to them is to opt to work in collaboration with a technical partner which makes it possible to curb the potential of a technical downward slide. The idea of collaboration is probably automatically driven, on a certain level, by the digital technologies themselves, because we can see that tools such as Processing or OF are distributed using open-source licenses and are the origin point of communities of users and developers who bring to the project as much as they benefit from it. However, the situation that interests me here is the autonomy of artists and designers in the writing of programs that create works, what will be the core of the work, their "engine". From my point of view, the knowledge and practice of programming results from a necessary literacy and a good understanding of the world we live in today. The ability to program machines provides a power over this that should not be left only to specialists and an ever-eager industry. To be a programmer of one's own works as an artist or a designer establishes a position that extends far beyond the field of interactive visual creation.

It goes without saying that everyone is free to choose their tools and that any of them could be the right one if it is suitable for a project in the midst of design and development. *Processing*, OF, C++, Objective-C, *JavaScript*, *Java* or any other platform, language or library make it possible to create an infinite number of interactive works. However, we can assume that it would be much more difficult for a novice to approach programming for the interactive arts through OF than through DBN. So, how can we explain this evolution that starts from a very simplified script language to arrive at C++? Maybe it consists of a generational effect: those who started with DBN continued on with *Processing* and wanted to get to something like OF, so they created it! If that is the case, are beginners today better equipped, better informed and better trained than before? This is probably not the case, because despite the increasing number of independent learning tools (such as https://openclassrooms.com and many other online tutorials, not including examples and guides, art-oriented libraries, specialized books, etc.), learning programming remains a continual challenge for those who engage in it, as I continue to today in teaching digital techniques to students in art and design schools. Have we made a mistake by introducing *Processing* into our schools? What are the alternatives?

5.2.4. *Art engine, an authoring environment possibility?*

As we saw above, *HyperCard* and *Director* allowed users new to programming to get involved in creation through the graphic interface and to move progressively toward programming. This progressiveness is largely lost with *Processing* and OF. The entrance into the matter remains difficult and the beginners seem to be forgotten. The heterogeneity of languages also poses a question here: from DBN to *Processing* and then to OF, three different languages are used and subtle difference exists in the principles of each environment. The succession does not make the environment itself, but rather binds the progression.

How can an environment offer a variety of levels of access without actually limiting the potential of the practices that it aims to support? Should we think up a strategy so that DBN is truly a simplified and very accessible version of *Processing*, which would itself be a kind of OF interface, to create these environments? The advantages of such a grouping maneuver would be the large scope of accessibility that it would offer to creators: for those who wish to "make their weapons" in programming for the arts, an adapted level of writing with a strong pedagogical harmony would exist (equivalent to DBN). The limited functionalities of this level of language would push them to go further to discover the potential that practice makes it possible to discover. A more complex language allowing for writing more developed and personalized program constructions would be a logical follow-up (equivalent to *Processing*). Finally, the original language of the tool, whatever it is, would be the lowest level and thus also the most permissive, because the library itself would be expanded, even modified by the user who would thus also become, in fact, a contributor.

This possibility of an authoring environment, which would be considered a kind of *Art Engine*, an art-oriented software engine whose design comes from artistic practices, leaves several questions open, such as, does such an authoring software environment not already exist?

Unity3D[28], a game engine that makes it possible to run executable programs on a wide variety of platforms (game consoles, computers, mobile screens, web, Oculus Rift, etc.), is increasingly used in the field of interactive creation. Its robustness and richness are among the main reasons for its success. *Unity*'s creation potential is so great that it is difficult not to observe that it is a potential candidate for the status of generic software environment *par excellence*. However, we note that outside of video games, it is a kind of *Game Art* in particular that naturally finds its niche as such a creation tool. Consider the works of the *Tale of Tales*[29] duo who undertook the creation of works of interactive art inspired by video games and using their technologies, some parts of which were created with *Unity*[30]. Here, the tool corresponds particularly well to the use that they make of it, even if it was for *Tale of Tales* to create works that only have the appearance of video games. In addition to being proprietary, which immediately endangers the durability of the works created with *Unity*[31], we have seen that the game engines are constructed from objectives whose needs are precisely determined and participate in their design event, including in their level of genericity. However, for their part, the artistic practices define their needs to each new action, to each new creation. If we take up the definition that Masaki Fujihata[32] gives for *new media art*, it suggests that artists do not implement new media (terminology that is debatable), but create new media by making works[33]. Considering the difficulty of technical anticipation brought on by the practices of art and design themselves, how can we design a tool that takes into account the fact that it will not know how to respond to all of its needs?

We have seen that the problems raised by designing an authoring software environment destined for artists and designers can quickly pile up. In an effort to provide an overview, we can summarize them as follows:

---

28 https://unity3d.com

29 Auriea Harvey and Michaël Samyn, http://conte-des-contes.com

30 For example, *Bientôt l'été*, http://tale-of-tales.com/bientotlete/index.html

31 In 2010, I wrote a text about the impact on my own practice of the slow disappearance of *Director* from the landscape of digital tools following its purchase by *Abobe*, in the online journal *So Multiples* (no. 4, Arts numériques). Reproduction and multiplication titled *Pratiques artistiques et nouvelles technologies: la faillite du multiple?* (http://www.so-multiples.com/wp-content/revue/pdf/numero4/ArticleDominiqueCunin.pdf)

32 Pioneering artist of new media: http://www.fujihata.jp

33 Jean-Louis Boissier [BOI 08, p. 8]

– How can we foster an artistic exploration of digital machines using a technical interface? This is the objective assumed by environments like *Processing* and that we also pursue. The question is thus to open the potential of the machines in and through the practices of art and design.

– How can we offer a variety of access levels to programming in the same environment? This concerns allows novices to learn by creating and advanced users to create more easily.

– How can we allow for compatibility between projects/works created with a wide variety of machines: computers with different OS, mobile screens, game consoles, etc.?

– How can we ensure the longevity of completed works, on the one hand, and their sources, on the other hand? Material obsolescence should not make us forget software obsolescence, which remains a major obstacle for the longevity of digital works. Maintaining source codes implies the possibility of executing them, which can no longer be assured for diverse and varied reasons.

– What methodology should we adopt to allow the practices of art and design to create the tool and not the other way around? If a software tool cannot respond to the needs of a specific work, should we abandon it or change it?

In an attempt to provide practical answers to these questions, we created the project *Mobilizing.js*.

5.3. *Mobilizing.js*: an attempt at a multi-paradigmatic authoring software environment

Mobilizing.js was directly followed *Mobilizing*, a programming language inspired by *Processing* intended for artistic creation on mobile screens, which was the technical core of my doctoral thesis[34] and developed with the assistance of Jonathan Tanant[35]. This first version of *Mobilizing* (2008–2013) was only compatible with iOS devices and contained many limitations because it was based on a *script* language written from zero. However, this experience of creating a *script* language and a graphic engine allowed me to better consider the impact of such work on my own practice and

---

34 From the University of Paris 8, available at: [CUN 14].

35 http://tanant.info

understanding of programming languages, but also the relationship that novices can have with this type of tool. Indeed, being at the origin of language and having complete control on the features of the engine below, the technical approach that I could offer to students was much more open than it would have been with another tool: if something was not possible for a particular project, it was possible for me to add to the required features in the *Mobilizing* engine and thus improve it over the course of the practice. This iterative methodology remains at the heart of my research-creation activities today. Because the evolution of the general technological landscape brought about a certain ubiquity of Internet users (most of the activities of a "lambda" user on a computer or a mobile screen pass through online services today, and thus through a kind of Internet browser), development with web technologies quickly became an alternative to the native technical sequences on mobile screens. That is why we reconsidered the *Mobilizing* project and began reconstructing it in 2014 with the script language used on the Web, *JavaScript*.

Mobilizing.js[36] is an authoring software environment project destined for artists and designers whose objective is to support the creation of interactive works on different kinds of device screens. The wide versatility that *JavaScript* currently offers, which shows a tendency to assert itself, allows *Mobilizing.js* to extend its field of application to various software contexts, which of course includes the Internet browser, the historical site of creation for the *JavaScript* language, *Node.js*[37] applications, a web server entirely scriptable in *JavaScript*, whereas Apache requires the use of PHP, or even contexts specific to certain machines (mobile screens – tablets and smartphones – iOS, Android, Windows, etc.). The core of *Mobilizing.js* has the form of a *JavaScript* library that defines a programming interface designed for interactive artistic creation in material and software contexts which are currently unified by the *JavaScript* language.

The fundamental features of *Mobilizing.js* are centered on graphic creation and propose a real-time 2D and 3D engine using the *Three.js*[38] library, itself built on *WebGL*, a standard successor of OpenGL-ES and specifically defined for the Web, which seems to be well established on the landscape of contemporary technologies with computed images. This choice,

---

36 http://www.mobilizing-js.net
37 https://nodejs.org/en/
38 http://threejs.org

in addition to being a gamble on the future of a standard in definition, relies on the ever-expanding availability of graphics processing units (GPUs) on various digital devices. It also consists of leaving open the possibility of implementing the graphic engine of *Mobilizing.js* on platforms different from the ones based on the *Document Object Model* (DOM)[39].

Because if, under the effect of the specifications of HTML5, the browser allows for ever more access to lower (material) layers in the host machine on which they are run, like WebGL does with the GPU, the many impossibilities of implementing device specificities (mobiles in particular) are still an obstacle for interactive artistic creation using web technologies: the time necessary for effective implementation of HTML5 specifications by large software publishers to allow for the application of technical elements recently integrated in the device (sensors) is inordinately long relative to the necessity of experimentation expressed by the artistic practices working with interactivity. That is why *Mobilizing.js* wishes to propose the possibility of applying these material specificities by integrated projects such as *Cordova*[40], which make it possible to create bridges with the native layers of the devices on which a web application is run. Thus, when a programming interface does not already exist in the web standards, an extension of the *JavaScript* context toward the native functionalities can be employed.

5.3.1. *Artistic technical conduct and critical technical practice*

Mobilizing.js is intended to become a library accessible for all and thus a part of the ocean of *Javascript* libraries. What distinguishes *Mobilizing.js* from any other project? A fundamental point is probably the methodology that we have adopted so far to move forward with the construction of the library and the design premises of the authoring environment. As with *Mobilizing*, we hope that *Mobilizing.js* will be driven by artistic creation, which is to say that when a project is constructed conceptually and

---

39 We will briefly recall that the *Document Object Model* is the standard that determines the abstract model of the documents that are interpreted by Internet browsers. HTML, CSS and *JavaScript* are the three most common modalities to describe the structure of the elements that make up the document (page layout), define the style of these elements and, finally, be manipulated with programming, respectively. In the context of the web, *Javascript* makes it possible to script Internet browsers.

40 https://cordova.apache.org

economically at the heart of our research-creation group[41], its realization is immediately thought out through *Mobilizing.js*, even if the state of the library does not yet contain all of the technical elements necessary for the project. It consists of an iterative method that starts from the specific needs of artistic projects and aims to create a base of generic developments, improving the potential of the library. This methodology, which passes through artistic creation as a construction vector of technical elements, is also dictated by what "theoretically" motivates the creation of *Mobilizing.js*.

The architecture that we are seeking to implement originates from a desire to encourage a kind of practice that artists can have in relation to digital machines. Indeed, by seeking to facilitate access to programming for novices involved in art and design, we are not only seeking to defend a certain autonomy of the "artists of interactivity". We also hope to encourage an "artistic technical conduct" in computer programming. We are borrowing this notion from the philosopher Pierre-Damien Huyghe, who said, "[...] the artistic behavior that I am trying to support is a behavior that is *a priori* searching in the technologies and not the means to make something exist that the artist has already seen, for example, but searching in the technologies for what possibilities there are, to push them. It, in fact, consists of discovering them, to say it in a very literal way"[42]. Starting from this thought, which suggests not considering technology as being put in the service of the arts as a separate step in the design of works, but more as being an activity that carries in itself a prospective aesthetic dimension in the technical practice, I suggested the figure of the artist in programming (as already stated in the introduction), so that it would consist of programming as an artist.

Mirroring this artistic technical conduct, which takes as a point of departure the practices of art, we find a similar thought process that is deployed under the name of "critical technical practice" of which one of the first definitions can be found in the text *Toward a critical technical practice* by Philip E. Agre[43]. Coming from the field of artificial intelligence, the

---

41 This is the line of research of *Reflexive Interaction*, under the direction of Samuel Bianchini, EnsadLab, laboratory of the Ecole Nationale des Arts décoratifs de Paris, where I am currently a researcher.
42 Pierre-Damien Huyghe [HUG 08], complete video available online at: http://www. mobilisable.net/2008/?page_id=9, 16 min 10 seconds (approximately).
43 [AGR 97].

author recounts his process and the difficulties that he encountered in his attempt to open his discipline to non-technical theoretical horizons[44]. Used to thinking through technical schemes that require the realization of an efficient and operating computer science program, the researcher became aware of the lack of critical distance from which the domain of artificial intelligence suffered. So, he attempted to define a technical practice that knew how to question itself, as much in its terms as in its more general philosophical challenges. From his point of view, the computer is a machine that demonstrates, more strongly than other technologies, a capacity to integrate, even reinvent, all of the sites of practice[45]. So a user must be able to remove themselves from the potential constraints that can be produced and to engage in a critical technical practice that "[...] will, at least for the foreseeable future, require a split identity – one foot planted in the craft work of design and the other foot planted in the reflexive work of critique"[46]. The artistic practices are precisely anchored in this work of self-criticism and are often based on a capacity to challenge the world, or in other words, a capacity to formulate questions around aesthetic objects. The relation of proximity that can be found between the attitude of the "creative technology experts" and artists in programming is discussed in an article by Kirk Woolford, researcher and artist-programmer, co-authored with people from various disciplines[47]. The artisanal part (a term to understand here in the sense of knowledge and the art of making) of the activity of a programmer is compared to the one that we find in the work of independent artists who produce their own programs to create works, even constructing their own tools (like, for example, the authors of *Processing*). Following Philip E. Agre, Kirk Woolford and his colleagues remark that a kind of hybridization happens more and more between the technical and critical capacities of creators of all kinds working with computer programming, resulting in the

---

44 This was very difficult because my technical training had instilled in me two polar-opposite orientations to language – as precisely formalized and as impossibly vague – and a single clear mission for all discursive work transforming vagueness into precision through formalization [AGR 97, p. 147].

45 "[Computing] aims to reinvent virtually every other site of practice in its own image". [AGR 97, p. 131].

46 [AGR 97, p. 155], personal translation.

47 [WOO 10].

fact that it is difficult today to work with digital technologies, including as a technician, without asking yourself how and why[48].

A kind of convergence of attitudes, practices or even behaviors is conducted through the digital and, more precisely, the implementation of computer programming. The notion of *craft* is here considered to be the center point between the figure of the artist, involved in a critical and reflexive practice continually seeking to situate their work in the field of art, and the figure of the engineer, who seeks to solve practical problems by technical measures. The notion of *bricodage*[49], introduced by David-Olivier Lartigaud, echoes this hybridization. The specialist historian of *Software Art* and teacher-researcher practicing art-oriented computer programming[50] supports an "aesthetic behavior" that is found mid-way between "bricolage" (i.e. DIY) and writing computer code: "the word play of 'bricoder' [...] can describe an 'aesthetic' attitude that consists of DIYing/programming the 'computer object.' 'Bricodage' is this curiosity, this desire to open a black box for reflective, artistic or aesthetic ends. An approach to computer science that is 'beyond' simple hacking that allows for 'capturing' the machine"[51].

But to act as an artist in the face of technology, it seems indispensable to practice with this technology, or, at least to have applied it. The difficulty of accessing technology is a considerable obstacle for artists to take charge of the machine and be critical of it. Therefore, access to the practice of the technology is an essential component of such an artistic technical conduct, which aims to incorporate the technology and its challenges in artistic practices. This is where *Mobilizing.js* comes in.

---

48 [WOO 10, p. 203], "Those technologists exposed to the forms of critical and contextual thinking so prevalent in Art and Design find it difficult to continue working without asking why as well as how".

49 David-Olivier Lartigaud [LAR 11].

50 This is a reference to the title of the international conference, "Programmation orienté art" organized by the author in 2004 around the uses of computer programming in contemporary artistic practices.

51 David-Olivier Lartigaud [LAR 11, p. 328].

5.3.2. *An engine with many speeds*

Mobilizing.js proposes a kind of program mobility designed for interactive works. While, in the first version of *Mobilizing*, the concern was mainly to allow for the prototyping of interactive works on mobile screens, *Mobilizing.js* hopes to create an authoring software environment with rich graphic (and, eventually, sound) capacities as close as possible to the start of the art, making it possible to deploy works in a wide variety of formats, mobile or not, while proposing a multitude of levels of access to the writing of the source code. That is why we are thinking of an architecture in layers – the image below shows the general organization.

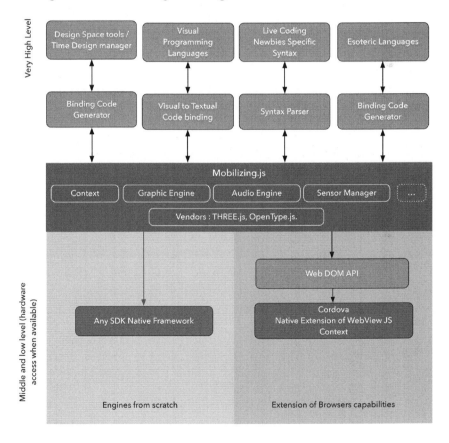

Figure 5.1. *General diagram of the architecture of Mobilizing.js. For a color version of this figure, see www.iste.co.uk/reyes/hypermedia.zip*

The base layer is written in *JavaScript*, for the reasons stated above. The lower layers are planned, in a hypothesis that consists of linking the *JavaScript* functions determined in *Mobilizing.js* to an engine written in an environment native to the platforms concerned (we are talking about *bridging*, making a bridge between the contexts of execution). This is conceivable through components like *JavaScriptCore* on iOS, which is nothing other than the *JavaScript* interpreter used by the *Safari Mobile* browser. This solution was tested in an experimental fashion in order to prove its technical validity, but it was not considered to be a priority. The other solution, effective today, passes through *Cordova* and was implemented during the *Surexposition* project, a work under the direction of Samuel Bianchini for the most part completed with *Mobilizing.js*[52]. *Surexposition* is a collective interactive work combining an installation and an application for *smartphones*. At the center of the urban space, a large black monolith produces an intense beam of white light in the sky. Visible from the whole city, this beam goes out, then is relit, emitting messages in Morse code. Using the mobile application, the spectators write their messages in the form of an alphabetic text and the system converts them into Morse code to transmit them to the monolith. On one side of the monolith, the white points and dashes composing the Morse code sentences march on, from bottom to top, on an LED screen: each time they reach the top of the monolith, the light is triggered as if these signs emptied into the light. We find these same signs marching by on the screen of *smartphones* of the public interacting with the work, in a rhythm, also emitting a light through their flash. It is this final point, the beginning of the flash of the mobile screens synchronized with the pulses of the monolith, which required access to the native layers of mobile devices. Indeed, the flash is not yet controllable from web browsers, so we had to make recourse to a *Cordova* plug-in that opens access to the flash through a *webview*.

The layers about the base can have different orientations. The pedagogical dimension is very present there with, on the one hand, a *Live Coding* environment and a visual programming language on the other hand.

---

52 http://surexposition.net/

5.3.2.1. *Live Coding*

Live Coding consists of writing a program while it is running. This "movement" is rooted in the artistic practices of performance, especially in musical interpretation[53]. It consists of writing the source code in front of the public, above the images and the sounds that it produces. At the origin of this unveiling of the program, which shows the design and writing "live", we find a desire to demystify creation through programming. The source code is shown "for the pleasure" of the spectators, but also in reaction to the figure of the electronic musician who faces their computer on stage, but whose screen does not face the public, making their actions, gestures and their very instrument totally unreadable. *Live Coding* introduces a transparency to the "kitchen" of the artist-performer who produces on stage. This transparency also brings to mind the notion of the "glass box" which was proposed in opposition to the black box of Pierre Rabardel in his work in relation to instruments[54]. Remember that the metaphor of the black box starts from the principle that the tool-machine[55] implemented must disappear as a technical object so that the user can focus on the task that they are in the midst of carrying out with and through this technical artifact. The internal functioning of the tool does not need to be known by its user; starting from the moment when it completely fills its functions, it is made technically opaque to offer a transparency of its application, to succeed in making it "forgotten" in practice.

"Obscurantism is dangerous. Show us your screens"[56]. This catchphrase stated in the manifesto of the *Live Coding* community evokes the opposite notion of the black box, the glass box, that refers to a transparency for the

---

53 On this subject, see: Adrian Ward, Julian Rohrhuber, Fredrik Olofsson, Alex Mclean, Dave Griffiths, Nick Collins, Amy Alexander [WAR 04].
54 Pierre Rabardel [RAB 95].
55 Rabardel is talking about the instrument; however, we prefer to focus on the definitions that Gilbert Simondon suggests. The tool is an effector and the instrument a sensor, and the machine is a complex set that unites the two functions all while having the capacity to function independently from an energetic as well as informational point of view (the user no longer intervenes in the work that the machine carries out once it is prepared – programmed).
56 http://toplap.org/wiki/ManifestoDraft

technical functioning of the machine used. Showing all or part of the internal technical principles, the machine opens up for the user in order to make it understandable, readable. Or, according to Rabardel, "the system must constitute [...] a glass box, in the sense that it exposes by itself what is pertinent on the subject"[57]. According to the technical object implemented and the use that is made of it, this transparency can vary. It does not only show its internal mechanic, its physical agency, but also puts in place strategies that make it possible for the object to make its actions and its internal state comprehensible at a given moment, in the context of a given use. The practice of *Live Coding* tends to offer this transparency not to programmers, who are *a priori* sufficiently conscious of the technical reality of the computer, but to the spectators in front of whom the source code is written and executed on the fly. We are thus at the opposite of a large part of the interactive artistic devices that have a tendency to mask certain material technical (for questions of presenting the work in a space, among others) and algorithmic aspects: the computer program, despite the fact that it is the function and operational heart of the work, is inaccessible to the public and only its "effects", its results, are perceptible. The programming languages that allow for *Live Coding* are increasingly numerous[58] and one of our inspirations is *LiveCode Lab*[59], created by Davide Della Casa in 2012, which consists of a real-time 3D graphic *Live Coding* environment constructed with web technologies and which proposes a very simplified programming language and a code editor on the fly designed specifically for that purpose. *Gibber*[60] is another *Live Coding* environment accessible online and another important reference, because it proposes using JavaScript itself as the *Live Coding* language. These two web-oriented projects supported by *JavaScript* strongly encourage us to introduce a layer of *Live Coding* in the environment of *Mobilizing.js* that could bring, in our opinion, a more important

---

57 Pierre Rabardel [RAB 95, p. 149].

58 For a list of *Live Coding* environments, visit the TOPLAP community site, http://toplap.org/

59 http://www.sketchpatch.net/livecodelab/index.html

60 http://gibber.mat.ucsb.edu/

pedagogical potential than the paradigm introduced by DBN. Indeed, it seems to us that for the visual creator who is a novice in programming, the flexibility and instantaneity of *Live Coding* encourages a certain pleasure in the act of creation that is generally interfered with by writing problems (algorithmic and syntactical design) in the more classical environments and programming languages.

It is important to specify here that we envisage this layer of *Live Coding* as using a textual programming language. Indeed, it is about implementing a potential learning sequence for programming in art and design leading toward programming at the lowest level that happens to be mostly textual. It is as a parallel that we want to propose environments based on visual programming languages, although it also allows a kind of programming on the fly.

5.3.2.2. *Visual programming*

Text-based computer programming uses successions of character sequences to form keywords (*tokens*, or key elements) assembled in expressions that make it possible to construct sequences of instructions whose objective is to describe the processes that can be executed by the computer. Although certain programming languages attempt to get as close as possible to natural languages – more specifically, English – like most of the "verbose"[61] style of script languages, the writing of a program does not seem to succeed in being as intuitive and flexible as the writing of a text in one of the languages that humans practice daily between themselves. Not long after its invention, the computer quickly showed a strong capacity of generation and manipulation of images, a capacity that would give rise to a specific domain of computer imaging (*Computer Graphics*). Interactivity also gave rise to a particular scientific field of research that questions the way in which a human being can enter into an interactive relation with a computer system: human–machine interface (HMI) research.

---

61 As we stated above about *Lingo* and *HyperTalk*, or even *AppleScript*, which are still commonly used on the Mac OS X platform today. The instructions of these languages tend to get as close as possible to the sentences in a mode close to the written imperative in English.

Visual programming is located at the intersection of two fields of research attached to computer sciences, because it consists of the creation of programming languages using manipulable (and thus interactive) graphic elements.

Visual programming is basically distinguished from textual programming by the fact that it uses more than one dimension to provide a semantics, which is to say to provide a certain meaning to the elements used in the formation of a program. In textual programming, the first dimension (on the x-axis, for instance) makes it possible to organize different symbolic elements (*tokens*), like keywords and punctuation signs, by aligning them one after another according to the conventions of Western writing that builds sentences starting with words (and works starting with letters) in a certain order and separated by spaces to create meaning. The second dimension (on the y-axis) is only used to facilitate writing and reading source codes and to distinguish the lines between them in order to sequence instructions, but does not really participate in the semantic realization of an algorithm.

In the majority of textual programming languages, the second dimension does not carry any semantic load, and the proof is that a large part of these languages (the standard ones are C, C++, Java, etc.) transform the programs into a large and unique line of code at the moment of their compilation. The multidimensional nature of visual programming languages is the characteristic that distinguishes them most clearly from textual programming[62].

Some authoring software environments are based on visual languages, such as Max/MSP, *Pure data*, *vvvv*, *Quartz Composer* and *Node Box*[63]. While these languages present a creative power similar to textual languages,

---

62 The difference that makes it possible to define visual programming languages in relation to textual programming can be found in a large number of publications of the *Journal of Visual Languages and Computing* (Elsevier edition, Amsterdam), and notably in Brad A. Myers [MYE 90] (original text from1989). See also the generalist text on the subject by Professor Margaret M. Brunett [BRU 99].

63 For a historical and technical study that is more expansive on the origins and paradigms of visual programming, see the text that I wrote on this topic: http://enjeuxdudesigngraphique.fr/ programmation-visuelle-etat-des-lieux/

the wide accessibility that they afford interests us greatly, especially in the contexts of familiarizing children with programming. Whether it consists of the *dataflow* paradigm (graphic nodes representing the functions are related to one another by cables and form a data processing flow) or an *assembly game* or *puzzle* paradigm (pieces cut according to a precise shape fit together to form an assembly that makes a program), we observe that the visual metaphors employed to build programs make it possible for young children to take control of the machine and develop a recreational practice of computer code. This simplified and visual approach seems to us to hold important pedagogical promises that must continue to be explored as much for young audiences, as the *Scratch*[64] project or its web implementation *Snap!*[65] shows, as for art school students beginning programming.

Before concluding this text, we believe it would be useful to observe the base layer of *Mobilizing.js* a bit more closely, represented in red in the architecture diagram above. Although it is not yet completely stabilized, the structure that we propose for this base layer is filled, on a technical level, with some of the ideas that we have evoked here. A quick description of the artistic works realized recently with *Mobilizing.js* will allow us to then approach certain questions concerning interactivity and, more particularly, collective interactivity, which is one of the unique elements of our authoring environment.

5.4. Structure and results of *Mobilizing.js*

5.4.1. *Overview of a technical sequence*

The development sequence that we use to produce *Mobilizing.js* is one that several contemporary *JavaScript* libraries implement: development environments integrated for compiled languages are copied using *Node.js* and a series of tools such as *gulp* or *grunt*, source file managers. A sequence

---

64 See the work by John Maloney, Mitchel Resnick, Natalie Rusk, Brian Silverman, and Evelyn Eastmond [MAL 10, p. 3], available at: http://web.media.mit.edu/%7Ejmaloney/papers/Scratch LangAndEnvironment.pdf

65 Previously called *Build Your Own Blocks*: https://snap.berkeley.edu/snapsource/snap. html

of rules makes it possible to automate the creation of a unique *JavaScript* folder in a version that is readable by a human being and another "minified" (and even "uglyfied" in such a way that it is no longer readable), which occupies the minimum memory space and makes it possible to accelerate its online transfer. It is one of these two files that users use in their projects. Here is an HTML base file that makes it possible to load *Mobilizing.js* and launch a user script.

```
<!DOCTYPE html>
<html>
  <head>
    <meta http-equiv="Content-Type" content="text/html; charset=utf8">

    <meta name="viewport" content="user-scalable=no"/>
    <meta name="apple-mobile-web-app-capable" content="yes">
    <meta name="apple-touch-fullscreen" content="yes">

    <link href="../style.css" rel="stylesheet" />

    <script src="../../vendor/three/three.min.js"></script>
    <script src="../../vendor/opentype/opentype.js"></script>
    <script src="../../dist/Mobilizing.js"></script>

    <script src="script.js"></script>
    <script>
      //Init a runner to execute the user script (required)
      var runner = new Mobilizing.Runner(new script());
    </script>

  </head>
  <body>
  </body>
</html>
```

The dependencies of *Mobilizing.js* are clearly identifiable here (*Three.js* and *OpenType.js*). We can also see a certain number of <meta> tags allowing for defining certain behaviors of browsers on mobile screens. It consists above all of being able to access *touch* events from *Mobilizing.js* in order to create interactive behaviors that are not those implemented by default in browsers (pinching to zoom, sliding to scroll, etc.). We also find a minimal script recorded in a <script> tag that serves to launch a user script with the help of an instantiation of the object. The reason for this script comes from the flexibility of integration in other environments that we wanted to give to *Mobilizing.js*. On the one hand, in order to be able to instantiate a *Mobilizing.js* script, we made it so that the execution context of scripts would be clearly separated from the global execution context that is imposed by *JavaScript*[66]. On the other hand, in order to control a *Mobilizing.js* script from outside of it, from another library, for example, we opened the possibility of accessing, initializing and refreshing functionalities of the scripts from an ordinary program. That is why a Runner was put in place, whose mission was to launch user scripts. These scripts are the object that must imperatively contain at least two functions: setup() and update(). These two functions are resurgences of the influence of *Processing* on *Mobilizing* (version 1.0 for iOS) and make it possible to completely separate the construction phase of the base elements of a scene and its logic of refreshing over time, during running. One of the advantages of this architecture is that a *Mobilizing.js* script can be used inside *Mobilizing.js* itself as an element that produces content: a conglomeration of scripts becomes possible encouraging a large reusability of codes. The diagram below attempts to show one of the possible usage bases of this conglomeration, a script producing images on a screen that becomes the texture applied to objects from another screen managed in another script.

The simplest example of script that can be made with *Mobilizing.js* makes it possible to display a cube in three dimensions rotating at a constant speed on two axes. The comments that we allow to appear in the source code below make it possible to clarify each instruction.

---

66 In the case of Internet browsers, this general context is nothing other than the *Window* object, to which every variable or function whose impact is not explicitly determined is attached automatically. It consists of avoiding all "pollution" of this general context, because the uses of a software library are generally led to produce by themselves the functionalities proper to their projects, and conflicts must be avoided. For example, if, for a specific project, the definition of an Input class must be implemented by the user, it can be substituted for the Input class that is part of *Mobilizing.js* if what belongs to *Mobilizing.js* is not located in its own *scope*. This is to avoid the type of confusions that we find in writings such as Mobilizing.Input to solve this type of problem, we can thus talk about *namespace*.

```
/* This is the Mobilizing.js user script.
 * For simplicity, we use "script" as a name for it.
 */
function script()
{
    //variable to hold the Mobilizing context
    var M = null;
    //variable to hold the camera object
    var camera = null;
    //variable to hold the cube object
    var cube = null;
    //variable to hold the light object
    var light = null;
    //Value to use for the rotation of the object
    var y = 0;
    //Value for the initial speed of the rotation
    var speed = 0;

    this.setup = function(){

        M = this.getContext();

        //construct a default perspective camera
        camera = new Mobilizing.Camera();
        camera.transform.setLocalPosition(0,0,0);
        M.addCamera(camera);

        light = new Mobilizing.Light();
        M.addToCurrentScene(light);

        cube = new Mobilizing.Mesh({primitive:"box", width:1, height:1, depth:1});
        //cube = new Mobilizing.Cube();
        cube.transform.setLocalPosition(0,0,-10);
        M.addToCurrentScene(cube);

        //Mobilizing.js includes some math methods
        speed = M.math.randomFromTo(1, 10);
    };

    this.update = function(){

        y += speed;
        cube.transform.setLocalRotation(45,y,70);
    };
};
```

Mobilizing.js

Context and runtime management scheme

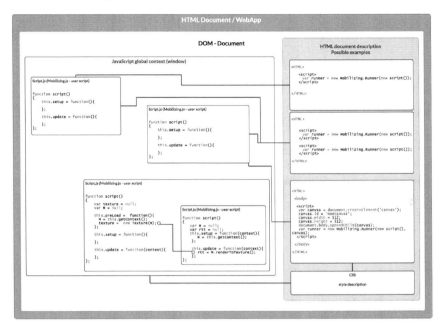

Figure 5.2. *Diagram representing the possible cases of the runtime stream of Mobilizing.js user scripts*

This basic script, whose visual result is in no way surprising (a white cube rotates on a black background), shows clearly that *Mobilizing.js* is based on a programming interface similar to many real-time 3D engines: the notions of the graph of the stage, camera, geometric object and linking of their transformation in space can be found here and are part of the "foundations" of the library. The default values are attributed to objects created when no argument passes at the time of the call to the builder, which allows for quick tests before consulting the documentation detailing the possible usages of each function (http://docs.mobilizing-js.net).

But because one of the contributions that we wish to bring to *Mobilizing.js* is the coexistence of a multiplicity of possible writings, the same example can be written in a completely different and more compact way using a *template*.

```
function script()
{
    var M = null;      //variable to hold the Mobilizing context
    var scene = null;  //variable to hold the main scene template
    var y = 0;         //Value to use for the rotation of the object
    var speed = 0;     //Value for the initial speed of the rotation

    this.setup = function()
    {
        M = this.getContext(); //get the Mobilizing context
        scene = M.createTemplateSimple3dScene();
        speed = M.math.randomFromTo(1, 10);
    };

    this.update = function()
    {
        y += speed;
        scene.cube.transform.setLocalRotation(45,y,70);

    };
};
```

This script assumes that the Context class contains the following elements of the program as well as the "shortcut" functions that are used in it:

```
//simple scene with one cam, one cube and one light
function TemplateSimple3dScene(M)
{

    this.camera = M.createCamera();
    this.camera.transform.setLocalPosition(0,0,10);
    this.camera.setClearColor(Mobilizing.Color.random());

    this.cube = M.createCube(2,3);
    this.cube.transform.setLocalPosition(0,0,0);
    this.cube.material.color = Mobilizing.Color.random();
```

```
this.light = M.createLight();
this.light.transform.setLocalPosition(10,0,10);
  };

Mobilizing.Context.prototype.createTemplateSimple3dScene = function()
{
  var scene = new TemplateSimple3dScene(this);
  return scene;
};
```

But this quest for density, which can lead to such a reduction that only some letters and syntactical elements are sufficient to make program, is only one aspect of our research. The more compact a code is, the more it can become simple to use and quick to write. The context of *Live Coding* is the most directly concerned with this effort of reduction, which passes through the implementation of "composite" functions because they themselves call upon a whole series of more "fundamental" functions. This consists of producing new layers of writing interfaces one on top of the other.

In the sequence of this work, we envisage exploring writing in natural languages in order to allow for a radically different approach to writing programs. My teaching activities at art school have reinforced my idea that the practice of programming for potentially resistant novices starts with the description of the project planned in natural language (in their mother tongue). From an intention expressed in a few sentences, generally very loaded with implicit elements that are however understood quite clearly by the human interlocutor, a user must be able to produce a more precise and refined description that leaves behind all kinds of ambiguity. This work stems from the design of the algorithm and is realized above all by language and can be accompanied by preparatory sketches. It consists of the first passage between the imagination of the author, their thinking and a formalization that tends to define with always more and more details and precision the technical and functional components of a project of creation. The textual descriptions that result from this first filter can then be "translated" into formal languages (this is where a tool like *Processing*, putting ahead the idea of the digital sketch, finds its place), and the resolution of the technical problems proper to the technology put to work can begin. This descriptive step is generally not carried out by experienced programmers, who demonstrate more of a tendency to directly code their projects and build them in an iterative manner by trial and error[67], because this phase of cutting and functional specifications of the project is completed mentally. However, the already old languages like those put to use in the *Inform 7* engine that creates interactive fictions demonstrate that "verbose" script languages can get even closer to natural languages[68].

The theoretical discussion guided by these approaches, comparing computer programming language and natural language, cannot go on without remembering the texts of Katherine Hayles[69] or Geoff Cox and Alex McLean[70], among others, but we will only enter into that discussion when our research and practices on the topic are sufficiently advanced. Now, we will approach the problem of interactivity, its theoretical bases and the way in which we propose implementations in *Mobilizing.js*.

5.4.2. *Constructing interactivities*

The notion of interactivity to which we are referencing in our research is linked to the technical system of the digital machines that we implement. "The very term itself of 'interactivity' appeared quite recently and was immediately obscured by social and ideological uses, beyond all references to the technologies that coined it to describe the activity of dialogue between a user and information provided by a machine"[71]. Jean-Louis Boissier, who researched on the notion of interactivity in contemporary arts working with digital technologies, correctly recalled this technological origin of interactivity. Computer science was transformed from the moment that computers acquired a manipulation terminal that was *interactive*. Before this, digital machines required fastidious preparation before they could execute any operation and produce results. The programs and data had to be "encoded" onto media that varied over time (perforated cards, audio cassettes, magnetic disks, etc.) and the result of the program was often returned on another medium that had to be "decoded".

---

67 At least, this is how I proceed for small-scale projects.

68 On this subject, consult the reference text on the language *Inform 7* by Graham Nelson [GRA 06], available online at: http://www.inform-fiction.org/I7Downloads/Documents/White Paper.pdf.

69 In particular, [HAY 05].

70 [COX 12].

71 Jean-Louis Boissier [BOI 09, p. 180].

In order to simplify and accelerate the dialogue between the programmer and the machine, the idea of a new type of control terminal appeared: a screen and a keyboard that made it possible to visualize in real time the text typed by the programmer, who could then enter the data required by the program that they wrote and command the execution at any time, and the result would be displayed on the screen immediately after their computation. This new situation provided a sense of instantaneous control over the machine. The actions of the programmer/user produced an immediate reaction on the machine's part and a certain interaction was created, establishing a human–machine relationship that we describe as interactive.

Incidentally, the term "relation" is alluded to in Jean-Louis Boissier's definition of interactivity, by referring to Gilles Deleuze: "Relations are outside of their terms. 'Pierre is smaller than Paul', 'the glass is on the table': the relation is not inside one of the terms that would subsequently be the subject, nor in both terms. In addition, the relation can change without the terms changing"[72]. If the relation has the ability to change because it is a third element that creates the liaison between the two parts, then we can assume that the relationship has a form. With this approach to the relationship, presented by Deleuze in the context of his studies on Hume's empiricism, Jean-Louis Boissier suggests that "if the relationship has a form, a form capable of transforming the whole that it structures, we understand that it has technologies and media, that it can work, that it can enter into an artistic process [...]"[73]. If interactivity makes it possible to formalize a relationship between an artistic medium and its audience, then this form is built using different components. "The interactive image is above all a *diagram*, a software structure"[74]. This structure is built using interactions that are captured (or seized, according to the terms of the author) with the help of peripheral devices. Parcels of the computer program make it possible to "replay" interactions inside an encompassing software structure that will not only produce and manage media put in place (images, sounds, text, etc.) but also regulate the relationship of the spectator to the whole system that was given to them to experience. The form taken by the relationships produced by an artistic interactive system is built using a set composed of as many material elements as software and abstract elements.

---

72 Gilles Deleuze and Claire Parnet, *Dialogues*, Flammarion, Paris, 1996, p. 69, cited by Jean-Louis Boissier [BOI 09, p. 264].
73 Jean-Louis Boissier [BOI 09].
74 [BOI 09, p. 182].

Jean-Marie Dallet suggests defining the figures of interactivity based on this foundational research about interactivity in new media art[75]. He poses "as a hypothesis that a figure structures a volume inside of which three levels of forms hierarchize the space: the responsive function, the relation function, and the program. These different stages fit together and make up the levels of concurrent reading"[76]. The three stages listed can be summarized as follows:

1) The responsive function, which represents the layer that is immediately perceptible by the senses (images, sound, etc.).

2) The relation function, which is a diagram of the possible relations between the elements that make up the system.

3) The program, or the implementation of all of the functions that make it possible to operate the modifications in the responsive form and also that give shape to relations.

This generic definition of a figure of interactivity insists on the fact that the term "interactivity", when it is used in the field of artistic practices that use digital machines, refers to a relation that takes shape between the spectator and the work, and that this form is made using three components cited by the author, which describes a kind of "global image" of the relation, like Jean-Louis Boissier already maintained, in his own way[77]. Boissier proposed a more concise approach to the notion of the figure of interactivity in one of his recent publications: "From the moment that we understand interactivity as falling under form, it is useful and necessary to attempt to establish the morphology in terms of figures. In interactivity, a figure is a relational structure capable of being repeated with some elements in different contexts all while preserving the same internal articulation and capacity to connect with others"[78].

Mobilizing.js, directly following its predecessor, proposes a sequence of functionalities that facilitate the use of sensors embedded in host devices.

---

75 Jean-Marie Dallet [DAL 03], online available at: http://www.sliderslab.com/pages_fr/PDF/TEXTES/03_dallet_Anomalie.pdf
76 [DAL 03, p. 2].
77 "I have put forward the idea [...] that an interactive application is built on a diagram of access, discovery, exploration and modification, which is itself an image, or more precisely an image included in the global image, the hyperimage" [BOI 09, p. 182].
78 Jean-Louis Boissier [BOI 16].

The Input class is responsible for many sensors and should improve over time and with practice. Today, it is mainly access to information provided by the sensors that is offered, and few treatments of this information are integrated ahead of time. The table below lists the methods and properties accessible by this class. The source code that follows makes it possible for a cube to be dragged by a finger or the mouse thanks to the getTouchX(touch_index) and getTouchY(touch_index) methods.

Methods		Properties	
1	getAcc	1	accAvailable
2	getDeviceOrientation	2	BatteryStatus
3	getGravityVector	3	compassAvailable
4	getLocation	4	context
5	getMousewheelDelta	5	GPSAvailable
6	getSmoothedAcc	6	mouseWheelAvailable
7	getTouch		touchCount
8	getTouchDelta		touchPressed
9	getTouchDeltaX		
10	getTouchDeltaY		
11	getTouchOffset		
12	getTouchOffsetX		
13	getTouchOffsetY		
14	getTouchPinch		
15	getTouchX		
16	getTouchY		
17	getUserAcc		
18	setAccStatus		
19	setCompassStatus		
20	setGeolocationStatus		

```
function script()
{
    //variable to hold the Mobilizing context
    var M = null;
    //variable to hold the camera object
    var camera = null;
    //variable to hold the cube object
    var cube = null;
    //variable to hold the light object
    var light = null;

    this.setup = function()
    {
        M = this.getContext();

        //construct a default perspective camera
        camera = new Mobilizing.Camera();
        camera.setFarPlane(10000);
        camera.setToPixel();//makes world's origin at top-left corner
        M.addCamera(camera);

        //make a light
        light = new Mobilizing.Light();
        light.transform.setLocalPosition(500,-100,500);
        light.setDistance(5000);
        M.addToCurrentScene(light);

        //make a cube
        cube = new Mobilizing.Mesh({primitive:"box", width:1, height:1, depth:1});
        cube.transform.setLocalScale(50);
        M.addToCurrentScene(cube);
    };

    this.update = function()
    {
        if(M.input.touchPressed){

            cube.transform.setLocalPosition(
                M.input.getTouchX(0),
                - M.input.getTouchY(0),
                0);
        }

    };
};
```

But more complex behaviors are undergoing integration based on these functions and an accumulation of several elements. It consists of determining a kind of model of interactivity that can be used with different data input (different sensors) in order to apply them to some graphic and sound objects. In other words, these *behaviors* are none other than figures of interactivity that are ready to use and potentially able to be configured by the user. As it happens, the behavior of being dragged by a finger can be applied to a graphic object using a function like setDraggable(set_object, touch_index)[79].

This potential for *Mobilizing.js* to construct interactivities is very significant, because it allows *Mobilizing.js* to become a software library for creation that stands out from the others, not because this way of building behaviors is not found anywhere else (other authoring software environments work like this), but because starting from "individual" interactivities, which only concern one spectator–interactor with one machine, we seek to build collective interactivities that rely on the interactions of a variety of spectators located in the same place and acting in coordination on a common object from mobile screens that they manipulate individually. This is one of the particularities – even a true originality of *Mobilizing.js*.

5.4.3. *Interactive, immersive and collaborative system*

In addition to proposing various types of figures of interactivity, the idea of *behavior* that we are attempting to strengthen in *Mobilizing.js* has the goal of allowing the automatic synchronization in a network with certain characteristics. Although this technical principle is, once again, very present in video game engines, it does not consist of creating simulated environments shared in networks that are multi-user or persistent, or with players dispersed in the world and alone behind the screen of their machine while being together in the virtual universe, but rather of proposing a new group of spectators who are physically present in a location and who collectively participate in the same experience. This desire has been reinforced following the implementation of the *Collective Mobile Mapping* –

---

79 One of the largest construction zones that we focus on in *Mobilizing.js* concerns the naming of various elements: functions, variables, behaviors, etc. The ambiguities and the recovery are not always easy to avoid, which slows down the stabilization of our API.

Montpellier (C3M) project, an event that is part of the CoSiMa[80] project and was welcomed by the Festival Montpellier Danse 2016[81] for its inauguration in June 2016. Two works were presented on this occasion, *Centon Digital*, by Christophe Domino, and *Espace puissance Espace* (*Espace^Espace*), of which I am the author. Combined in a 360° immersive video projection system, these two works assume a particular interactive system: faced with a large image[82], a crowd of spectators each uses a mobile screen (*smartphone* or tablet) to interact with the representation that surrounds them. Their respective actions are taken into account according to the different scenarios and influence the large image in a certain way, defined by the work and its intent. It consists of exploring and evaluating a certain number of modalities of collective interactions in this immersive system in a context of artistic creation. C3M is a research action that could only be realized on a scale of one. Indeed, the work of collective interactivity requires holding an event to gather enough people ready to "play the game" and thus reach a certain critical mass that allows the experiments to leave the protected context of the laboratory. So we had to put our hypotheses to work, create effective software implementations and test them on the public to move our research forward. On this occasion, *Mobilizing.js* became as much a 3D engine as a *projection mapping*[83] engine as well as an environment to create collective interactive experiences.

---

80 Software platform project for the creation of localized collective interactive experiences supported by the ANR (Agence Nationale pour la Recherche), derived from Icram and whose organization includes Orbe, EnsadLab, IDScènes, NoDesign and Esba TAML. Certain components of *Mobilizing.js* are intended to be integrated into the CoSiMa platform. http://cosima.ircam.fr

81 http://www.montpellierdanse.com/spectacle/collective-mobile-mapping-montpellier; http://www.ensadlab.fr/fr/c3m-montpellier-danse-2016/

82 This "large image" terminology was supported for several years by the Grande-Image Lab at the École Supérieure des Beaux-Arts du Mans, an art research laboratory led by Christophe Domino. http://lemans.esba-talm.fr/recherche/grande-image

83 The technique of *projection mapping* makes it possible to transform an ordinary built space into a 360° video projection screen onto which a scene in 3D is broadcast. It is fundamentally an anamorphic method that uses a reproduction that is as faithful as possible to the projection location in order to produce images of a virtual scene observed from a single point of view, from which a coherent perspective is re-established and "cancels out" the particularities of the architecture (reliefs, reinforcements, protrusions, etc.). Virtual cameras are then placed in this simulation at the location and with the exact orientation of the video-projectors that are broadcasting the images onto the physical space. If the spectator is in the location from which the anamorphic panorama of the 3D scene is realized, they will have the

Espace^Espace proposes as a starting point a simple idea: the projection of a space onto itself. Metatheater, which conceptual artists have grown accustomed us to, is the pretext for the exploration of architecture through the projection of its 3D model on its own walls. On each physical wall, the corresponding wall is projected in a 3D model, so that the two instances of the building overlap perfectly in the space. The spectators, equipped with mobile screens, use a special application that proposes different interaction scenarios with the projected architecture. Because the walls of the building become screens, a simulation of the architecture in three dimensions, generally produced for design and preview purposes, encounters the real wall on which it is projected. The constructed space becomes the very location of a meeting with its own projection – an architecture project simulated using digital technologies that aids design, the image and projection of the "large image" using a large-scale video *mapping* system where a group of spectators is invited to "manipulate" through strategies created at that moment, and in great number.

One of the three scenarios that have been proposed to the public presents a 3D model of the building in *wireframe*, thus giving a feeling of transparency to the construction, which can be found right behind the walls that are immediately observable. The mobile screen displays a kind of level with several bubbles, an instrument *a priori* intended to verify the tilt of the mobile screen in relation to the ground. Each spectator must find the correct tilt of the screen so that all of the bubbles center on each other so that they all become concentric. Once they are centered, all of the bubbles progressively turn red and, if the person maintains their position, the system "petrifies", the bubbles turn white and immobilize, marking the success and the end of this sequence of the "game". If all of the participants manage to stabilize their level (which is to say to find the tilt that centers the bubbles), the simulated architectural space carries out a movement (animated in real time) to appear under new angles, impossible to design outside of a simulation.

---

feeling of being in a spherical screen. For a complete explanation of this complex procedure and its implementation in *Mobilizing.js*, see the document I produced in the framework of the deliverables of the CoSiMa project: http://www.mobilizing-js.net/cosima/livrable_5.3/ Livrable5.3_screen.pdf

Figure 5.3. *Interaction interface on the Espace level. For a color version of this figure, see www.iste.co.uk/reyes/hypermedia.zip*

The bubble level of each participant is reproduced on the walls, and the projection and their state (their movements) are updated in real time. Thus, everyone can see who managed to center their level (who "finished the game") and who is struggling to do so. We were able to observe the spectators impatient to see the next movement of the space. Because they had managed to center their own level, they could see in the projection how many people had not yet managed to stabilize their own. So they physically sought out who were the late people to try to understand why they were unable to finish this little game, and so conversations took place between them: "No, no, no, more to the bottom. Yes, there, it's turning red, you have to stay like that... ah! Too bad, almost, try again...". This behavior would be very difficult to find among spectators of an interactive work that does not allow for collective interactions. A collaborative and playful dimension switches on and becomes a condition of the relation to the work. Because the bubble level, individually manipulated on a mobile screen, is projected as a large image, everyone can recognize the effects of their actions on the object shared by all. When all of the participants have succeeded in their mission and the space suddenly moves, it becomes possible to understand that the sum of the individual acts, the "small victories" of each person, transform the common object, which in this case is the 3D model of a building in which we are present, which becomes shared by each person in their aesthetic understanding as in their control.

The software architecture that was introduced in *Mobilizing.js* to make this kind of interactive and collective experience possible is totally generic. Its basic component is a communication system through network publication and subscription (*publish/subscribe*, or *pubsub*) using *WebSocket* and requiring the execution of a generic *Node.js* server whose role is to distribute network messages between different clients. Beyond this very open system, a programming interface specific to *Mobilizing.js* makes it possible to define the role of each script, which can then act like a server or like a client as a function of the "network design" required by the project. On this base, we built a structure making it possible to define the interactive and collective experiences starting from the recurrent technical elements that we identified: each experience needs "mobile" and "video" clients as well as a server. The "video" clients are the scripts that produce images that will be displayed on video projectors, and they integrate the organization of the cameras in such a way that a single script can be written, the cameras corresponding to the physical video projectors linked to the machine being able to be chosen on the fly. The "mobile" clients make it possible to manage the mobile screens and their content, and the servers allow for regulating the relation between the two types of clients by introducing specific logics. The base principles of the network communication between the different clients are encapsulated in the *Mobilizing.js* behaviors that facilitate the creation of new interactive and collective experiences.

In the case of the bubble level, the mobile client is a standard *Mobilizing.js* script that defines the center of gravity of the five colored disks at its launch; the information from accelerometers are used to define the distance of the disks in relation to the center. Their positions are transmitted continuously to video clients so that the level is accurately reproduced in the projection. When the center is attained and the disks turn from red to white, network information is sent to the server that stores the "success" of the participants in a dynamic list. When all of the connected mobile clients are recognized as having succeeded, the server triggers the transition from one point of the transformation to another (translation and rotation) from among the video clients.

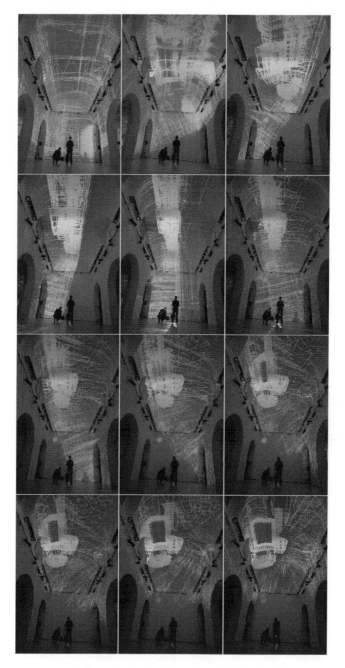

Figure 5.4. *For a color version of this figure, see*
www.iste.co.uk/reyes/hypermedia.zip

5.5. Conclusion

Mobilizing.js is a project that effectively applies our hypothesis concerning authoring software environments for interactive artistic creation intended for art and design and whose conception and architecture are guided by them. This "art tool", which can also be called an *Art Engine*, is distinguished from other authoring environments and from *Game Engines* in several ways while sharing many structural elements with them. From a technical point of view, most of the basic principles of video games can be found in authoring environments and vice versa: separation between the functional bricks of the base and the media that are used in one particular project, modular architecture allowing for a large reusability of the base components, the possibility of using a graphic interface and a programming interface, etc. The programming paradigms (textual/visual, but also object-oriented, functional, etc.) used by the different creation tools are added to more general paradigms that determine the design methods and writings that end up creating the environment, as we observed with the evolution from *Design By Number*, *Processing* and *Open Frameworks*. These authoring libraries can be considered engines inasmuch as they propose a set of functions that are accessible by the users from a programming interface. If a contrast must be put forward between game engines and these authoring libraries, which are intended for artistic creation, we should not look to their technical nature but rather their purpose and their audience. The pedagogical desire of programming tools for the arts and design is not found in game engines. However, we observed a contradictory movement in the evolution of tools intended for art practices: accessibility has lost ground in favor of a greater proximity to the tools of the software industry that also ensure a greater efficiency and a faster running speed.

This contradiction seems to make it difficult to encourage a certain *artistic technical conduct*, or a certain *critical technical practice* that we consider fundamental to the position that artists and designers can take relative to digital technologies. Actor practitioners of artistic creation working with the digital need not take on the role of computer engineer, but can instead practice computer programming as an artist or as a designer. A critical or theoretical engagement cannot disregard a technical practice that fosters reflection, just as this reflection is transformed by the technical application. This cycle of mutual influence drives the innovative nature of the tool's evolution and the projects made possible by it. That is why the capacity to adapt the tool used must be anticipated, because the needs of future works and projects cannot themselves be entirely predicted. It consists of proceeding by iteration, both in the creation of artistic systems that evolve at each opportunity of presentation and exhibition and in the construction of the tool that an application will continually put back into question. Finally, the accessibility offered by the software environment must also be taken into account. If a base layer can be implemented by the authors of the tool itself, the pedagogical dimension cannot be ignored because it is a condition for opening creation software tools so that the black boxes that are digital machines always become a bit more transparent. This mission, which springs from a kind of literacy, must be completely accepted and integrated into the software tools in order to propose various layers of accessibility without forcing users/creators to change tools as a function of their level of expertise or their needs.

5.6. Bibliography

[AGR 97] AGRE P.E., "Toward a critical technical practice: lessons learned in trying to reform AI", in BOWKER G.C., LEIGH STAR S., TURNER W. *et al.* (eds), *Social Science, Technical Systems and Cooperative Work: Beyond the Great Divide*, Erlbaum, 1997.

[BOI 08] BOISSIER J.-L., Remarques sur les Field-Works de Masaki Fujihata, p. 8, available at: http://www.arpla.fr/canal20/adnm/wp-pdf/Fujihata_lineaire_actif. pdf, 2008.

[BOI 09] BOISSIER J.-L., *La relation comme forme: L'interactivité en art*, Les Presses du réel, Mamco, 2009.

[BOI 16] BOISSIER J.-L., "For a dramaturgy of interactivity", BIANCHINI S., VERHAGEN E. (eds), *Practicable: From Participation to Interaction in Contemporary Art*, Cambridge, MIT Press, Cambridge, 2016.

[BRU 99] BRUNETT M.M., *Visual Programming*, Wiley Encyclopedia of Electrical and Electronics Engineering, 1999.

[COX 12] COX G., MCLEAN A., *Speaking Code: Coding as Aesthetic and Political Expression*, MIT Press, 2012.

[CUN 14] CUNIN D., Pratiques artistiques sur les écrans mobiles: création d'un langage de programmation, Thesis, University of Paris 8, available at: http:// theses.fr/2014PA080045, 2014.

[DAL 03] DALLET J.-M., *Figures de l'interactivité*, Anomalie, 2003.

[FRY 07] FRY B., REAS C., *Processing: A Programming Handbook for Visual Designers and Artists*, MIT Press, 2007.

[GRA 06] GRAHAM N., Natural Language, Semantic Analysis, and Interactive Fiction, White Paper, St Anne's College, Oxford, 2006.

[GRE 14] GREGORY J., *Game Engine Architecture*, 2nd ed., A K Peters/CRC Press, 2014.

[HAY 05] HAYLES K., *Speech, Writing, Code – Three Worldviews*, in *My Mother Was a Computer*, University Of Chicago Press, 2005.

[HUG 08] HUYGHE P.-D., "L'art comme conduite technique", *Conférence donnée dans le cadre de l'opération Mobilisable 2008*, available at: http://www. mobilisable.net/2008/?page_id=9, 2008.

[HUT 11] HUHTAMO E., PARIKKA J. (eds), *Media Archaeology – Approaches, Applications, and Implications*, University of California Press, 2011.

[LAR 11] LARTIGAUD D.-O., "Bricodage", in LARTIGAUD D.-O. (ed.), *Art++*, HYX, 2011.

[LOW 14] LOWOOD H., "Game Engines and Game History", *History of Games International Conference Proceedings*, available at: http://www.kinephanos.ca, 2014.

[MAL 10] MALONEY J., RESNICK M., RUSK N., *et al.*, "The scratch programming language and environment", *ACM Transactions on Computing Education*, vol. 10, no. 4, 2010.

[MYE 90] MYERS B.A., "Taxonomies of visual programming and program visualization", *Journal of Visual Languages and Computing*, no. 1, pp. 97–123, 1990.

[RAB 95] RABARDEL P., *Les hommes et les technologies; approche cognitive des instruments contemporains*, Armand Colin, 1995.

[WAR 04] WARD A., ROHRHUBER J., OLOFSSON F. *et al.*, "Live algorithm programming and a temporary organisation for its promotion" in GORIUNOVA O., SHULGIN A. (eds), *read_me - Software Art and Cultures*, Aarhus University Press, 2004

[WIN 96] WINOGRAD T., *Bringing Design to Software*, Addison-Wesley, 1996.

[WOO 10] WOOLFORD K., BLACKWELL A.F., NORMAN S.J., *et al.*, "Crafting a Critical Technical Practice", *Leonardo*, vol. 43, no. 2, pp. 202–203, April 2010.

Clues. Anomalies. Understanding. Detecting Underlying Assumptions and Expected Practices in the Digital Humanities through the AIME Project

6.1. Abstract

Imagine a collective inquiry presenting its results before the collaboration has even started; an academic book without footnotes and references; an open, on-and-off-line platform to collaborate with peers where all must subscribe to a strict protocol to express their ideas. This is the AIME (An Inquiry into Modes of Existence) project. It is an experimental intertwining of analog and digital practices that often contradict the norms and formats they belong to, thus creating expectations and objections from different communities of users. By adopting a critical position toward the project, we multiplied the listening devices to collect these reactions. We propose here, to reframe them as *clues* to identify the different practices and assumptions at work in collaboration-based projects, design, and Digital Humanities communities. This paper details the methodical activity of collecting *clues*, grouping them in specific *anomalies* and then explaining the choices that generated them. In a situation where Digital Humanities are still delineating their position and role in the wider academic environment, our study on the AIME project will help reframe the role of experiments in the

Chapter written by Donato RICCI, Robin DE MOURAT, Christophe LECLERCQ and Bruno LATOUR.

Digital Humanities. This study about AIME enables an *understanding* of some underlying assumptions and expectations in Digital Humanities.

This chapter has a digital component available at http://bit.ly/dhanomalies[1]

6.2. Introduction

The AIME[2] project tried to explore the many discrepancies between the description that the Moderns are offering of their values and the ways they are defended in practice. For instance, there is a huge gap between Science, capital S, and the scientific institutions. There is almost no relationship between technology as it is hyped and the ways they are defended in practice. This gap also exists in law, politics, religion, etc. Such discrepancies raise the question of deciding which version of their values the modernists are ready to defend: the official one or the more practical ones? In order to pursue such a vast inquiry, we needed to transform the inquiry of a lone ethnographer into a collective undertaking of a community of co-inquirers. In order to achieve this transformation, in addition to the publication of a book, we produced a series of workshops and meetings and the design of a digital platform with the intention of testing and expanding the preliminary results of the inquiry.

This is where AIME project overlaps with innovative practices in Digital Humanities (DH). This meant we had to build, technologically speaking, an on-the-fly experiment that depended as much on the scholarly practices of philosophy and anthropology as on the many new skills and habits of the emerging DH field. Over a four-year timespan, a vast and diversified *set-up* of technologies has been designed, developed, tested, and modified[3]. Some of them clearly achieved the foreseen objectives, whereas others did not. For most of them, we struggled to design their features and to understand their agency. Although challenging from a management and scholarly point of view, this was not completely unexpected. AIME provided the rare opportunity to craft all at once a new method of inquiry in philosophy, its own content and format, and a way to disseminate its results, all the while striving to build an innovative relationship with a diversified spectrum of readers. In

---

1 The first version of this chapter appeared in *Visual Language*, vol. 49, no. 3. Reprinted by permission, copyright University of Cincinnati.
2 See http://modesofexistence.org/
3 Here, the term *set-up* refers to the network of complementary instances of the project: interconnected material artifacts (i.e. print, Web interfaces, meeting rooms) as well as people with their skills supporting an ecosystem of distributed practices.

a more than chaotic trajectory, design practices played a major role, acting as critical and speculative agents[4]. To understand the role of AIME in the field of DH, as well as what has to be retained as good practices and what should be avoided in similar future projects, we offer here a thoroughgoing analysis. It is an empirical observation – to this extent we will try to adopt the same research posture as the AIME inquiry itself – based on the different feedback collected with heterogeneous strategies: from digital methods of research to web analytics; from qualitative interviews to an online questionnaire.

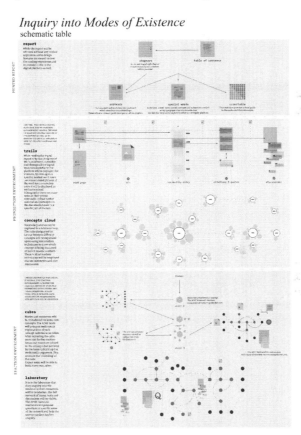

Figure 6.1. *AIME schematic table. In this poster the main features of the different instances of the project are shown to highlight their connection and interactions. For a color version of this figure, see www.iste.co.uk/reyes/hypermedia.zip*

4 Lukens' definition [LUK 11] perfectly describes our design attitude in engaging with the project: "Speculative design is an approach to design that emphasizes inquiry, experimentation, and expression, over usability, usefulness, or desirability. A particular characteristic of speculative design is that it tends to be future-oriented".

6.3. AIME and its digital humanities set-up

Johanna Drucker [DRU 13] stated that finding a vocabulary – and we would also add finding the meaning (what it is) and the sense (what it does) – of a new technology (and here the new technology is the entire AIME set-up) takes time. During the initial development of the AIME set-up, only a few components were presupposed and could be identified via a specific nomenclature. One of these components is the principal investigator (PI): Bruno Latour. In one of the first public presentations of AIME, delivered in late 2011[5], he defined AIME as a collective procedure triggered by a series of troublesome anthropological and philosophical questions. AIME's ambition was to invent a specific medium for an empirical[6] inquiry. The inquiry had started 25 years earlier as a personal endeavor[7]. Given the huge scope and impact of the topic, it had to be opened to other researchers willing to use the AIME protocol and method (borrowed from William James) in order to validate and expand the results. In this presentation, the moments of hesitation about the medium are clear, and the names for designating technologies and procedure are shaky, signaling something still to invent. Leaving the philosophical community to judge the relevance and quality of the AIME arguments, in this paper, we dedicate ourselves, instead, to describing the evolution of these hesitations. They evolved into a chimera whose body parts do not have a clear identity, becoming one of the "strange beasts" described by Ludovico [LUD 12]. Thus, here was a collaborative inquiry presenting some results before the collaboration was even started; an academic book without footnotes and references; an open, on-and-off-line platform to collaborate with peers where subscribing to a strict protocol was required. It is a set-up that was composed before it was able to be described[8].

---

5 The presentation was given to students in the SPEAP Master program at Sciences Po on 17 November 2011. See https://vimeo.com/36089028
6 It is empirical in the sense that the demonstration and discussion of the philosophical arguments are grounded on anthropological experiences fostered by diverse types of documents (e.g. iconic, audio visual, textual, etc.).
7 For an historical account of the project, see [LAT 13].
8 Obviously, this does not mean that we had no plan or strategy. It is simply that these were anticipated as achievements of the philosophy itself. Figure 6.1 is among the very first comprehensive depictions of the project.

Eventually, we identified some BUILT-IN EXPECTATIONS where the produced artifacts did not present all of the features required from the general type of media they belonged to.

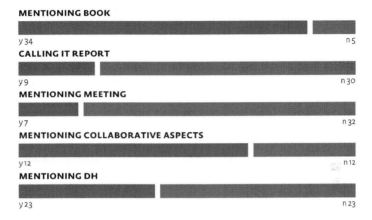

MENTIONING BOOK

y 34   n 5

CALLING IT REPORT

y 9   n 30

MENTIONING MEETING

y 7   n 32

MENTIONING COLLABORATIVE ASPECTS

y 12   n 12

MENTIONING DH

y 23   n 23

Figure 6.2. *Count of the pages mentioning the different components and naming of the AIME projects. For a color version of this figure, see www.iste.co.uk/reyes/hypermedia.zip*

Observing how people described AIME is enlightening. By analyzing 39 web pages retrieved by employing five different search-engine queries[9], selected according to their relevance and pertinence [ROG 09], almost all the pages are mentioned in the book[10] but only a few of them called it a report. While it is easy to label a printed academic artifact as a book, "the very best 'interface' ever designed" [LUD 12] to convey arguments, it has been fairly impossible to reinforce its unstable nature by associating it with the word

---

9 The queries, carried out on the search engine duckduckgo, were as follows: "latour+digital", "latour+humanities", "latour+website", "latour+meeting", "latour+conference", "latour+design", "latour+augmented", "latour+platform".

10 The first community-oriented instance of the project is a printed artifact called the "preliminary report". However, designating it as a philosophical book may be dangerously misleading. It does not present the conventional cognitive and cultural features expected from a philosophical book. It features neither footnotes or glossary, nor any critical apparatus. It presents additional characteristics atypical of philosophical book templates, such as expanded margins and a report-like index that provides the reader with a very precise overview of the contents. This first printed instance is, therefore, an incomplete or defective version of a philosophical book. This incompleteness is intentional; it is a call for reworking the project along with the other instantiations of the inquiry, especially the digital interfaces of the project.

"report". It is a kind of MISMATCHING OF LEXICAL REFERENCES where the labels used for an established artifact did not fit with "new" experimentation.

Another interesting element of reflection emerged from the relatively small number of pages mentioning AIME as an experiment in DH, even though, looking at Twitter activity during the DH2014 meeting, Latour's keynote speech received a great deal of attention. These initially high expectations were quickly frustrated by the clumsiness of the first version of the online platform and by the type of DH activities conducted on it. Aren't these clues of a kind of MISALIGNED SET-UP PRACTICES for DH, where data visualization and large datasets are supposed to be the "new" norm, whereas the close reading of large numbers of documents is not?

Almost all the pages retrieved above mentioned the collaborative aspects of the AIME digital platform[11], but only a few cited the face-to-face meetings[12] that had been widely communicated. This lack of citation is a marked contrast to the other digital methods analysis [ROG 13] that we conducted using Twitter. Having a look at the graph produced by connecting hashtags and users certainly gives the impression of a complete contrast. (Figures 6.3 and 6.4).

---

11 The digital interfaces of the project find their unity in a shared URL: modesofexistence.org. This accesses a blog-like home page and two interfaces for the inquiry contents. The first interface (modesofexistence.org/inquiry), named "book entry", features the elements of the project in a layout composed of four columns: the first presents the preliminary report (txt), then comes a vocabulary discussion and definition column (voc), then contextual documents along with bibliographical references (doc) and, last but not least, collective contributions pointing at elements from the three previous columns (cont). The reader is then left free to navigate through a nonlinear logic by clicking through the links bounding the diverse elements of the inquiry, reassembled through specific visual agencies depending on the main element read by the visitor. The second interface (modesofexistence.org/crossings), called "crossings entry," displays the elements of the investigation as sorted through the theoretical framework of the enquiry, that is modes and their crossings. It allows for the building of alternative and nonexclusive pathways, called scenarios, into the network of contents (book paragraphs, vocabulary entry, documents), each scenario intended to shed new light on the meaning of modes and their crossings.
12 Another instantiation of the project consisted of physical meetings gathering various people interested in specific modes and responding to a call for contributions on the digital version of the inquiry.

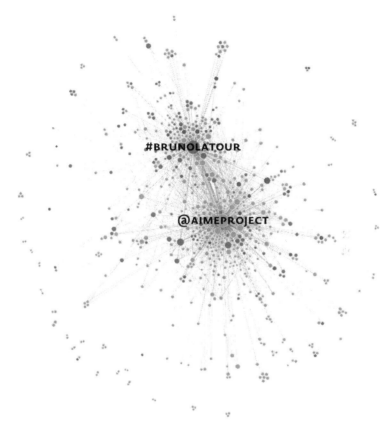

Figure 6.3. *Graph depicting the link between users (@) and hashtags (#) for the AIME project. For a color version of this figure, see www.iste.co.uk/reyes/hypermedia.zip*

Evident at first glance is a polarization between AIME and its PI. It is probably the clue of a personality and status refraction where the reputation of a specific project actor multiplies engagements with the project itself. If we remove the two main nodes, (Figure 6.4), a clearer view of the discussion around AIME arises. Some discussions are shown to be revolving around DH memes (e.g. #digitalhumanities) and various related AIME workshops and side events (e.g. #thatcamplyon). As would be expected, discussions appear around the usual fields of study with which the PI is associated (#sociology, #ANT, #STS)[13] as well as other projects conducted by him (#mooc, #cop21). Here

13 ANT stands for Actor-Network Theory, while STS stands for Science and Technology Studies.

we can see a sort of AMALGAMATION OF THE HETEROGENEOUS PUBLIC, where the composition and scale of the communities being formed do not fit with what had been expected. The projected audience did not conform to a single discipline/community, which engendered some confusion, thereby leading to misunderstandings.

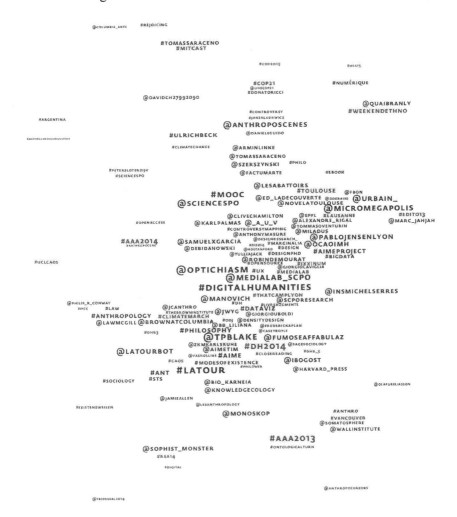

Figure 6.4. *Graph depicting the link between users (@) and hashtags (#) for the AIME project. The nodes @aimeproject and #brunolatour have been removed to show how the network is organized around the events #. For a color version of this figure, see www.iste.co.uk/reyes/hypermedia.zip*

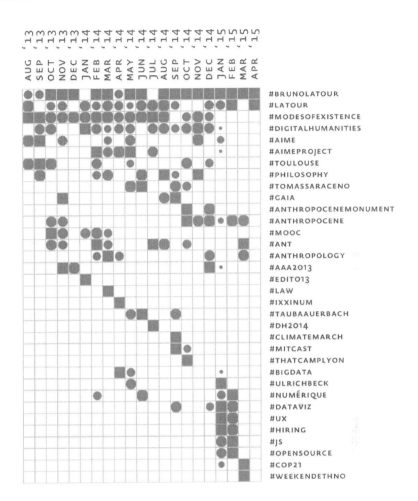

Figure 6.5. *Heatgraph depicting the relevance of the different # during the time of the project. The first five are present during all the time of the observation; all the others are clustered in specific moments. For a color version of this figure, see www.iste.co.uk/reyes/hypermedia.zip*

6.4. Methodology: multiplying listening devices

This is a shallow *understanding* of what the AIME project did, trying to recombine inventive and classic intellectual technologies. With a different timing in each case, the project created different expectations from various communities[14], philosophers, designers and DH researchers as well as created a wide range of frustrations and protestations.

We are proposing to reframe these different elements as *clues*, allowing us to detect different *analogous*[15] practices and assumptions at work in philosophy, collaboration-based projects, design and DH communities. In order to do so, this paper will:

– detail the methodical activity of collecting different criticisms and analyzing the data produced by the project;

– interpret them as *clues* signaling *anomalies* (expressed in SMALL CAPS) grouped into three main families[16];

– look for an understanding by eliciting, using an insider point of view, the choices which eventually generated them;

– evaluate each AIME project anomaly as: (a) a future norm (innovation), (b) a useful mistake for similar experiments in the future or (c) an uncertain anomaly, which reveals underlying assumptions in the audience and participants.

What is at stake here is the evaluation of the process of building set-ups central to the DH hermeneutics [RAM 11]. In a situation where the DH is still delineating its position, shape and role [SVE 10], our way of studying the AIME project – focusing on what has been done and said than on what it is – will help to produce a wider understanding of some assumptions and expectations about DH itself.

---

14 For a thorough, qualitative analysis of AIME project's outsiders diverging expectations, see [NYR 15].

15 Here, the word *analogous* is in contraposition to the word *anomalous* as per the linguistic quarrel of ancient started in ancient Greece and then developed in Rome. While the doctrine of the analogy fostered the idea of a rational language stemming from regular fixed grammatical rules, the doctrine of the anomaly saw language as a spontaneous phenomenon crafted by its living use, evolving and modifying itself, thus admitting divergences and irregularity. The meaning of the term should not be taken in contraposition to digital.

16 A further family has been identified as well. We have temporarily dubbed it DEVELOPING THROUGH PUBLISHING, which refers to the peculiar process of developing a project while having already constituted an audience around its first instance, and to the role of different team members in such an endeavor. Since it is still under elaboration, we prefer not to publish it here and develop it in future contributions.

Figure 6.6. *Graph depicting the various names and adjectives used to address the digital platform of the AIME project. The graph is based on a set of web pages harvested with different search-engine queries. The nodes are connected when two words appear in the same description. The size is proportional to the overall mentions of a specific word*

The DH field is increasingly heading to a certain stabilization of formats, methods and goals[17], supported by the development of shared standards and infrastructures[18]. This tendency toward a "conventionalization" is motivated by the need for technical interoperability and methodological comparability of research programs and projects. It is also driven by empirical, trial-and-error procedures toward new research methods: a lot of projects are trying to establish a more stable basis stemming from previous experiments and available for further projects. This incremental approach could be described as a *conventional* [MAN 15] – we would rather say an *analogous* – way of solving problems that is opposed to a *design* – we would rather say *anomalous* – mode grounded in our ability to "imagine something that is not

17 Although not in a strictly rigid normative sense, it could be cited as a clue toward this need of standardization noted in a passage from the book *Digital Humanities* [LUN 12]: "Curation, collection, and data management are cohering around shared standards, while concrete rationales for the production and deployment of Digital Humanities methodologies have emerged in the academy".

18 See, for instance, the DARIAH European infrastructure: dariah.eu and the Research Infrastructures in the Digital Humanities from ESF: esf.org/fileadmin/Public_documents/ Publications/spb42_RI_DigitalHumanities.pdf

there". Acting in this mode, the highly idiosyncratic (or *anomalous*) activity of AIME could be a useful instrument to observe which *conventions* are populating, in terms of practices as much as values, the communities of Digital Humanities. Our investigation could then inform us about how the AIME project has been an anomaly in these emerging conventions and analogies. *Anomaly* here is not opposed to normativity (*nomos*) but to regularity (*omalos*) [CAN 91]. This notion is flexible enough to compare the project with its hosting environments while avoiding too sharply edged distinctions (normative vs. exceptional) and respecting the highly empirical statements of digital humanists while questioning them. We argue here that these two approaches – analogous/conventional and anomalous/design – are complementary in order to understand the activity patterns of an object of concern such as Digital Humanities. However, as analogies rarely provoke reactions and are thus difficult to trace, focusing our attention on which DH *anomalies* the AIME project has produced, would allow for a richer and softer interpretation of DH's implicit and explicit emerging analogies.

In order to detect AIME's anomalies, we designed a series of listening devices, both inquiry methods and visual instruments that enabled us to grasp reactions and practices produced by the project. They were purposed for both design research and for more pragmatic project management reasons. These devices harvested data from October 2013 to April 2015:

– a systematic analysis of the project's mentions over the Web;

– an analysis of AIME-related Twitter activity;

– a questionnaire analysis, based on a study involving 249 out of the ~6000 users registered in the project's platform at the time of collection;

– a platform's database analysis featuring recordings about enlisted co-inquirers and their writing and annotating activities;

– an analysis of Google Analytics data about the digital platform;

– a series of interviews with team members conducted by an external researcher during the most active phase of the project.

The above-mentioned devices allow us to make use of quantitative and qualitative, enunciative and practical, and insiders' and outsiders' data. We analyzed each of these sources, considering all the traces collected after the passage of the project as *clues* requiring an inferential explanation.

6.5. Anomaly family #1: displacements in acknowledging on-and-offline practices ecosystem

Since its objective was to test the same theoretical hypothesis within diverse media and toward diverse audiences, AIME has been conceived to support a series of complementary on- and off-line, textual and visual, specific and generic media-scholarly practices. Looking at the project reviews and external online reports, some reactions were aligned in their understanding of this multimodal[19] strategy. However, others revealed that this distributed media organization ended up with some MISSING CONNECTIONS between the components of the project. Some descriptions simply did not take into account one or several of the project instances, pointing out, in their critique, a lack of consistency or solidity, while other ones found fault in one instance, not to propose the functionalities that were aimed at being fulfilled by another one. Hence, the printed instance was blamed for not providing contextual references – they were available in the "book entry" of the digital platform; the "book entry" of the platform was accused of not allowing enough discussion and debate, which were designed to be held during physical events, and so on. What had been conceived of as a distributed environment of complementary workplaces was received in these cases as a hegemonic and constraining factory for digital intellectual labor[20].

Another source of displacement in the understanding of the project came from BUILT-IN EXPECTATIONS and the deceptive, although natural, comparisons they made explicitly or implicitly between AIME-specific artifacts and more widespread new media formats[21] with which they shared some features or methodological resonances. Indeed, while the printed artifact has been criticized for being flawed as a defective version of a "philosophical

---

19 As McPherson [MCP 09] stated, a multimodal scholar should make profit of a variegated array of literacy forms. She goes further in posing a question that was at the very core of AIME: "How do you 'experience' or 'feel' an argument in a more immersive and sensory-rich space?"

20 This latter feeling could also have been favored by the technical problems faced by the site, which made it slow and irritating, due to its experimental and evolutionary history. The lack of seamlessness may have engendered some doubts about the relevance of such an ecosystem of instances: "In any case, it is faster and easier to negotiate the book via a PDF file than through the Web interface, or certainly it is better to keep ready to hand the PDF or the paper copy when waiting for the Website to slowly grind back into life" [BER 14].

21 Namely social media platforms, blogging platforms, wiki Websites, academic documents, online repositories and digital archives.

book" due to its lack of critical apparatus, more subtle analogies were made regarding the digital instances.

The principle of a collective endeavor supported by digital means and framed through systematic guidelines often caused the project to be likened to an encyclopedia[22]. This has been reinforced by some AIME platform features, such as its extended glossary (voc column of the "book entry"[23]), its systematic organization through modes of existence, and as a network of linked entries. Therefore, these latter similarities caused multiple, related protestations about the absence of some topics judged as mandatory in the AIME database (e.g. feminist history, petro-chemicals) or, more broadly, a supposedly exhaustive and thus hegemonic approach to AIME's philosophical project, namely the description of the moderns, contradictory to the scope of the project.

We also noticed that the project has been recurrently compared to the archetype of Wikipedia and its corresponding principles of organization. Wikipedia's approaches to *crowdsourcing, source citing* or *content mutability* were projected on AIME's own principles, and seem to have produced misaligned requirements about its content management policy and collective organization[24].

Another recurrent comparison was with blogs, from the PI's argument about blogs being the opposite of the project's principles of collaboration, to external critiques emphasizing the similarities between the two forms, and thus the lack of "originality" of the set-up[25], contradicting its claims of exceptionality. Comparison with blogs provoked the evaluation of the project in terms of innovation, and its distance from the conventional point of reference of blogs. It also imported false expectations regarding a presumed easiness to comment upon and discuss user contributions.

---

22 This distinction has been underlined several times in different writing; for further discussion, see [RIC 13] and [KEM 14].
23 See http://modesofexistence.org/
24 See also anomaly family #3.
25 See http://www.boiteaoutils.info/2015/06/latour-humanites-numeriques/

We could try to explain the MISSED CONNECTIONS provoked by the project as a clash between the tradition of the humanities to use (one) text as the main (and only) medium for intellectual argument, and AIME multimodal shifts through several complementary instances. But if we then try to understand them in the specific context of DH experiments, some BUILT-IN EXPECTATIONS may also have been caused by the heterogeneity of the AIME set-up in terms of templates' compliance or divergence: on the one hand, the various generic media and tools used for the project life (Twitter, AIME blog, mailing list, shared on-line meeting materials) and, on the other hand, the parts that were specifically designed for the inquiry. The latter presented a strong visual and organizational homogeneity (e.g. book and interfaces were presented with the same typesetting and colors, dialoguing with similar visual codes). It could be stated first that their peculiarity asked for some linking with existing templates, provoking the displacements that we have described. Second, the specifically new artifacts were perceived as designed to fulfill *every* cognitive and intellectual expectation of such a project, while some of them, like project discussion and scholarly debate, could and have also been fulfilled by more generic media such as Twitter or blogs.

6.6. Anomaly family #2: interface-driven methodology and its encounters with scholarly publics

Once the different reactions provoked by AIME were observed and analyzed, we could focus on the very activity of people engaged with it. The possibility of contributing to the inquiry was meant to be open to diverse practitioners and scholars able to witness the clashes between the "modes of existence". This process required AN EVOLVING SET OF SKILLS: the co-inquirers should have known the main inquiry narrative by having read the report (traditional humanities literacy skills), and then navigated through the extended contextual contents on the "book entry" ("digital literacy" skills). There, they could bookmark some excerpts through a specific functionality. Eventually, they were encouraged to propose a "contribution" to the inquiry by attaching to one part of existing content a production of their own in order to amend/expand the original PI work (philosophy and anthropology-related skills). In this process, a huge role was also played by the face-to-face meetings, mainly aimed at discussing, accompanying and encouraging contributions on the platform. Comparing reading and contribution activity of the platform overall and the project events agenda (Figure 6.7), it seems that the digital platform activity was correlated with the AIME workshops and events agenda.

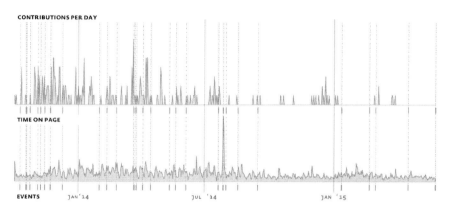

Figure 6.7. *Timelines depicting the number of contributions created per day (top chart), and the cumulative time spent by readers on the website (middle chart), in relation to the AIME events agenda preceding or following a peak in activity. For a color version of this figure, see www.iste.co.uk/reyes/hypermedia.zip*

Looking, then, at project reading metrics in more detail (Figure 6.8), it can be seen that the "contributions column" was proportionally more and more consulted as workshops were deployed. These correlations show that the co-inquirers subscribed rather well to the proposed sequence of activities. Accordingly, when looking at the questionnaire sent to platform subscribers, it can be seen that people participating in workshops were more likely to write contributions and to get published (Figure 6.9). Furthermore, most of those who declared having actually read the report happened to own or use a hardcopy of the inquiry and also to have read the documentation of the project (voc and doc columns). These findings are a good indication of some success in the AIME multimodal plan of action. However, they also reveal that this multimodal awareness was the main condition for having people successfully engaged in the project methodology, whereas "single-medium" participants were left behind.

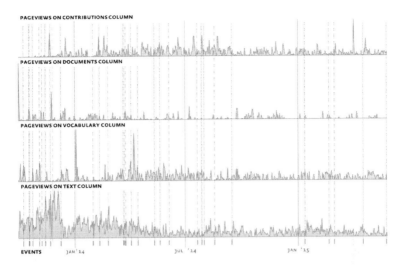

Figure 6.8. *Timelines depicting, per day, the number of consultations of each of the four columns of the "book entry". Namely: text column – featuring content of the printed instance, vocabulary column – acting as a glossary, documents column – featuring bibliographical references and media documents, and contributions column – featuring co-inquirers productions. These are compared with the project agenda of events. It can be seen a proportional rise in consultation of "contributions" as compared to "text" that correlates with AIME events. For a color version of this figure, see www.iste.co.uk/reyes/hypermedia.zip*

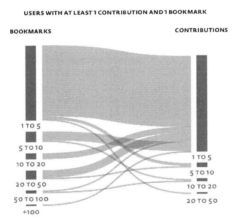

Figure 6.9. *Alluvial diagram, based on the AIME Web platform database of users, depicting the correlation between contribution activity and bookmarking activity among the sub-set of co-inquirers who have used both of these functionalities. An important correlation between active bookmarking profiles and prolific contributors can be observed*

The UNUSUAL BLEND OF PRACTICES required by the project online contribution scenario asked the participants to pass through a series of particular steps designed to make their work become an empirical contribution fitting into the AIME methodology. To do so, following the suggestion to react to specific parts of the text rather than addressing general remarks, they were first supposed to select an anchor point, being a report or vocabulary word or paragraph, and then attach to it a "contribution"[26]. It is clear that a first condition for being able to contribute was to know how to navigate and get acquainted with the contents available on the web. Users declaring to have the highest digital literacy level were also the ones who declared to have profited from the writing and bookmarking functionalities (Figure 6.10). However if we look more deeply into the platform database of co-inquirer activity[27], it can be seen that the diverse, demanding practices were deployed by a rather small part of the community composed of participants who used most of the platform's functionalities together: people who had discovered/used one of the website features were more likely to enter the complete scenario of use that was proposed to them.

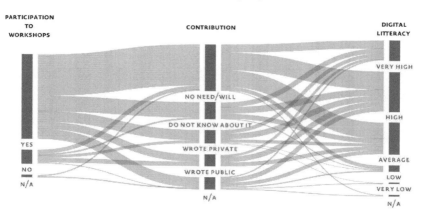

Figure 6.10. *Alluvial diagram, based on AIME web platform database of users, depicting the correlation between contribution activity and bookmarking activity among the subset of co-inquirers that have used both of these functionalities. An important correlation between high bookmarking profiles and prolific contributors can be highlighted*

26 In order to emphasize the role of empiricism, the "contribution" was a composite and constrained format composed of a short abstract and a series of slides presenting commented documents.

27 Collecting personal anonymized information declared at sign-up, and information related to bookmarking and annotation/contribution activity.

Digital literacy [GIL 98] proved as well to be an important factor for subscribing to the methodological affordances of the project interface. An insightful clue to the digital literacy required by the project is the observation that almost none of the few questionnaire respondents declaring to have a low or very low level in this skill wrote a contribution. It seems that the overall project set-up was well fitted for a very specific category of users, those who presented both content and research-related skills and familiarity with digital environments[28]. Having a look at the qualitative feedback from the person in charge of managing contributors[29], some explanations can be found. In addition to the difficulty of finding, understanding, and using such features[30], a strong intellectual compliance to the contribution format (an abstract followed by a series of commented documents) was required: it has been as much a practical as an intellectual obstacle to some of the people willing to participate to the project.

Another explanation may lie in the ways of presenting the project features to the reader. While the Website was designed to focus attention and to help navigate inside a dense network of neatly packed content, it produced at the same time a certain intimidation for the potential contributors; such a feeling has been recurrently reported to the team. The design of *rhetorical expression* [BUC 85] developed in the AIME platform granted access to a huge amount of very sophisticated content and simultaneously asked for contributions and discussions about that content, and simultaneously asked for contributing to and expanding that content.

While multimodal inquiry and composition seem to be one of the most discussed and experimented topics of the DH field [EYM 15], we have experienced how such an endeavor needed to take into account various DH public literacies, and how it sometimes collided with them: encouraging a specific mindset through very specific interfaces requires a long learning curve and inevitably excludes some users. However, mixing digital activities with other types of undertaking helps to strengthen on-screen practices, commitment, and the valorization of online contributions.

---

28 We are also aware that some scholars presenting a low or very low level of digital literacy were enabled to contribute, thanks to the team's help.
29 It has to be said that the UI/UX elements for performing these actions are pretty similar to the ones present in the vast majority of reading/annotation software and annotations.
30 Pierre-Laurent Boulanger, acting as "meta-mediator", was in charge of coordinating the revision of contributions submitted to the Web platform and helping contributors to get acquainted with the process and rules of contributions.

6.7. Anomaly family #3: the shock of collaboration's ethoses

During a French Digital Humanities event[31], the collective and collaborative nature of the AIME project was challenged as presenting a certain non-reciprocity between the main author and contributors: co-inquirers were asked to dedicate a huge amount of time while not being acknowledged clearly enough as genuine contributors to the inquiry. During the latter meeting, the very principle of contribution was under discussion as a matter of intellectual work reward.

If we compare the project idea of a contribution to that of the *analogical* academic publishing habitus, the AIME contribution activity is indeed somehow perturbing: it could be framed, on the one hand, as an open reviewing process where co-inquirers propose modifications and improvements, and, on the other hand, as a journal call for contributions through which accepted submitters get to the status of author. This hybrid, peculiar finality of the contribution activity, that fit with none of the established ways of recognizing and acknowledging scholarly work, has caused various aural and written protestations that we could frame as the sign of an AMBIVALENT STATUS IDENTIFICATION anomaly. Besides the very format of the contributions, a sort of *middle-state publishing*[32] between traditional academic contribution and academic blog argumentation may have fed and complicated this latter anomaly.

It has to be said that the PI considered contributors to have specific and autonomous interests in the project and a shared, though limited, status of author. Even if limited, this acknowledgement of the co-inquirers' authorship has been emphasized by featuring them on platform credits[33]. The contribution validation process itself has been under discussion as well (Figure 6.11). The contributions followed a definite process of mediation and review as a result of their compliance with a specific research methodology, strategy and empirical protocol. They were evaluated and followed by a small collective of scholars acquainted with certain intellectual regions of the inquiry: these particular reviewers were labeled as mediators. This distribution provoked some concern. Some co-inquirers

---

31 THATCamp Saint-Malo, held in Saint-Malo (France) from 17–20 October 2013. See books.openedition.org/editionsmsh/2203
32 This expression is borrowed from "The New Everyday" experiment in academic publishing. See http://mediacommons.futureofthebook.org/tne/about
33 See http://modesofexistence.org/#the-network/contributors.

criticized the lack of transparency of the process and questioned the "testability" of AIME methodology as a closed process. Here we face an intellectual critique highlighting an ETHICAL DISJUNCTION between design project choices and an intellectual debate about philosophical inquiry.

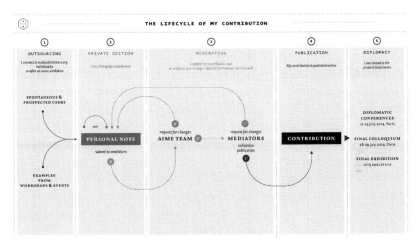

Figure 6.11. *The life cycle of a contribution showing the mediation and review process. From a private edition, progressively and with the help of the AIME team, the submitted contribution reaches the "status" of being public and part of the AIME official documents*

Another similar ETHICAL DISJUNCTION can be detected regarding the very discourse supporting the DH dimension of AIME, thanks to the reactions responding to some public presentations of the project to DH audiences that repeatedly framed *closeness* as one of the core values of the project. Closeness was presented as *distance*: a close arguments analysis also required a *close reading* rather than *distant reading* [MOR 13]. This first claim provoked reactions[34] about the relevance of such an undertaking in the context of "post-digital" research, implicitly assuming that because the set-up of AIME was making use of digital instances, it should have specifically addressed the question of digitality in its very contents and intellectual scope, and thus used distant reading activities, the most

_____

34 In his book [BER 15], Berry states: "The use of the 'digital' in such a desiccated form points to the limitations of Latour's ability to engage with the research program of investigating the digital, but also the way in which a theologically derived close-reading method derived from bookish practice may not be entirely appropriate for unpacking and 'reading' computational media and software structures".

appropriate methodology for activities such as "unpacking and 'reading' computational media and software structures" [BER 15][35].

Closeness was also presented as *focus*: producing philosophical argument required a non-distracting environment[36]. This declaration provoked strong reactions inside DH communities since openness[37] is one of the key values allowing humanities to address contemporary issues and reframe their role inside society [SPI 12]. Although this gap between web ethos of collaboration and closeness claims could be minimized by the fact that the whole inquiry content is freely available to anyone, and that its generated contents (not being formerly copyrighted) are published under Creative Commons license[38], the question of controlling the process of collaboration remains under question. While the team members interviewed unanimously valued the opening of access as mandatory, others also argued for the need of a protection to maintain homogeneity and coherence within the inquiry. Underneath the value statements discussion lay also a practical tension between the need for methodological quality and the broader political expectations about the formation of scholarly community in the digital age.

From an ethical point of view, we have seen that the complex process of constituting a collective body of inquiry provoked important reactions among its publics, responses motivated by several cultural references and agendas (advocates of an alternative academy, of open access, of open software, etc.). We see through this anomaly how DH projects may gather under the same roof a broad variety of ethical guidelines and value systems. While openness is a shared value of digital humanists, it seems to us that the expression of such a notion would need somehow to be precisely cast

---

35 The amalgamation of the PI's discourse about the AIME project's peculiar choices, and its broader positions about the philosophy of digital and software in general, while legitimate, could also be the sign of a PERSONALITY AND STATUS REFRACTION. See [BER 15].

36 This concern has been expressed through design choices such as not pointing to external Websites inside the digital instances of the project while allowing the embedding inside this protected workplace of a variety of media and contents coming from external sources.

37 "The digital is the realm of the open source, open resources. Anything that attempts to close this space should be recognized for what it is: the enemy." The Digital Humanities Manifesto 2.0. Online: manifesto.humanities.ucla.edu/2009/05/29/the-digital-humanities-manifesto-20/

38 The Websites were nevertheless password protected because of legal reasons concerning quoted documents such as texts and videos, and the source code of digital interfaces was not published at first because it was not reusable as is. At the moment of this writing, interfaces are in the process of being open sourced.

regarding the several underlying meanings it is given [TKA 15] and modeled according to the specific needs and methodological goals of one's project.

6.8. Qualifying anomalies for a better understanding of Digital Humanities projects

By collecting clues and spotting anomalies, our AIME critical review helped us to get a better understanding of the feedback coming from different communities of users. In this last part, we will focus on operationalizing these anomalies to debrief and assess the AIME project itself, hopefully transforming the anomalies into recommendations, warnings or observational remarks, and then reframing our approach within the broader Digital Humanities field.

To perform this anomaly detection activity, we draw our methodological framework from an ancient dispute about the nature and evolution of language [DOU 91]. This opposed, during the 2nd century B.C., the stoics of Pergamon (the anomalist school) and the philologists of Alexandria (the analogist school). While analogists were looking for proportional repetitions to be instituted into grammatical rules, anomalists were looking for exceptions that would bring these rules into question. The situation ended up with a very fruitful debate where the description of language was as much at stake as the ethical rules for its further development. In other words, the question was whether to assess language in terms of conventional rules or relevance inside a specific context.

Here, some anomalies we detected could be seen as *future analogies* and *future conventions*, becoming a base for future norms if they reached a certain level of dissemination[39]. Anomalies like MISSED CONNECTIONS could be attenuated by the proliferation of multimodal and distributed projects, and the BUILT-IN EXPECTATIONS that the project faced could be eluded and eventually replaced by its own medial peculiarities after a longer period of use.

It is inevitable to consider some AIME anomalies as mistakes or evitable transgressions of justified emerging conventions. These are not able (and for

---

39 We would here follow Canguilhem's definition [CAN 91] of anomaly regarding biological life, as a successful mutation that "spreads into space rather than time" and is sometimes eventually recast as a normativity producer.

our case, not wished) to come back into any normative status. Such anomalies as AMBIVALENT STATUS IDENTIFICATIONS could have been handled in a clearer way[40]. The understanding of their genesis will inform other projects that would want to follow similar paths.

Some other anomalies could be qualified as specific, undecidable features. These cannot be cast into the former categories or linked to any guidelines or recommendations, either because they are caused by the encounter of irreconcilable viewpoints or because they are completely idiosyncratic to the project. For example, the ETHICAL DISJUNCTIONS provoked by the project remain still to be discussed, as the UNUSUAL BLEND OF PRACTICES issue remains attached to a peculiar methodological wager of the project. These are therefore anomalies of epistemological interest, informing "the ways" Digital Humanities publics expect and preconceive the artifacts they are dealing with.

Our reflective study helped to provide some feedbacks for a certain approach to Digital Humanities focusing more on the methodological renewal of Humanities through experimentation and design practices, than on the new intellectual and methodological challenges arising from the encounter between the digital and humanities topics and methods. In the introduction of his book, David M. Berry [BER 12] framed DH latest developments as anomaly-producing agents that allow us to question and challenge the traditional values, expectations and methodologies of the humanities[41]. Although this assertion is probably crucial for framing DH inside the broader humanities, we could also admit that DH are themselves in a process of normalization or "conventionalization", following necessarily not only the installation of shared standards and infrastructures, but also values and practices grounded in the feedbacks given from the first experiments in the field.

In that sense, DH could be addressed as an anomaly themselves, as the temporary and preliminary sign of an imminent shift within the humanities. However, we argue that this conception is a perilous move, because it would

---

40 We could have, for instance, tried to feature inquiry's contents through a wider range of points of view, acknowledging the work of particular contributors. We could as well have put a priority on providing co-inquirers with a way to reference their work and embed it on other places on the Web.

41 "Indeed, we could say that third-wave digital humanities points to the way in which digital technology highlights the anomalies generated in a humanities research project and that leads to a questioning of the assumptions implicit in such research, e.g. close reading, canon formation, periodization, liberal humanism, etc." [BER 12].

wipe out the privileged capacity of DH to continuously interrogate, through an experimentation dealing with technical, social and experiential *means*, the very *ends* toward which research is conducted. As Lunenfeld *et al.* [LUN 12] stated:

> "When new norms establish themselves, when new procedures and techniques become naturalized, assumptions can become invisible. [...] the new routines that structure this world of practice have the potential to become just as sedimented and automatic as those of the print era, and when they do, they sound the death knell for Digital Humanities as a practice that is both critical and experimental."

The anomaly-tracking endeavor performed in this paper seems to be a good way to prevent this risk. Anomalous dimensions of DH experiments are essential features for their critical approach to the contemporary condition of humanistic knowledge. We advocate that they should not be left out of the future developments of the field, but rather deliberately produced and then observed for their reflective qualities. The interest of DH lies less in essential regulating principles than in a corpus of irregularities, tropes or spontaneous moves that give its reflective and transgressive value to Digital Humanities practice.

6.9. Bibliography

[ADE 12] ADEMA J., "On Open Books and Fluid Humanities", *Scholarly and Research Communication*, vol. 3, no. 3, available at: http://src-online.ca/index.php/src/article/view/92/128, 2012.

[AND 11] ANDERSEN C. U., POLD S. B. (eds), *Interface Criticism: Aesthetics Beyond Buttons*, Aarhus University Press, Aarus, 2011.

[BER 12] BERRY D., *Understanding Digital Humanities*, Palgrave Macmillan, 2012.

[BER 14] BERRY D., "On Latour's notion of the digital", available at: http://stunlaw.blogspot.fr/2014/08/on-latours-notion-of-digital.html (Retrieved 24 July 2015), 2014.

[BUC 85] BUCHANAN R., "Declaration by design: rhetoric, argument, and demonstration in design practice", *Design Issues*, vol. 2, no. 1, pp. 4–22, 1985.

[CAN 91] CANGUILHEM G., FOUCAULT M., *The Normal and the Pathological*, Zone Books, New York, 1991.

[DOU 91] DOUAY F., PINTO J., "Analogie/anomalie. Reflet de nos querelles dans un miroir antique", *Communications*, vol. 53, no. 1, 1991.

[DRU 13] DRUCKER J., *What Is? Nine Epistemological Essays*, Cuneiform Press, Victoria, 2013.

[EYM 15] EYMAN D., BALL C., "Digital humanities scholarship and electronic publication", in RIDULFO J., HART-DAVIDSON W. (eds), *Rhetoric and the Digital Humanities*, University of Chicago Press, Chicago, 2015.

[FAL 12] FALLEN C., *L'anomalie créatrice*, Kimé, Paris, 2012.

[GIB 12] GIBBS F., OWENS T., "Building better digital humanities tools: toward broader audiences and user-centered designs", *Digital Humanities Quarterly*, vol. 6, no. 2, 2012.

[GIL 98] GILSTER P., *Digital Literacy*, John Wiley & Sons, New York, 1998.

[KEM 14] KEMMAN M., KLEPPE M., "Too many varied user requirements for digital humanities projects", *3rd CLARIN ERIC Annual Conference*, 24 and 25 October Soesterberg, The Netherlands, 2014.

[LAT 13] LATOUR B., "Biography of an inquiry: on a book about modes of existence", *Social Studies of Science*, vol. 43, no. 2, 2013.

[LUD 12] LUDOVICO A., *Post-Digital Print: The Mutation of Publishing Since 1894*, Onomatopee, 2012.

[LUK 11] LUKENS J., DISALVO C., "Speculative design and technological fluency", *International Journal of Learning and Media*, vol. 3, no. 4, 2011.

[LUN 12] LUNENFELD P., BURDICK A., DRUCKER J. *et al.*, *Digital Humanities*, MIT Press, Cambridge, 2012.

[MAN 15] MANZINI E., *Design, When Everybody Designs – An Introduction to Design for Social Innovation*, MIT Press, Cambridge, 2015.

[MAR 13] MARRES N., WELTEVREDE E., "Scraping the social?", *Journal of Cultural Economy*, vol. 6, no. 3, 2013.

[MCP 09] MCPHERSON T., "Introduction: media studies and the digital humanities", *Cinema Journal*, vol. 48, no. 2, pp. 119–123, 2009.

[MOR 13] MORETTI F., *Distant Reading*, Verso Books, 2013.

[NYR 15] NYRUP T., THOMSEN J., *AIME* – Perceptions and Experiences, IT University of Copenhagen, 2015.

[PRE 09] PRESNER T., SCHNAPP J., LUNENFELD P., "The Digital Humanities Manifesto 2.0", available at: http://humanitiesblast.com/manifesto/Manifesto_V2.pdf, 2009.

[RAM 11] RAMSAY S., "On building", available at: http://stephenramsay.us/text/2011/01/11/on-building/, 2011.

[RAM 12] RAMSAY S., ROCKWELL G., "Developing things: notes toward an epistemology of building in the digital humanities", in GOLD M.K. (ed.), *Debates in the Digital Humanities*, University of Minnesota Press, Minneapolis, 2012.

[REN 08] RENEAR A.H., "Text encoding", in SCHREIBMAN S., SIEMENS R., UNSWORTH J. (eds), *A Companion to Digital Humanities*, Wiley-Blackwell, New York, 2008.

[RIC 13] RICCI D., *Documenti di scena*, Progetto Grafico, 2013.

[RIC 14] RICCI D., DE MOURAT R., BOULANGER P.-L., "AIME: opening the context of a humanities inquiry", *Digital Intelligence Conference Proceedings*, Nantes, 2014.

[RIC 15] RICCI D., DE MOURAT R., "An account of digital humanities from the AIME Project", *Échappées*, available at: http://echappees.esapyrenees.fr/numeros/numero3/an-account-of-digital-humanities-from-the-aime-project, vol. 1, no. 2, 2015.

[ROG 09] ROGERS R., "The Googlization question, and the inculpable engine", in BECKER K, STALDER F. (eds), *Deep Search: The Politics of Search Engines Beyond Google*, Studien Verlag, Innsbruck, 2009.

[ROG 13] ROGERS R., *Digital Methods*, MIT Press, Cambridge, 2013.

[SPI 12] SPIRO L., "This is why we fight: defining the values of the digital humanities", in GOLD M.K. (ed.), *Debates in the Digital Humanities*, 2012.

[SVE 10] SVENSSON P., "The landscape of digital humanities", *Digital Humanities Quarterly*, vol. 4, no. 1, 2010.

[TKA 15] TKACZ N., *Wikipedia and the Politics of Openness*, University of Chicago Press, Chicago, 2015.

List of Authors

Nasreddine BOUHAÏ
Paragraphe
University of Paris 8
Paris
France

Stéphane CROZAT
Costech
University of Technology Compiègne
France

Dominique CUNIN
EnsadLab
Paris
École Supérieure d'Art et Design de
Grenoble
Valence
France

Robin DE MOURAT
Arts : Pratiques et Poétiques
University of Rennes 2
France

Orélie DESFRICHES-DORIA
ELICO
University of Lyon 3 - Jean Moulin
France

María Inés LAITANO
Paragraphe
University of Paris 8
France

Bruno LATOUR
Médialab
Sciences Po
Paris
France

Christophe LECLERCQ
Médialab
Sciences Po
Paris
France

Leslie MATTÉ GANET
Paragraphe
Intuitive World
Paris
France

Donato RICCI
Médialab
Sciences Po
Paris
France

Everardo REYES-GARCIA
Paragraphe
University of Paris 8
France

Index

Other titles from

in

Information Systems, Web and Pervasive Computing

2016

BEN CHOUIKHA Mona
Organizational Design for Knowledge Management

BERTOLO David
Interactions on Digital Tablets in the Context of 3D Geometry Learning
(Human-Machine Interaction Set – Volume 2)

BOUVARD Patricia, SUZANNE Hervé
Collective Intelligence Development in Business

EL FALLAH SEGHROUCHNI Amal, ISHIKAWA Fuyuki, HÉRAULT Laurent,
TOKUDA Hideyuki
Enablers for Smart Cities

FABRE Renaud, in collaboration with MESSERSCHMIDT-MARIET Quentin,
HOLVOET Margot
New Challenges for Knowledge

GAUDIELLO Ilaria, ZIBETTI Elisabetta
Learning Robotics, with Robotics, by Robotics
(Human-Machine Interaction Set – Volume 3)

HENROTIN Joseph
The Art of War in the Network Age
(Intellectual Technologies Set – Volume 1)

IAFRATE Fernando
From Big Data to Smart Data
(Advances in Information Systems Set – Volume 1)

KRICHEN Saoussen, BEN JOUIDA Sihem
Supply Chain Management and its Applications in Computer Science

NEGRE Elsa
Information and Recommender Systems
(Advances in Information Systems Set – Volume 4)

POMEROL Jean-Charles, EPELBOIN Yves, THOURY Claire
MOOCs

SALLES Maryse
Decision-Making and the Information System (Advances in Information Systems Set – Volume 3)

SAMARA Tarek
ERP and Information Systems: Integration or Disintegration
(Advances in Information Systems Set – Volume 5)

2014

DINET Jérôme
Information Retrieval in Digital Environments

HÉNO Raphaële, CHANDELIER Laure
3D Modeling of Buildings: Outstanding Sites

KEMBELLEC Gérald, CHARTRON Ghislaine, SALEH Imad
Recommender Systems

MATHIAN Hélène, SANDERS Lena
Spatio-temporal Approaches: Geographic Objects and Change Process

PLANTIN Jean-Christophe
Participatory Mapping

VENTRE Daniel
Chinese Cybersecurity and Defense

2013

BERNIK Igor
Cybercrime and Cyberwarfare

CAPET Philippe, DELAVALLADE Thomas
Information Evaluation

LEBRATY Jean-Fabrice, LOBRE-LEBRATY Katia
Crowdsourcing: One Step Beyond

SALLABERRY Christian
Geographical Information Retrieval in Textual Corpora

2012

BUCHER Bénédicte, LE BER Florence
Innovative Software Development in GIS

GAUSSIER Eric, YVON François
Textual Information Access

STOCKINGER Peter
Audiovisual Archives: Digital Text and Discourse Analysis

VENTRE Daniel
Cyber Conflict

2011

BANOS Arnaud, THÉVENIN Thomas
Geographical Information and Urban Transport Systems

DAUPHINÉ André
Fractal Geography

LEMBERGER Pirmin, MOREL Mederic
Managing Complexity of Information Systems

STOCKINGER Peter
Introduction to Audiovisual Archives

RIVARD François, ABOU HARB Georges, MERET Philippe
The Transverse Information System

ROCHE Stéphane, CARON Claude
Organizational Facets of GIS

2008

BRUGNOT Gérard
Spatial Management of Risks

FINKE Gerd
Operations Research and Networks

GUERMOND Yves
Modeling Process in Geography

KANEVSKI Michael
Advanced Mapping of Environmental Data

MANOUVRIER Bernard, LAURENT Ménard
Application Integration: EAI, B2B, BPM and SOA

PAPY Fabrice
Digital Libraries

2007

DOBESCH Hartwig, DUMOLARD Pierre, DYRAS Izabela
Spatial Interpolation for Climate Data

SANDERS Lena
Models in Spatial Analysis

2006

CLIQUET Gérard
Geomarketing

CORNIOU Jean-Pierre
Looking Back and Going Forward in IT

DEVILLERS Rodolphe, JEANSOULIN Robert
Fundamentals of Spatial Data Quality